THE DILEMMA OF
QUALITATIVE METHOD

The dispute over the value of qualitative versus quantitative approaches to social research originated in nineteenth-century debates about the relationship between the methods of history and natural science. Within sociology, this dispute first arose in the United States during the 1920s and 30s, between adherents of 'case study' and 'statistical' methods. One of the main advocates of case study was the Chicago sociologist, Herbert Blumer. His influential writings on methodology provide a link between this earlier controversy and the debates of the 1960s, 70s and 80s. However, Blumer's arguments for qualitative, or 'naturalistic', method retain a central ambivalence: does that method share the same logic as natural science, or does it represent a different form of inquiry characteristic of history and the humanities? That issue continues to underly discussions of qualitative method, and provokes fundamental questions about the procedures employed by qualitative researchers.

The Dilemma of Qualitative Method is a stimulating guide to this key area of social research methodology. The author sketches the historical context of the dispute and provides a detailed account and systematic analysis of Blumer's methodological writings, including his doctoral thesis. The strategies for qualitative research advocated by Blumer and others within the Chicago tradition are reviewed and assessed. The author's conclusions about the current status of qualitative method are likely to be controversial.

THE DILEMMA OF QUALITATIVE METHOD

Herbert Blumer and the Chicago Tradition

MARTYN HAMMERSLEY

London and New York

First published in 1989
by Routledge
11 New Fetter Lane, London EC4P 4EE

Simultaneously published in the USA and Canada
by Routledge
a division of Routledge, Chapman and Hall, Inc.
29 West 35th Street, New York, NY 10001

Reprinted in paperback in 1990

© 1989 Martyn Hammersley

Typeset by LaserScript, Mitcham, Surrey
Printed and bound in Great Britain by
Billings & Sons Limited, Worcester

British Library Cataloguing in Publication Data
Hammersley, Martyn
The dilemma of qualitative method: Herbert
Blumer and the Chicago tradition.
1. Social sciences. Blumer, Herbert
I. Title
300'.92'4

Library of Congress Cataloging in Publication Data
Hammersley, Martyn.
The dilemma of qualitative method: Herbert Blumer and the
Chicago tradition / Martyn Hammersley.
p. cm.
Bibliography: p.
Includes index.
1. Sociology—Methodology. 2. Blumer, Herbert, 1900-1987.
3. Chicago school of sociology. I. Title.
HM24.H355 1989
301'.01'8—dc19
88-25962
CIP
ISBN 0-415-01772-6

This book is dedicated to the memory of Herbert Blumer who, had he lived to read it, would have written a robust reply.

I also offer this book to Joan, Rachel, and Paul, in recompense for time that might have been spent otherwise.

At least knowing where the difficulty lies, we should be prevented from engaging in the practice of the ostrich or in expecting some form of magic to make the problem vanish.

Herbert Blumer

CONTENTS

FIGURES

ACKNOWLEDGEMENTS

In writing a book one always incurs numerous debts. My family have had to put up with my absences and absent-mindedness. For their tolerance, and everything else, I thank them. Many colleagues have played an important role, wittingly or unwittingly, in the development of the ideas that make up this book: I thank Stephen Ball, Barry Cooper, Andy Hargreaves, Donald MacKinnon, Andrew Pollard, Pat Sikes, and Peter Woods. John Scarth must be singled out for his sustained interest and encouragement, and for our many discussions of methodological issues. He has been true colleague. Thanks also to Jaya and Donald for being interested despite having their own books to write, to Colette for insisting that it was worth doing, and to Sheila Hill for sundry help and encouragement. I would also like to thank Marcia Blumer for granting me permission to quote from Herbert Blumer's 1928 PhD thesis. Material from Herbert Blumer's *Symbolic Interactionism: Perspective and Method* (1969) is reprinted by permission of Prentice-Hall Inc., Englewood Cliffs, New Jersey. Finally, I must thank the librarians of the Open University Library for their help over many years, and particularly for tracking down some rather obscure items. They continue to provide an excellent service in increasingly difficult circumstances.

INTRODUCTION

In the social sciences over the past thirty years there has been a tremendous growth in the use and acceptability of what has come to be called 'qualitative method': research using 'unstructured' forms of data collection, both interviewing and observation, and employing verbal descriptions and explanations rather than quantitative measurement and statistical analysis. One of the features of this recent period of growth is that qualitative method has become institutionalized as a largely self-sufficient approach to social research, with its own literature, both substantive and methodological.[1]

The attitude of qualitative researchers to quantitative method varies considerably, from tolerance to outright rejection. Often, though, quantitative research is criticized on the grounds that it is committed to a conception of research method that is modelled on the natural sciences and which neglects the distinctive character of the social world. Qualitative researchers claim that operationalization of sociological concepts in terms of quantitative indicators squeezes the meaning out of those concepts. Similarly, they argue that conceptualizing the social world in terms of variables and the relationships among them abstracts away the character of social life and produces distorted, inconclusive, irrelevant, banal, or even plainly false results. They suggest that if we are to understand the social world, rather than merely aping the natural sciences, we must attune our methods of inquiry to its nature. Human behaviour is complex and fluid in character, not reducible to fixed patterns; and it is shaped by, and in turn produces, varied cultures. Adopting this conception of the social world, qualitative method often involves an emphasis on process rather than structure, a devotion to

1

the study of local and small-scale social situations in preference to analysis at the societal or the psychological levels, a stress on the diversity and variability of social life, and a concern with capturing the myriad perspectives of participants in the social world.[2]

The sources of qualitative method, and of the ideas surrounding it, are various, but one of the most important is what has come to be called 'Chicago sociology'. This originated in the Chicago Department of Sociology in the 1920s and 1930s, and was transmitted to and developed by several generations of students at Chicago, and elsewhere. Members of this tradition have not only produced studies that have served as exemplars of qualitative research, but have also written articles and books about qualitative methodology that have been used as guides by many neophyte qualitative researchers.[3]

In this book I want to examine the methodological ideas that underlie the Chicago tradition of qualitative research, and to do this I shall focus on the writings of one representative of this tradition who has given particular attention to methodological issues: Herbert Blumer. Blumer's long career links the Chicago sociology of the 1920s and 1930s to the resurgence of interest in qualitative method in more recent times, after a period in which it had been eclipsed by quantitative approaches. Blumer joined the Chicago sociology department as an instructor in 1925, became a full professor in 1947 and remained there until 1952, when he moved to the University of California at Berkeley. Through his teachings at Chicago and at Berkeley, and through his writings, Blumer was a leading figure in US sociology and beyond. His name is closely associated with symbolic interactionism, a distinctive approach to sociological theory. Indeed, he invented that term in 1937 and, as he says, 'somehow it caught on' (Blumer 1969b:1). Equally important, and closely related, has been his advocacy of what he calls 'naturalistic research', a form of qualitative method. His presentation of these metatheoretical and methodological ideas in a collection of articles published in 1969 was especially influential (Blumer 1969b).

Symbolic interactionism and naturalistic method achieved particular prominence in the USA and Britain in the 1960s and 1970s. At that time they formed part of the reaction against those kinds of sociology that had become dominant in the 1940s and 1950s. The attack on these orthodoxies involved political, theoretical and methodological arguments. At the heart of the

2

critique was the claim that the dominant theoretical tradition – notably, structural functionalism – portrayed human society as a natural object independent of and controlling human behaviour. This, it was argued, contradicted the nature of human social action, as well as serving to support the status quo by implying that people could not change society. Similarly, the dominant methodological approach, survey research, was criticized as dehumanizing, as eliminating the most significant elements of human life, and thereby producing a distorted picture of the world.

Blumer's theoretical and methodological arguments were an important resource drawn on by many of the critics of sociological orthodoxy in this period. Symbolic interactionism grew popular as a theoretical counter to functionalism, and the 'naturalistic' methods advocated by Blumer became one of the most common alternatives to survey research. On both sides of the Atlantic, there was considerable growth in the amount of interactionist ethnography in many fields, but especially in the study of deviance, medicine, and education. Blumer was an important, though by no means the only, influence on those adopting this approach. Most of the arguments currently used to legitimate qualitative research are to be found in his writings.

This book is not an intellectual biography of Herbert Blumer. It focuses almost exclusively on his methodological writings, and it is framed within my own concerns about qualitative methodology. More than most books, this one is centred on the obsessions of its author.

My interest in Blumer's work stems from a dissatisfaction with the methodological arguments currently used to support qualitative research. I find the criticisms that qualitative researchers direct against quantitative research cogent in many respects. What is more problematic is the implication that qualitative research resolves or avoids these problems. Twenty years ago when I began social research I believed that it did; today I am no longer convinced.

If one looks closely at the methodological rationales for qualitative research, and at empirical work within this tradition, I believe that serious doubts appear about its capacity to deliver what its advocates promise.[4] Fundamental questions abound: Is ethnography devoted to description or is it also concerned with developing valid explanations and theories? If the latter, what are the means by which the validity of explanations and theories are assessed? If operationalization of concepts in terms of concrete indicators is to be avoided, how can concepts be clarified and related to data? And, perhaps most fundamental of all, how do ethnographers know that quantitative research fails to capture social reality, what access do they have to the latter? If that access is through everyday experience of the social world, what justification is there for taking this to represent the true nature of that world?

These questions are not novel, but I find them increasingly troublesome. Even more troubling is what seems to me to be complacency on the part of qualitative researchers towards these questions. When they are not effectively dismissed as founded on the assumptions of an alien paradigm (Williams 1976), or treated as imponderables generated by the anti-philosophical temperament of symbolic interactionism (Rock 1979), the answers that are given are disturbingly vague and inconclusive. The latter is sometimes true of the work of Blumer himself. However, that work has the virtue of posing the fundamental problem that faces qualitative research; and in most of what he writes Blumer does not pretend that the problem has been resolved. He identifies what he refers to as a 'dilemma' facing social research: on the one hand, social phenomena cannot be understood without taking account of subjective as well as objective factors; yet, at present we have no way of capturing subjective factors that meet the requirements of science (Blumer 1939). The central question I shall address in this book is whether qualitative method can resolve Blumer's dilemma, and if so how.

I approach answering this question by means of a detailed investigation not just of Blumer's own writings but also of the intellectual context from which they emerged. However, this is not primarily a historical study. I am not concerned so much with documenting the influences on or impact of Blumer's ideas as with exploring the variety of arguments that have been used to support qualitative method and analogous approaches. What I offer is, in effect, an immanent critique. By outlining some of the diverse intellectual background to Blumer's writings, of which Blumer tells us little, I want to show that the issues underlying the advocacy of qualitative research are more complex, diverse, and problematic than is sometimes recognized.

The history of debates about qualitative and quantitative method is rather neglected by researchers today. There is a tendency to pick out Malinowski, Max Weber, phenomenology, Chicago sociology, and so on as sources of the methodological ideas supporting qualitative research, these being contrasted with positivism in the form of the quantitative sociology that dominated US sociology in the 1950s. But this is to ignore not only the variety of views about key issues to be found among those labelled as positivists (see Halfpenny 1982), but also the diversity of perspective among nineteenth-century writers from whose work those regarded as the precursors of qualitative method drew many of their ideas.[5]

Furthermore, our historical awareness is sometimes distorted by present concerns and assumptions. In the case of Weber, there has been much debate about interpretations of his methodological views and this has raised questions about the relationship between these interpretations and the theoretical assumptions of the interpreters (Runciman 1972; Bruun 1972; Burger 1976; Bauman 1978; Manicas 1987). Similarly with Schutz (Gorman 1977; Thomason 1982). In the case of Chicago sociology several authors have claimed that there are inaccuracies in contemporary understandings of its history. Some have challenged Blumer's claim that his arguments for naturalistic method derive from the work of the Chicago philosopher George Herbert Mead (Lewis 1976; McPhail and Rexroat 1979; Lewis and Smith 1980). Jennifer Platt has shown that, contrary to what is often assumed today, the Chicago research of the 1920s and 1930s did not use participant observation in the modern sense of that term (Platt 1983). Similarly, Lee Harvey has demonstrated that the usual picture of the early Chicago sociologists as symbolic interactionists engaged in research that was primarily qualitative is mythical (Harvey 1987; see also Bulmer 1984).

Neglect or mythologization of the past can have the effect of narrowing the range of theoretical and methodological resources available to us. For this reason, I have provided detailed accounts of nineteenth-century debates about the relationship between the natural and social sciences, about the philosophical pragmatism that underlies a considerable amount of current social research methodology, quantitative and qualitative, and about discussions within US sociology in the first half of this century about case study and statistical methods. What will become clear from these accounts, I hope, is that these arguments cannot be reduced to two contrasting positions, quantitative versus qualitative; or even to a single set of polar types. The debates involve multiple issues, and a wide variety

5

of positions have been adopted. Several of these issues recur throughout this book. Among the most important are the following:

(a) Realism versus phenomenalism. Is there a reality independent of our ideas and experiences whose character we can come to know; or must our knowledge always and forever be only of phenomena as they appear in our experience?

(b) The priority of epistemology or ontology. Must we found our investigation of the world on assumptions about how knowledge is possible or on assumptions about the nature of the world that we seek to understand?

(c) Is science the only source of knowledge; or is it only one, and perhaps even an inferior one, among many sources?

(d) Unity of science versus diversity of science. Are all the sciences fundamentally similar in methodology, or do they differ profoundly in both assumptions and techniques?

(e) The pursuit of abstract knowledge versus the attempt to portray reality in its immediacy and wholeness.

(f) The search for laws versus the identification of limited patterns. Is human behaviour governed by universal laws of the kind often assumed to operate in the physical world? Or is the most that we can expect the identification of limited patterns, culturally specific and/or probabilistic in character?

(g) Is knowledge acquired by inventing hypotheses and testing them (the hypothetico-deductive method); or by unearthing relations among phenomena (a more inductivist or discovery-based approach)?

Over the past 200 years, those advocating what we would today call qualitative methods have adopted a variety of views about these issues, as have the critics of these approaches. Like writers today, they have also sometimes been unclear about where they stood in relation to these issues or have conflated them. For all these reasons, one does not find a simple contrast between two fixed positions.

I should perhaps warn the intending reader who is tempted to turn to the end of this book to discover my solution to Blumer's dilemma: none will be found there. In my view, there are no convincing solutions currently available. To make that clear is, indeed, one of the main purposes of this book. However, I do discuss a number of ways in which a resolution might be achieved. My hope is that this book will move us towards a solution by placing the issues with which it is concerned higher up the agenda, and by making more accessible some of the resources that might contribute to a solution.

Chapter One

PHILOSOPHY AND THE HUMAN SCIENCES IN THE NINETEENTH CENTURY

At the heart of Blumer's metatheoretical and methodological work is the question of the relationship between the methods employed by the natural and those appropriate to the social sciences. Of course, the idea of a science of human social life has a long history, going back beyond the point in history when the concept of science began to be distinguished from philosophy.[1] With the striking developments in physical science in the seventeenth century, the proposal that the same methods be applied to the study of human social life gained ground. Then and later there were also reactions against the encroachment of the new science on areas that had hitherto been the domain of theology, philosophy and the humanities. By the nineteenth century, as a result both of further rapid progress in the natural sciences (not just in physics but also in chemistry, physiology, and biology) (Knight 1986) and of the growing influence of the Romantic reaction against Enlightenment thought, the question of the relationship between the social and natural sciences reached crisis-point.

Before the nineteenth century much thinking about society had been based on the ideas of natural law or natural rights. The central concern of this tradition was with the common good and with how society might best be organized to achieve this. Initially, the common good was conceptualized in terms of the realization of the essential character of humanity. For Aristotle and those who followed him, every kind of thing, including animal species, had its own nature or end, and the good was defined as anything that was conducive to the achievement of that end. In the case of humans, the good was sometimes conceived as a life spent in pursuit of philosophic truth, though politics was viewed as a more distinctively human activity (Lobkowicz 1967). Among later natural right theorists, such as Hobbes and Locke, the common good became redefined as peace in the war of all against all, and as the satisfaction of human needs and wants.

Natural law, the law of the perfect society, was distinguished from the laws of actual societies, and regarded as probably unattainable. Nevertheless it was the ultimate standard by which human societies were to be judged, and it represented a combination of what we would today distinguish as legal and scientific laws. Natural law was held to be discernible by reason, and the discovery and clarification of natural law was the function of the philosophers. Richard Wollheim (Wollheim 1967) usefully summarizes the core of natural law doctrine as follows:

> The whole universe, on this view, is governed by laws which exhibit rationality. Inanimate things and brutes invariably obey these laws, the first out of necessity, the second out of instinct. Man, however, has the capacity of choice and is therefore able at will either to obey or to disobey the laws of nature. Nevertheless, owing to the character of these laws, it is only insofar as he obeys them that he acts in accord with his reason. 'Follow nature' is therefore, on this view, the principle both of nonhuman behavior and of human morality; and in this last category justice is included. The laws which apply to man and which he can and should obey are not identical in content with those which apply to, for example, planets or bees and which they cannot but obey. Nevertheless, since the universe is a rational whole, governed by a unitary principle of reason, the analogies between the laws of nonhuman behavior and those of human morality are very strong and readily penetrated by the rational faculty with which man has been endowed.
>
> (Wollheim 1967:451)

This concept of natural law remained central to the work of writers on society up to and including Rousseau (Strauss 1953), but its meaning was gradually transformed until it came to be descriptive rather than normative, picking out causal relations or at least regularities in the natural world. Eventually the concept of natural law came to be understood in the context of the modern sciences of nature, and its application to the study of human society became seen in analogous terms (Zilsel 1942; Needham 1951; but see also Ruby 1986).

The success of the natural sciences in the nineteenth century highlighted the question of the limits of scientific knowledge. It not only raised the issue of the proper relationship between scientific knowledge and religious belief, but also challenged assumptions about the connection between science and our everyday experience of the world. Was science the only source of true knowledge, and would it expand to deal with all aspects of our experience of the world, including our understanding of human life itself? Or was science only able to help us understand the material world? Indeed, was it able to do even this except in a partial and inadequate manner?[2]

Sometimes, these issues were conceptualized in terms of the clash of two contrasting positions: for example, idealism versus realism.[3] However, the terms 'idealism' and 'realism' are treacherous, since they are used to refer to a variety of positions that differ in important ways. A particular problem is that they conflate epistemological and ontological issues, questions about how we know with questions about the existence and nature of reality. Nonetheless, they are a useful starting point for an analysis of trends in nineteenth-century thinking about the study of human life.[4]

I shall apply the term 'realism' to the claim that there is a reality independent of our ideas or experiences, and that we can gain knowledge of it. Very often, though not necessarily, realism is associated with the idea that science is the only true source of knowledge. In the nineteenth century, realism was also usually associated with materialism. This complex of ideas formed a key element of much Enlightenment thought.

Materialism has had a curious history, as Bertrand Russell remarks in his preface to what is still one of the major philosophical texts on the subject, Frederick Lange's *History of Materialism* (Lange 1865):

> Arising almost at the beginning of Greek philosophy, it has persisted down to our time, in spite of the fact that very few eminent philosophers have advocated it. It has been associated with many scientific advances, and has seemed, in certain epochs, almost synonymous with a scientific outlook.
>
> (Russell 1925:v)

For the materialist, the world is made up of matter: that is the substance from which all else is constructed. Furthermore, everything in the world obeys the laws of matter, including human behaviour and consciousness. For most eighteenth- and nineteenth-century materialists, science was the only true form of knowledge and could in principle explain everything. Materialists often regarded their views as anti-philosophical: they believed that science would replace both religion and philosophy, and, in any event, it was felt that the success of science removed any need for philosophical justification.[5]

An early advocate of materialism, realism and science was Francis Bacon. He argued that science was the most important source of knowledge, condemning the scholastics' interminable arguments and the humanists' reverence for ancient texts. He believed that the nature of the world, both physical and human, was to be discovered by observation and experiment. From facts about the world established in this way, the laws governing the world could be induced by rigorous method. Bacon conceived the process of acquiring knowledge in terms of the overcoming of various obstacles to true perception that he referred to as 'idols': universal or idiosyncratic mental weaknesses (the idols of the tribe and the cave), errors arising from language (the idols of the market), and those deriving from philosophy (the idols of the theatre). In order to discover the nature of the world, Bacon suggested, paraphrasing the New Testament, we must become as little children, ridding ourselves of the various idols that we have acquired in the course of our lives and that obscure our vision.

In reaction to materialism and realism, some philosophers – for example, Descartes – identified different realms, matter and mind, and in so doing both emphasized and placed limits around the power of scientific knowledge. Descartes viewed animals as machines, and therefore as subject to materialistic forms of explanation. Some human behaviour was treated as mechanistic too, but for the most part it was subject to reason and therefore not open to scientific explanation. Descartes also represented a contrast with Bacon in his conception of method. Where the latter stressed the role of induction from observational data, Descartes advocated a more deductivist approach, seeking to deduce scientific findings from a small number of first principles which were taken to be ideas innate to reason, and therefore indubitable.[6]

The issue of the limits to science and to its application to human social life took on particular importance in Germany in the late eighteenth and nineteenth centuries, perhaps because at that time Germany witnessed both a flowering of the natural sciences and of the study of history.[7] Furthermore, as we shall see, the German intellectual scene was a very important influence on philosophers and social scientists in the United States in the late nineteenth and early twentieth centuries, many of whom studied there and were familiar with the German debates (Herbst 1965).

The most extreme reaction against the materialism associated with the development of the natural sciences in the eighteenth and early nineteenth centuries was the absolute idealism of Fichte, Schelling, and Hegel. They sought to combine, on the one hand, the stress on spiritual or cultural diversity to be found in German Romanticism with, on the other, the emphasis on the freedom of the human will deriving from the Reformation, and brought to fullest expression in Kant.

The Romantics – for example Lessing, Herder, and Goethe – rejected the Enlightenment view of humanity as representing a single, universal rationality and as governed by material needs, and of society and nature as mere resources for the fulfilment of human desires. They dismissed the associated view of science as analytic, as concerned with breaking nature down into its components and treating the world as a vast machine. Rather, humanity was for them an expressive unity, each part only finding its true meaning in its relations with other parts; just as the elements of a work of art find their expression in the whole. And, indeed, for the Romantics, art was the highest form of human activity. They rejected the analytic stance of modern science in favour of a more spiritual approach concerned to enter into communion with nature. They were also opposed to the individualism of the Enlightenment. For them, humans were expressive beings because they belonged to cultures developed and transmitted within communities; and there were many such communities, each bearing a distinctive form of life, valuable in its own right.

Absolute idealism also drew on Kant, and particularly on Kant's notion of individual freedom as the pursuit of rational ideals. Kant sought to clarify and justify the grounds of natural scientific knowledge, adopting much of the empiricist critique of metaphysical speculation to be found in Hume. However, he departed from

Hume in arguing that our experience is structured by categories that are *a priori*, such as space and time. According to Kant, then, our experience is a joint product of reality and of the categories of mind. We can never know reality independently of those categories, but science can discover causal laws within our experience. In this way, Kant sought both to secure the foundations of natural science, and to place limits on it. Science could not tell us about reality as such. Furthermore, Kant was particularly concerned to preserve ethics from the determinism of science. While he recognized that human beings are part of nature and are to that degree subject to the operation of natural laws, he insisted that they are also part of a higher, supernatural world that lies beyond the sensible world with which science deals. While he believed that the nature of that higher world could not be known in the manner of science, Kant sought to show that it was rational for us to act as members of that world. This implied exercising freedom of choice by following moral imperatives, rather than submitting to our natural inclinations. From this perspective, those who obey the moral law rise above the world of sense and the necessity and order that govern nature, and enter the realm of freedom and reason that transcends the realm of phenomena. Thus, as Kroner (1914) remarks: 'science conveys theoretical information only about a subordinate part of the world, a part whose metaphysical insignificance appears most clearly when we consider that from it originate just those sensuous impulses and desires which undermine the dominion of moral reason'. For Kant, the realization of human freedom in moral action is humanity's highest ability and duty. It was this aspect of Kant's work that most strongly influenced the absolute idealists.

The attempt of absolute idealism to combine Romanticism with Kantianism was not without problems. To integrate these two philosophical tendencies it was necessary to assume that the ethos of a culture would match the rational commitments of its individual members. For Kant the expression of true freedom was to follow the dictates of reason, and these were conceived as transcendental. Yet, the Romantics stressed the culturally variable character of ideals. Hegel sought to overcome this conflict by treating reason not as fixed in character but as developing over time and as immanent in the world. He believed that humanity had been in harmony with nature and society in classical Greece, a unity that was destroyed by the development of reason in the form of Greek philosophy. There was no possibility of a return to this earlier harmony. Modern humanity was, for the moment, condemned to conflict between inclinations, desire, and sensibility on the one side, and ideals, reason, and morality on the other; and as a result between individual and society. However, Hegel believed that these conflicts could be overcome in a new cultural synthesis that would mark the end of history, and humanity's realization of its true nature. It would overcome the traditional philosophical antinomies: between matter and spirit; between the earthly and the divine; and between the individual self and world.

The idealists went further than Kant, claiming a form of philosophical knowledge more penetrating than that characteristic of natural science. They argued that Kant had violated his own rule that knowledge cannot go beyond experience in claiming that there is a supersensible world. They sought to render him consistent by reinstating metaphysical inquiry as the true source of knowledge; giving modern analytic science, at best, a subordinate role. For Hegel, it was philosophy, and in particular his own philosophy, not physical science that epitomized true knowledge.[8] Equally, Hegel's work contributed greatly to making history central to nineteenth-century thinking. As Ermarth comments:

> History, which had previously been regarded by most secular thinkers as the sphere of contingency, chaos and error, became in Hegel's system the very process of reason itself. In history the mind discovers and recovers the record of its own operation; it thereby comes to itself by overcoming its initial self-alienation.
>
> (Ermarth 1978: 49)

The absolute idealists were very influential in the early nineteenth century, but by the 1840s even Hegel's influence began to wane. This was partly because his philosophy had become identified with the Prussian state at a time when that state was under attack, partly the result of the progress of science and the failure of absolute idealism to take effective account of natural scientific ways of thinking. As we have seen, materialism was closely associated with the development of science, it was a view adopted by many working scientists, and in the 1840s and 1850s, in the wake of the collapse of idealism it experienced a revival in Germany (Gregory 1977). However, ironically, developments in one of the sciences also posed a serious challenge to it. Research on the physiology of human perception began to suggest that our experience of the world, including scientific observations, is dependent on the physical structure of our senses. This reinforced earlier arguments to be found in Kant and the British empiricists that rejected realism, at least in its most naïve form, denying that we could have knowledge of a world independent of our experience. This conflict was brought to a head in the Materialism- usstreit of 1854: during a scientific convention Helmoltz and some other leading scientists attacked materialism, calling for a revival of Kant's critical philosophy. This was one of the first signs of the revival of interest in Kant that was an important feature of the century.

As a result of these developments, neither idealism nor materialism dominated the philosophical scene in Germany in the latter half of the century. Positivism, a point of view that had begun its development in Britain and France, gained considerable support in Germany as the century progressed. Like materialism it took science as an epistemological ideal, but it differed from materialism in rejecting realism. Equally important was the historicist movement which developed out of German Romanticism. While it shared the idealists' rejection of the view that natural science was the only form of true knowledge, it did not accept what it saw as their reduction of the human spirit and its history to a single process of rational development. Instead, like Romanticism, historicism stressed the diversity of human cultures. Also important at this time, as we have seen, were calls for a return to Kant, and there developed a substantial neo-Kantian movement. It was believed that Fichte, Schelling and Hegel had misread Kant's work and that this was one reason for the failure of their systems. But the interpretations of Kant that resulted were diverse, some quite close to positivism, others sharing much with historicism, yet others approaching Platonism.

Positivism, historicism, and neo-Kantianism were extraordinarily influential in Germany, and subsequently for US intellectual life in the early twentieth century. Many of the arguments used by Blumer and by qualitative researchers today can be found in these three nineteenth-century intellectual movements. For this reason, I shall discuss them in some depth.

POSITIVISM

Positivism is a much abused term.[9] I shall use it to refer to the combination of three ideas. The first concerns the concept of scientific law. The positivists retained from natural law theory the idea that the central aim in the study of the social world was to identify universal laws. However, under the influence of developments in both philosophy and the natural sciences these laws came to be reinterpreted as regularities describing human behaviour rather than as political ideals used to judge the value of existing political arrangements.

A second important element of positivism is the restriction of knowledge to experience, in the form of elemental sensations. This is a form of phenomenalism: the claim that we only have knowledge of the phenomena available to our senses. This does not necessarily involve a denial of the existence of an external world: questions of the existence or non-existence of such a world are simply placed outside the boundaries of the knowable. An important feature of the phenomenalism of the positivists was a rejection of the concept of causality. They denied that laws involve necessary connections. Instead, laws were treated as summaries of regular patterns of occurrence experienced among phenomena.

A third component of positivism is the view that science represents the most valid form of human knowledge. Much of the impetus of positivism arises from the desire to apply the methods of the natural sciences to other areas, in the belief that this will produce similar benefits to those already visible in the physical realm, notably advances in technology. Furthermore, for positivists, all scientific inquiry shares the same methodological principles, and perhaps ultimately is reducible to a single science, most commonly physics.

The beliefs of the nineteenth-century writers who are usually regarded as positivists vary considerably, not just in how they interpret the concept of law, phenomenalism and the primacy and unity of science, but also in how strongly they adhere to these principles. None the less, these three ideas, in some combination, are to be found in the work of some of the most influential nineteenth-century philosophers, in particular Comte, Mill, Spencer, and Mach.

Positivist thinking was stimulated by the scientific developments of the seventeenth century, though there were earlier precursors

(Kolakowski 1972). Although Newton's views were predominantly realist, in the sense that he believed in the existence of atoms, and even of forces like gravity that were independent of our perceptions of them, his concern to distance his work from speculative metaphysics led to statements of a positivist cast. The most famous is 'hypothesis non fingo', variously translated as 'I feign no hypotheses' or 'I frame no hypotheses' (Mandelbaum 1964; Hanson 1970; Manicas 1987). Newton claimed that his findings were induced 'from the phenomena', that is from experimental observations.

However, the emphasis on experience as the true basis of knowledge was taken further by Locke, Berkeley, and Hume. For them there was no other source of knowledge about the world than experience, and they subjected commonsense beliefs, philosophy, and/or religion to criticism on this basis. Ironically, Berkeley used phenomenalist arguments to attack the Newtonian world view and thereby to protect Christian belief, a fact that illustrates the threat that phenomenalism can pose to science. However, positivist arguments were generally used in attempts to reconstruct knowledge on a sound footing in line with the findings of modern science, and sometimes thereby to clear the way for social reform.

A famous quotation makes clear the radical nature of empiricism in its most developed Humean form:

> If we take in our hand any volume; of divinity or school metaphysics, for instance; let us ask, *Does it contain any abstract reasoning concerning quantity or number?* No. *Does it contain any experimental reasoning concerning matter of fact and existence?* No. Commit it then to the flames: for it can contain nothing but sophistry and illusion.
>
> (Hume 1748: section 12, pt III; 1975:175)

As with materialism, positivist ideas were often conceived as an anti-philosophy, as an attempt to get rid of philosophical obfuscation by adopting the model of science.

Auguste Comte invented the term 'positivism', though not the ideas to which it refers. He believed that he had discovered the law of the development of mind. Like Hegel, he viewed human inquiry as developing through stages. However, his view of these stages and their culmination was very different. He argued that, initially, inquiry had been framed in religious terms: people had sought to understand the world, nature included, as the product of the activities of one or more gods. Later, in the metaphysical stage, these gods were transformed into abstract forces or causes. Only in the final, positive, stage do human beings recognize the limits of what can be known and restrict their study to the recurrent patterns among phenomena, the only area where sound knowledge is to be attained. This knowledge was exemplified in natural science and was to reach its apogee in sociology, the study of the human social world. The sciences were ranged in a hierarchy, with sociology the last to experience the positive stage and viewed as the queen of the sciences.[10]

The driving force behind Comte's work was a concern with the reform of society. The reconceptualization of knowledge and inquiry that he set about was a necessary preliminary to this. Following the anarchy of the French Revolution, what was necessary, he believed, was an organic period of reconstruction. However, whereas the conservative reaction to the revolution – for example, the writings of Bonald and de Maistre – looked for a restoration of the old regime, Comte envisaged the development of a new society, but one based on a clear, scientific understanding of the nature of human life and its development, and the limits that this imposed.

Perhaps even more influential than Comte, even in the nineteenth century, was John Stuart Mill. His ideas were a bench-mark for those concerned with the possibility of a science of human behaviour, whether they were in favour of or against that proposal. Mill's views were a development of the empiricism exemplified in the writings of Locke, Hume, Bentham, and Mill's own father James Mill, combined with the influence of the French positivism of Comte.

For Mill, all knowledge comes from experience, and experience consists of sensations linked together by association. It is from sensations organized by association that an individual constructs her or his perceptions and understanding of the world. Similarly, scientific laws emerge from the observation of regularities in the patterning of phenomena. For Mill, as for Bacon, induction is the source of all knowledge, but he conceives it in more phenomenalist terms than Bacon as the observation of associations between sensations. Mill argues that simple observation of regularities is not an adequate method for the production of knowledge, since it often leads to false generalization; though he recognized that all induction rests on the assumption that nature is uniform, a claim that can only be justified by simple induction. Mill proposed that methodological or experimental induction is the method of science, and indeed is the only sound means of producing knowledge. He summarized this method in a discussion of the canons of induction, identifying four main methods for identifying causal relationships: the method of agreement, the method of difference, the joint method of agreement and difference, and the method of concomitant variation (Cohen and Nagel 1934; Mackie 1967). Mill conducted vigorous campaigns against what he called intuitionism, attempts to found knowledge on bases other than experience, and against those who in his view assigned too great a role to deduction and too small a role to empirical evidence in science.[11]

In Mill's view there were no limits to the application of scientific method, though he argued that its manner of application had to be different in the social as compared with the natural sciences. Where natural scientists were able to experiment, the social scientist was forced to rely on the observation of naturally occurring regularities. However, he believed that the effects of the development of social science would be as great as, if not greater than, the impact of natural science. Mill saw contemporary society as in a process of change towards a more liberal state, and positivism, or what he called the philosophy of experience, was an essential guide in this process.

Mill's writings were treated as an exemplification of positivist epistemology. His ideas were developed and modified by many subsequent writers. One of the most influential, especially in North America, was Herbert Spencer. For Spencer, as for Mill, all knowledge comes from sense experience. Our ability to make sense of our experience is an evolutionary product that allows us to gain control over our environment. Science is the most sophisticated and developed form of this natural intelligence that all humans use in adjusting to the world. Spencer's view of science is very similar to that of Mill: it requires the induction of laws from the observation of empirical regularities. The role of philosophy, for Spencer, was to synthesize the findings of the social sciences. He believed that previous philosophical systems had been speculative, but that Darwin's theory of evolution provided the foundation for the first philosophical world-view that incorporated scientific data and was justified by inductive procedure. That was what he endeavoured to produce in encyclopedic writings ranging across cosmology to psychology and sociology. Like Comte, though he rejected many of the latter's views, Spencer sought to present an account of the place of humanity in the world, with science itself as part of that world. For Comte, the framework was historical; for Spencer, it was more biological in character and origin, with social phenomena undergoing a similar process of structural differentiation to that found in the biological sphere.[12]

As I noted earlier, positivism became very influential in Germany after the collapse of absolute idealism and with the rapid development of science and technology. Mill's ideas, though also those of Kant, stimulated the views of radical positivists like Ernst Mach, Richard Avenarius, and (in Britain) Karl Pearson, which were developed in the second half of the century. These writers were much more consistent phenomenalists than most earlier positivists. For them science did not provide explanations but simply economical descriptions of experience, the latter being conceptualized, once again, in terms of sensations and the relations to be found among them. They regarded sensations as neither physical nor mental in character, but as philosophically neutral; and argued that scientific accounts must be restricted to the registering of regularities that occur within experience. Moreover, many of these radical positivists rejected the concept of the self on the grounds that it was a construct imposed upon sensations. The result was that for them experience took on a character independent of individual subjectivity. Here the parallels between positivist phenomenalism and idealism are most striking. However, the positivists were, none the less, vehemently opposed to 'metaphysics', by which they meant claims about the true nature of some reality independent of our experience. They believed that such metaphysical ideas were even present in science – for example, in the concepts of the atom, force, absolute space, and so on, and that these must be eliminated if future progress was to be assured. While these writers were primarily concerned with physics, Mach was himself an eminent physicist, the general philosophy was to be applied to all science, including the social sciences, as Pearson made explicit in his very influential book *The Grammar of Science* (Pearson 1892). There was no limit to the reach of scientific method.

Similar in some respects to this radical positivism were the ideas of conventionalists like Hertz, Poincaré, and Duhem, writing at around the same time. However, rather than rejecting theoretical ideas because they referred to an unknowable reality, the conventionalists viewed them as potentially useful fictions that were to be retained or discarded, in part at least, according to considerations of convenience, purpose, simplicity, or elegance. While the central concern of these writers was sometimes to protect religion from the claims of science (as in the case of Duhem, for example), their views of the data of science corresponded closely to those of the positivists.

Nineteenth-century positivist ideas provided a foundation for the subsequent development of logical positivism and operationism in the early twentieth century. These, as we shall see, strongly influenced trends within social psychology and sociology that Blumer opposed. At the same time, however, they shaped pragmatism, the philosophical movement that had the greatest impact on Blumer's methodological ideas.

HISTORICISM

Historicist ideas can be traced back to Vico and beyond, but they rose to particular prominence in Germany in the late eighteenth and early nineteenth centuries in the Romantic movement and then in the work of Ranke, Savigny, Droysen, and other members of the 'historical school'.[13] For the historicist, history is the key discipline in the humanities, rather than, for example, the political philosophy of the natural law theorists. This emphasis on history was in reaction against the idea, central to natural law theory and to the Enlightenment, that there is a single human nature and that it is what people or societies share in common that is most important. Hume provides an example of such a view: 'Mankind are so much the same, in all times and places, that history informs us of nothing new or strange in this particular. Its chief use is only to discover the constant and universal principles of human nature' (Hume 1748, section 8, pt I; 1975: 83-4).

It was precisely such assumptions about the uniformity of human nature that were rejected by the historicists. It was not that they were the first to discover cultural variety in human societies. This had long been recognized. But for many Enlightenment thinkers tradition and local custom were merely evidence of ignorance and an obstacle to progress. The historicists not only emphasized the natural diversity of belief and practice but also insisted that these must be interpreted and evaluated in their own terms, and indeed were to be valued for their own sake. Human phenomena are unique, it was suggested, they do not fit neatly into abstract categories. Attempts to reduce them to such categories involve loss of their most distinctive features.[14] This signalled an approach to understanding the world at variance with Enlightenment views of reason modelled on the method of the natural sciences.

One of the most influential of the early historicists was Johann Gottfried Herder. Although at one time a student of Kant, Herder rejected the abstraction and universalism of Kant's philosophy. He stressed the unity of thought and feeling, of the physical and the mental, of fact and value. He put the concrete above the abstract, the particular before the universal. Berlin (1976) sums up three key elements of Herder's work under the headings of populism, expressionism, and pluralism.

'Populism' refers to a belief in the importance of belonging to a cultural group. Herder placed particular emphasis on the value of 'natural' relationships such as those to be found within the family, as opposed to the artificial relationships imposed by the state. Herder's populism was not political, and he was internationalist rather than nationalist. He was, for example, a bitter critic of western imperialism.[15] Later historicists, notably Ranke, adopted an explicit political nationalism, treating the state as natural, though retaining a belief in the value of a plurality of nations.

Berlin's second summary concept – 'expressionism' – refers to the belief that human actions express the entire personality of the individual actor or of the group to which the individual belongs. Every form of human self-expression is viewed as in some sense artistic, and self-expression is the essential character of human beings.

Finally, 'pluralism' refers to the belief:

> not only in the multiplicity, but in the incommensurability, of
> the values of different cultures and societies and, in addition,
> in the incompatibility of equally valid ideals, together with the
> implied revolutionary corollary that the classical notions of an
> ideal man and of an ideal society are intrinsically incoherent
> and meaningless.
>
> (Berlin 1976:153)

In this respect, Herder was a relativist.

These three ideas lead to the historicists' characteristic emphasis on the diversity and changeability of human cultures, and the need to understand human behaviour in its cultural context and in its own terms. A major element of Herder's writings is the description of other cultures in their peculiar, complex, historically changing manifestations:

> He was inspired by the possibility of reconstructing forms of life as such, and he delighted in bringing out their individual shape, the fullness of human experience embodied in them; the odder, the more extraordinary a culture or an individual, the better pleased he was.
>
> (Berlin 1976:155) [16]

Historicism distanced itself not only from the concept of rationality embedded in most Enlightenment thinking, but also from Hegelianism. Hegel was criticized for imposing categories on history instead of seeking to discover them through rigorous historical inquiry. For the historicist, each age or culture was to be studied in its own terms, not slotted into some schema of the development of human rationality or society. Like positivists, historicists rejected 'metaphysics' in favour of the study of phenomena, but while some of them agreed with the positivists about the nature of natural science methodology, all rejected the application of that methodology to the study of human social phenomena. They adopted a very different approach. Herder's view of the process of understanding other cultures was close to that of many contemporary ethnographers:

> To grasp what a belief, a piece of ritual, a myth, a poem, or a linguistic usage meant to a Homeric Greek, a Livonian peasant, an ancient Hebrew, an American Indian, what part it played in his life, was for Herder to be able not merely to give a scientific or common-sense explanation, but to give a reason or justification of the activity in question, or at least to go a long way towards this. For to explain human experiences or attitudes is to be able to transpose oneself by sympathetic imagination into the situation of the human beings who are to be 'explained'; and this amounts to understanding and communicating the coherence of a particular way of life, feeling, action; and thereby the validity of the given act or action, the part it plays in the life and outlook which is 'natural' in the situation.
>
> (Berlin 1976:154)

The task of the historian was to understand diverse forms of life, and to do this it was necessary to go beyond the physical expressions with which natural scientists were content to infer the underlying and distinctive spirit or culture that had produced those expressions. This process of understanding, or *Verstehen*, was conceptualized in different ways, sometimes as 'the pure seeing of things', sometimes as a constructive process drawing on the whole person of the interpreter. On the one hand, *Verstehen* was regarded as rigorous, like the methods of natural science; on the other hand, it was treated as creative. Ranke, for example, is sometimes represented as a positivist or empiricist because of his emphasis on the rigorous analysis of texts as the foundation of historiography. But while he certainly did insist on the importance of careful analysis of sources, he also talks of the 'genius' of historical interpretation. The historian, unlike the natural scientist, had to go beyond the expressions he or she could perceive to recreate the culture that had produced them. At a fundamental level, for Ranke, *Verstehen* is human self-understanding: it is humanity understanding itself through its own diversity. Ranke suggests that the historian is 'the organ of the general spirit which speaks through him' (Iggers 1968:77). In this respect, and despite protestations to the contrary, the historicists often shared similar metaphysical assumptions to those of the absolute idealists (Geyl 1955; Schnadelbach 1984). Indeed, some historicists sought to identify historical tendencies in the growth and decay of cultures, though these were not usually regarded either as the march of reason in history or as having the same character as natural scientific laws.[17]

The historicists often believed that by understanding our past we would be able to discover principles that would be as objective as natural law theory had claimed to be. Unlike the latter, though, they would be concrete and particular, appropriate to the particular culture or nation concerned. This possibility was underpinned, for many historicists, by the assumption that God was immanent in history.

One of the most influential exponents of historicist ideas was the historian and philosopher Wilhelm Dilthey. Dilthey produced a huge body of published and unpublished work in which he struggled with the task of clarifying the methodological foundations of the study of history and of the emerging social sciences, much as Kant had sought to identify the basic categories involved in our understanding of the physical world. However, Dilthey was not in any simple or narrow sense a Kantian. His work was structured not only by his reading of Kant, but also by the influence of Hegel and of earlier historicists such as Ranke, and even by the positivism of Mill. Over the course of his long life, Dilthey sought to integrate a wide range of philosophical perspectives in a critical way.[18]

Ermarth (1978) has characterized Dilthey's philosophy as 'ideal-realism', as an attempt to overcome the conflict between idealism and realism, taking as his starting-point life experience, conceived not as an individual, subjective phenomenon, but as a cultural, social world. Dilthey argued that the natural sciences abstract from this life experience, but that the human studies do not need to and must not do so. The goal of these sciences is to clarify and understand the nature of human experience, seeking to identify the structures implicit in it:

> The human studies are distinguished from the sciences of nature first of all in that the latter have for their objects facts which are presented to consciousness as from the outside, as phenomena and given in isolation, while the objects of the former are given originaliter from within as real and as a living continuum. As a consequence there exists a system of nature for the physical and natural sciences only thanks to inferential arguments which supplement the data of experience by means of a combination of hypotheses. In the human studies, to the contrary, the nexus of psychic life constitutes originally a primitive and fundamental datum. We explain nature, we understand psychic life. For in inner experience the processes of one thing acting on another, and the connections of functions or individual members of psychic life into a whole are also given. The experienced whole is primary here, the distinction among its members only comes afterwards. It follows from this that the methods by means of which we study psychic life, history, and society are very different from those which have led to the knowledge of nature.
>
> (Dilthey 1894:27-8)

Like the positivists, Dilthey rejected speculative metaphysics, but, like other historicists, he did not accept that the methods of natural science were an appropriate model for history and the social sciences. He argued that human social life is more complex than the physical world, but that whereas natural science must rely on observation of the external features and behaviour of phenomena, in studying human social life we have access to the thoughts, feelings, and desires that motivate action. This is achieved by the process of *Verstehen*, in which we draw out of our experience the ideas and beliefs from which the expressions and behaviour we are studying arose.

For Dilthey, the process of understanding is not simply a matter of following a set of rules; it is not even an entirely cognitive process. Indeed, he sometimes suggests that one understands only what one loves (Ermarth 1978:250). At the same time, he believed that *Verstehen* was a rigorous process, not purely idiosyncratic. Crucial here is the idea of the hermeneutic circle, the fact that in understanding the parts of a text, the acts of an individual, or the elements of a culture, we must draw on ideas about the text, individual, or culture as a whole; and yet our knowledge of the whole is also based on understanding of the parts. Sometimes Dilthey writes as if this rendered understanding a mysterious process, quite distinct in character from the observational processes employed by natural scientists; at other times he approaches treating it as a special case of the hypothetico-deductive method (Krausser 1968).

Dilthey distinguishes between different forms of understanding. At the most basic level, mutual understanding is a routine feature of everyday life. But scholarly work requires a higher understanding that, while fundamentally similar in character, demands that the scholar meets the canons of rigorous inquiry. The primary model of rigour drawn on here was not that of the natural sciences, but hermeneutics, the discipline concerned with identifying the principles underlying our understanding of the meaning of texts. Hermeneutics was developed by Schleiermacher as a general theory of understanding human cultures, on the basis of earlier efforts to theorize the interpretation of classical and biblical texts by humanist and Protestant scholars. He emphasized the ever-present possibility of misunderstanding, and sought to develop a method to overcome this problem. Dilthey developed and extended Schleiermacher's work in this respect (see Palmer 1969).[19]

Dilthey did not believe that *Verstehen* produces a perfect reproduction of the original experience: the understanding would be schematic and always fallible. However, he did believe that it could produce objective accounts of meanings, even though historians were themselves part of history and shaped by it. His goal was to show how such objectivity could be achieved. He believed this to be an urgent requirement in order to resolve the crises that he saw facing German culture. Along with some of the neo-Kantians, and in contrast to the conservatism of many historicists, Dilthey was active in the liberal reform movement that flourished in mid-nineteenth-century Germany. He believed that a new philosophy based on history and the human sciences would provide the basis for rational, peaceful reform.

In summary, then, Dilthey argued that history and the social sciences, including psychology, while scientific in the broad sense, must none the less adopt a different approach from that of the natural sciences. They are not reliant solely on the observation of external features. Moreover, their aim is not the identification of universal laws, but the description of patterns found in experience. Dilthey believed that, through the identification of such patterns, history and the social sciences could provide knowledge that would resolve the cultural crisis arising from the collapse of traditional ideas and values.

Historicist ideas were important not only for the development of philosophy and historiography, but also for the emerging social sciences, as we shall see later. Indeed, the parallels between historicism and modern ideas about qualitative research are particularly striking: there is the same emphasis on diverse cultures valid in their own terms, the same distrust of abstraction and preference for detailed descriptions, the same reliance on *Verstehen* rather than external description of behaviour, the same appreciative stance.

NEO-KANTIANISM

While Dilthey had in some respects returned to Kant, the cry of 'Back to Kant' was much more widespread, and from the mid-century onwards there emerged in Germany a loosely structured neo-Kantian movement. Neo-Kantianism was a diverse movement, and I shall focus primarily on the south-west German neo-Kantians, Windelband and Rickert.[20] Their fundamental stance was to reject both materialism and idealism as transgressing the proper limits of what can be known. The neo-Kantians argued that one of the most important failings of idealist philosophy was its slighting of empirical science, and of the growing power of science to produce knowledge of the physical world. They paid close attention to these scientific developments; and this stimulated a reassessment of the proper role of philosophy. Neo-Kantianism represented a turn to philosophical modesty as against what was seen as the speculative excesses of both idealism and materialism. In this sense, neo-Kantians shared some ground with positivism. Both rejected claims about the nature of a hidden reality beyond our experience. For the neo-Kantians the primary concern of philosophy was to analyse the conditions under which knowledge could be produced, both in the physical and historical sciences.

The neo-Kantians viewed the world of experience as continuous and heterogeneous; in other words, as formless, or at least as open to multiple descriptions. The patterns that we perceive, and the cognitive structures that we use to make sense of our perceptions, were regarded as human constructions devised on the basis of human values. While they are presumably limited by the nature of reality, their character was thought to derive, for the most part, from the human activity that went into their construction. The neo-Kantians criticized the positivists for taking too restrictive a stance, denying the value of myth, religion, and history. They sometimes argued that although these do not provide knowledge of reality in the same sense as science, they embody their own forms of truth, and are no less important as human creations than science. None of these modes of apprehending reality can claim, legitimately, to capture the one and only reality.

Many neo-Kantians also rejected positivist and materialist arguments that reality can only be studied by the methods of the natural sciences. Unlike Dilthey, however, they did not base their arguments on the claim that social life is different in character to the physical world. For them all science, all knowledge, refers to the same reality; and that reality is not divided up into areas with different natures. Depending on the values they adopt, observers structure their interpretation of their experience in different ways. From this point of view, science and history have different methods because they have different concerns, and approach reality in different ways. Thus, Windelband distinguished between idiographic disciplines like history, that study the unique character of particular events, from nomothetic disciplines, like the natural sciences, whose aim is the identification of universal laws:

the empirical sciences seek, in their pursuit of knowledge of reality, either the general in the form of laws of nature or the particular in the form of what is historically determined: they study on the one hand the permanently identical form, on the other hand the once-for-all and completely determinate content of the real event. The one kind of science is concerned with laws, the other with events; the one teaches what always is, the other what once was. Scientific thought, if new and artificial expressions may be permitted, is in the one case 'nomothetic', in the other 'idiographic'.

(quoted in Schnadelbach 1984:57)

Robert Park, perhaps the key figure in the Chicago sociology of the 1920s and 1930s, was a student of Windelband, and this distinction is enshrined in the opening chapter of the so-called 'green bible', the text that Park wrote with Ernest Burgess for their students.

One of the most influential of the neo-Kantians who sought to justify the method of history as distinct from that of the natural sciences was Heinrich Rickert. His major work, *The Limits of Concept Formation in Natural Science* (Rickert 1902), is cited in Blumer's dissertation and clearly shaped the latter's conception of science.

Rickert's starting-point was the illimitable character of phenomena. He argues that the phenomena of experience are composed of elements that are in turn made up of smaller elements, and so on, *ad infinitum*. Similarly, every phenomenon forms part of a larger phenomenon. As a result of this structure, phenomena do not compel any interpretation of themselves on the part of an observer. Rather, the manner in which they are approached depends on human values. The value that motivates scientific research is truth, the concern to establish objective knowledge. Since phenomena are heterogeneous and continuous, the assertion of a fact requires the imposition of a form on the phenomenal content. A fact is a segment of experience singled out from the mass of dimly experienced states of consciousness and given the status of being real. What people treat as concrete reality is simply those contents of consciousness judged by everyone to be facts.

Given the nature of phenomena, the number of possible facts is unlimited, both extensively (there are an indefinable number of them) and intensively (each one can be divided into an infinite number of parts and sub-parts). Rickert assumes that the goal of science is total factual knowledge – in other words comprehensive knowledge of phenomena. However, this is not possible since, whereas phenomena are inexhaustible, the human mind is finite. This poses a problem for science: how can it be ensured that all scientists select the same facts? Some standard of selection must be employed, and this must be objective – in other words accepted as valid by everyone. Rickert argues that if we examine science (in which he includes not only the natural sciences but also the historical, social and linguistic sciences) we find that there are two methods that, although not achieving the ideal of comprehensive knowledge, approximate its achievement.

The first is the *generalizing method*, which Rickert identifies with the natural sciences, though he recognizes that this is not the exclusive method of those sciences. (This conforms broadly to Windelband's 'nomothetic' method.) Here the focus is on the common features that many phenomena share. The aim of natural science is to form a system of general concepts that allows every event, including those that will occur in the future, to be subsumed under general concepts. Furthermore, it is assumed that in each case phenomena can be assigned unambiguously to a particular concept. Rickert recognizes that in practice this is not possible because the conceptual image is too vague, being a combination of the images of many particulars. However, he argues that, for practical purposes, a sufficiently precise statement of what is assumed by a concept can be given in a definition. This indicates what elements have to be present in a specific combination in a concrete fact for it to be subsumed under that concept. Through comparison of phenomena, general concepts are formed at a relatively concrete level, but in time these are subsumed under more and more abstract concepts. These concepts relate both to things and to relations, the latter including causal relations: Rickert believed that all phenomena are meshed in the causal nexus. Concepts concerned with causal relations are built up in precisely the same way as those relating to things, and at the more abstract levels they constitute laws of nature.

The generalizing method solves the problem of the inexhaustible character of phenomena by selecting only those aspects of phenomena that are shared with other phenomena. While this does not provide knowledge of the intensive inexhaustibility of reality, it does deal with its extensive inexhaustibility: a large number of phenomena are studied and the laws produced are held to apply to all phenomena. It is this feature of them that makes them objective, by which Rickert means that they are of interest to everyone.

The alternative approach that Rickert identifies is the *individualizing method.* (This matches Windelband's idiographic approach.) Here, by contrast, the focus is on an individual fact; and in particular those elements of it that, in their combined occurrence, make it unique. This is the method that is characteristic of history. Through artful presentation historians attempt to evoke an impression of actual concreteness, to re-create the phenomenon as it existed. History tries to provide an unambiguous account, not through definitions but through images that are as precise and clear as possible. For instance, in studying the French Revolution, historians focus on its distinctive features rather than what it shares with other revolutions.

The question remains, though, of how we select individual facts to study. Rickert argues that this is done on the basis of values. He notes that not all individual phenomena are valued, and draws a distinction between two types of phenomena. First, there is nature: those things that originate and persist without human interference and concern. Second, there is culture, objects produced directly by humanity in pursuit of values, or phenomena that are given value by humans. History, given its value orientation, is concerned with the study of individual cultural phenomena. The cultural values within a society designate a certain range of phenomena as of common concern. This is true both of the values characteristic of the period under study and those of the historian's own time. The historian using the individualizing method focuses on phenomena identified by those values. Rickert also claims that some of these values are universally valid: valid for all people at all times. This gives the individualizing method its objectivity. Here, then, we have a principle of selection that approximates solution of the problem posed by the fact that phenomena are unlimited, this time by giving greater emphasis to the intensively infinite character of phenomena.

Rickert draws a sharp distinction, then, between science and history. However, the place of sociology and the other social sciences within his scheme is somewhat ambiguous. He portrays the generalizing and individualizing methods as polar types, and recognizes that in practice many sciences combine the two methods.

He does not, though, provide much clarification of the implications of this for the social sciences.

The neo-Kantians are, perhaps, the most neglected of the three traditions discussed here, often being given attention today only as precursors of Max Weber. They were, however, very influential in the late nineteenth and early twentieth centuries, and their attempts to identify the similarities and differences between natural and social sciences offer an important corrective to both positivism and historicism. The diversity of views about the methodology of the human sciences to be found among philosophers in the nineteenth century was paralleled within those sciences themselves. In the final section of this chapter I shall examine developments in those disciplines.[21]

THE SOCIAL SCIENCES AT THE TURN OF THE CENTURY

Before the First World War, the boundaries between philosophy and the various social sciences, and among these sciences themselves, were not as strong or as clear as they are today. The philosophical ideas that I have discussed in this chapter arose at a time when the study of the social sciences was developing rapidly. The latter were in the process of becoming institutionalized within universities. The debates arose in part from problems within the human sciences, and in turn they had a profound effect on developments in those disciplines. Here, I want to sketch very briefly the methodological tendencies within some of the most important of the human sciences at this time.

Psychology

In the nineteenth century psychology developed in large part under the influence of materialistic and positivistic ideas. A major influence was the associationist psychology of empiricists like Locke, Hume and the Mills – and British psychology in the nineteenth century remained associationist but largely non-experimental. Here psychology was concerned solely with establishing the laws of association between ideas. In general the possibility that these associations might be caused by something outside the organism was ruled out by phenomenalism. In Germany, however, experimental psychology emerged out of physiological work, in the form of the psychophysics of researchers like Ernst Weber, Fechner, Helmholtz, and Wundt. Associationism was influential here too, but ideas were also drawn from a wide range of other sources, including idealism and the work of Kant. The aim was to identify the basic psychological elements of consciousness and the regularities underlying their combination, and these were investigated experimentally by means of controlled introspection.

Even before the emergence of behaviourism in the United States in the early twentieth century, then, psychology was already a discipline very much oriented towards the model of the natural sciences. Dilthey (1894) sought to rectify this, criticizing experimental psychology for its atomistic approach to consciousness. He argued that experimental psychology had failed in its own terms since it had produced no psychical laws, and that this stemmed from the fact that psychologists did not recognize that the study of the mind was not an appropriate field for the application of natural science method. As we saw, for Dilthey the correct approach for psychology was descriptive, aimed at detecting the patterns or structures within human experience, the latter being viewed as cultural rather than individual and subjective. Ebbinghaus, one of the leading figures in the new experimental psychology, replied to Dilthey, arguing that Dilthey's proposed descriptive psychology was not even viable in its own terms and that it did not provide an effective alternative to experimental psychology (Makkreel 1975:207-9).

There was also some variation in orientation among experimental psychologists. For example, one of the pioneers of the discipline, Wundt, regarded psychology as both a natural and a human science, and he pursued both physiological psychology and what we would today call cultural anthropology (under the title 'Volkerpsychologie') (Danziger 1979; Leary 1979). However, as far as the development of Anglo-American psychology in the twentieth century is concerned, it was the more positivistic approach of Ebbinghaus, Kulpe, and Titchener that carried the day. Psychologists have remained more strongly committed to the natural science model, conceived in a broadly positivistic manner, than practitioners of the other human sciences; though in recent years there has been increasing criticism of this model (Joynson 1974: Harré and Secord 1972; Valle and King 1978; Rosnow 1981; Ashworth, Giorgi and de Koning 1986).

Economics

In economics the classical approach of Smith, Mill, and Ricardo of the late eighteenth and early nineteenth centuries was based on a mixture of natural law and positivist ideas, and this continued to dominate economic thinking in Britain until the marginalist revolution of the 1870s. However, in Germany the influence of classical political economy was limited by the development of a more historical approach on the part of such writers as Hildebrand, Roscher, Knies, and, later, Schmoller. Their concern was not with the discovery of economic laws but with the economic conditions of particular nations, these being taken to be diverse in character, reflecting their particular political and social histories. In line with the principles of historicism, these writers argued that economic behaviour could not be understood as following universal principles but only as the product of the particular history and wider culture of the society in which it occurred. They rejected the concept of 'economic man' as an abstraction that did not accurately reflect the motivation of human beings and did not provide a sound basis for national policy.[22]

This historical school of economics was one of the parties to what has become the best-known nineteenth-century controversy about social research methodology, the '*Methodenstreit*' (or battle of the methods) in the 1880s and 1890s, in which a generalizing and deductive approach was opposed to the individualizing and inductive method of the historical school. The debate was sparked off by an attack on the historical school by the Austrian economist Carl Menger (Menger 1883). Although Menger rejected some key features of classical economics, as one of the developers of marginalism his approach retained its concern with developing abstract economic theory intended to apply to economic processes in all times and places. He attacked the work of the German economists for neglecting the analysis and testing of such principles, while necessarily using them in an implicit and sometimes ill-conceived manner. Ultimately, the Austrians had the longest-lasting effects on the development of economics, but in the early twentieth century the historical school was an important influence on US economics, and particularly on what came to be referred to as the 'institutional' school, whose influence prevailed in the early part of the century.

Sociology

The term 'sociology' was, of course, invented by Comte, and its development in the nineteenth century was strongly influenced by positivism, most obviously in the work of Spencer, but also Durkheim. Within this tradition the goal was to discover sociological laws by the application of methods broadly similar to those employed by other sciences, especially biology. However, an almost entirely independent development of the discipline occurred out of historicism and neo-Kantianism in the work of Georg Simmel and Max Weber, and this was particularly important for Chicago sociology, and for the emergence of ideas about qualitative method generally.

What Simmel provides is a method rather than a system of thought. Levine (1971:xxxi) summarizes this method as follows:

> [Simmel's] method is to select some bounded, finite phenomenon from the world of flux; to examine the multiplicity of elements which compose it; and to ascertain the cause of their coherence by disclosing its form. Secondarily, he investigates the origins of this form and its structural implications.

Much of Simmel's sociological work consists of essays on diverse topics, from the role of money in social life to the characteristics of secret societies. Moreover, he writes in a manner that makes the attempt to identify his philosophical position difficult. It is quite clear, though, that his approach to sociology was strongly influenced by neo-Kantianism. Like the neo-Kantians he emphasizes the role of mind in constructing and reconstructing experience. Thus he criticizes the 'historical realism' of the historicists (Simmel 1905). Simmel was particularly concerned with identifying the categories through which we understand and thereby constitute social life, much in the manner that Kant sought to identify the categories that structure our experience of the physical world. Indeed, he shares some of the same motives as Kant, interpreted under the influence of the absolute idealists:

> It is necessary to emancipate the self from historicism in the same way that Kant freed it from naturalism. Perhaps the same epistemological critique will succeed here too: namely, to establish that the sovereign intellect also forms the construct of

mental existence which we call history only by means of its own special categories. Man as an object of knowledge is a product of nature and history. But man as a knowing subject produces both nature and history.

(Simmel 1905:viii-ix)

Simmel emphasizes that while history must begin from the understandings of the people under study, it goes beyond these, and does so on the basis of particular angles of vision. He believed that there is no single true account of history, there are multiple accounts that may be valid in their own terms.

The parallel with Kant, while true in one sense, hides the very different modes of philosophizing characteristic of these two writers, the one systematic and concerned with identifying transcendental truths, the other eclectic, impressionistic, and searching for historical, social, and cultural forms. Moreover, for Simmel forms were not immutable. Indeed a key concern of Simmel's was to trace the *emergence* of social and cultural forms. He argues that they arise from the exigencies of practical everyday life, but that once established they take on a life of their own and are cultivated for their own sake. This results in the emergence of various worlds (of art, religion, science). These worlds are distinct from the everyday world, that framework of assumptions required for us to adapt to our environment in such a way as to satisfy the biological requirements of our species.[23] These different ways of organizing the contents of life are in conflict, but are all equally valid for Simmel. He adopts a relativist stance (see Spykman 1925): 'In radical contrast to Comte and Marx, who envisioned the goal of evolution to be the production of a homogeneous culture for one humanity, Simmel saw the generation of increasingly specialized cultural products ordered in fundamentally discrete and incommensurable worlds' (Levine 1971:xvii).

Sociology is itself one of these worlds, so that its concerns are independent of the demands of politics or practical affairs. As for Weber, so for Simmel, sociology must strive to be value-neutral. As he comments at the end of *The Metropolis and Mental Life*: 'It is our task not to complain or to condone, but only to understand' (Levine 1971: 339).

The distinctiveness of sociology lies not in the contents that it organizes – these can be viewed from many perspectives – but from its mode of apprehending human experience. The contents organized by sociology are the needs and purposes that draw individuals into interaction with one another, the social forms that it studies are the 'synthesizing processes by which individuals combine into supraindividual unities, stable or transient, solidary or antagonistic, as the case may be' (Levine 1971:xxiv).

Park was a student of Simmel, and the latter's work seems to have had a considerable impact on Chicago sociology, more than that of any other European, with the possible exception of Spencer. However, the importance of Simmel for Chicago sociology seems to have been in large part as a source of specific sociological ideas, for example about the nature of urbanism as a way of life or about social marginality: there is little sign that his general philosophical viewpoint had much influence on the Chicagoans, even on Park.

Weber seems to have accepted most of the epistemological framework provided by Rickert (Burger 1976; Oakes 1987); though he was also strongly influenced by Simmel (Frisby 1987). His only major departure from Rickert was in rejecting the latter's assumption that universal values can underpin historical inquiry. For Weber, as for Simmel, there is an ineradicable conflict among values: we cannot assume or justify consensus on any single consistent set of value principles. As a result, history can always be written from different perspectives, there can be no one single true history. It will be rewritten at different times on the basis of different values.

Much of Weber's work was historical in character, focused on individual phenomena, most famously the spirit of western capitalism and the Protestant ethic. He viewed sociology as an adjunct to historical work, refining the general concepts that historians need in studying individual phenomena. However, Weber argued that these general concepts are not, and cannot be, the same as the general concepts developed in the natural sciences. Whereas the latter summarize common features shared by all the phenomena they subsume, the general concepts used by historians are idealizations: they specify features that phenomena share only to varying degrees, and from the point of view of a particular set of values; they are generalizations about an idealized world, or ideal types. For Weber, then, sociology provided the conceptual resources necessary for the idiographic work of historians.

Weber doubted the value of a nomothetic science of social phenomena, on the grounds that the more abstract the knowledge in this field the less significant it was. As he says, 'the most general laws, because they are most devoid of content are also the least valuable' (Weber 1903-17:80). Certainly, the task of historical explanation could not be executed by subsuming an event under a sociological law: there are always a plurality of causes of any event, and judgement about whether an explanation was effective depended on assessing the effects of different causes through thought experiments, eliminating those putative causes that seemed unlikely to have been significant in the case under study. Weber recognized that historical explanations relied upon causal generalizations, but he did not see nomothetic science as the only, or even the most significant, source of these generalizations: they also derived from our general experience and knowledge of the social world.

Of course, an important element of Weber's sociology was the need to interpret the subjective meanings attached to human actions. Like Dilthey, Rickert, and others before him, Weber was concerned to find a way of providing for a scientific understanding, in the broadest sense, of subjective phenomena:

> Weber's life-work, at least in its methodological aspect, derived
> its dynamics and purpose from a tension between his view of
> reality, the subject-matter of sociology as irretrievably
> subjective, and his determination to find a way of knowing it
> objectively. The task Weber set himself with unprecedented
> determination was nothing less than an objective science of the
> subjective.
>
> (Bauman 1978:72)

Weber adopted a distinctive perspective on this problem. He recognized that we could understand most human actions in the sense of being able to make plausible sense of them. However, he regarded many of these interpretations as having a weak claim to knowledge compared to the observations of physical scientists. This was particularly true of empathetic understanding, where we rely on imagining how we would react in the same circumstances as those in which the people whose actions we wish to understand are placed. Weber believed that the success of empathetic understanding depended heavily on the degree of similarity between the experience of the observer and that of the people he or she is studying. But he argued that sounder knowledge was available where action could be portrayed as rational. Here the links between goals and means were logical in character. Furthermore, he claimed that the application of such rational models to human behaviour was becoming more and more appropriate given the process of rationalization that western societies were undergoing. To the extent that the logic of rationalization continued to play itself out, more and more human behaviour would approximate rational models and therefore would be amenable to scientific understanding.

However, in Weber's view neither empathetic nor even rational understanding in itself provides adequate explanations for human actions. Each can tell us only whether a proposed explanation is 'adequate at the level of meaning' – that is, whether it makes those actions intelligible to us. Equally important is causal adequacy. In the case of rational understanding, we must show that our identification of the objectives of those whose behaviour we seek to explain is correct and that it was because they had those objectives and regarded the actions in question as the best means of achieving them that the actions were performed. With empathetic understanding we must show that a person did have the emotions or attitudes we are ascribing to her or him, and that it was these that led to the actions being performed. Weber regarded the task of establishing causal adequacy as difficult and rarely conclusive. It involves checking whether the pattern of action that we would expect to occur given the motivation ascribed does actually occur. In the case of his attempt to explain the rise of the capitalist spirit, for example, he provided comparative evidence to show that in the sixteenth and seventeenth centuries capitalist forms of enterprise arose more frequently among Protestants than among Catholics. He also argued that they did not arise in India and China, even when the necessary material conditions were present, because the forms of religion to be found in these areas were not such as to produce the spirit of capitalism. In this way he sought to show that the Protestant ethic was not only an intelligible cause of the spirit of capitalism, but a causally adequate one.[24]

Weber's work seems to have had little impact on the Chicago sociologists, though Blumer discusses the ideal type method in his dissertation as one of the alternatives to the attempt to create a science of social psychology. However, the influence of Weber has been important for later exponents of qualitative sociology, and his discussions of methodological issues parallel those of Blumer at many points.

Anthropology

Within anthropology, one of the most important developments was Franz Boas's criticisms of speculative theorizing and his advocacy and practice of a 'historical' approach. Boas is often regarded as a critic of evolutionism and a proponent of diffusionism, but his primary concern seems to have been to improve methodological standards within anthropology, and his advocacy of detailed descriptions of cultures and reconstructions of their histories was intended to counter the excesses of speculation to be found among his contemporaries, both evolutionists and diffusionists. He was influenced by historicism, neo-Kantianism, and the *Volkerpsychologie* of Wundt in his conception of the historical method, emphasizing the detailed study of unique phenomena. But, for much of his career at least, he regarded this method as paving the way for the application of comparative method and the discovery of laws:

> When we have cleared up the history of a single culture and understand the effects of environment and the psychological conditions that are reflected in it, we have made a step forward, as we can then investigate how far the same causes or other causes were at work in the development of other cultures. Thus by comparing histories of growth, general laws may be found. This method is much safer than the comparative method, as it is usually practised, because instead of a hypothesis on the mode of development, factual history forms the basis of our deductions.
>
> (Boas 1940:279; originally published 1896)

Here Boas is advocating an inductive approach to scientific inquiry, in contrast to the speculative method adopted by many of his contemporaries. In this respect his views show affinities with those of Bacon and the positivists (Harris 1969).

From Boas's perspective, then, science had both individualizing and generalizing components. Indeed, he was criticized by two of his students, Kroeber and Radin, for retaining a concern with science and the discovery of laws, instead of adopting a thoroughgoing historical or idiographic approach (Radin 1933; Kroeber 1935). Furthermore, it seems that over the course of his career Boas gradually abandoned the belief that it was possible to discover laws in the cultural realm, moving towards an exclusively idiographic approach.

Within British social anthropology there was also a reaction against the speculative excesses of the nineteenth century; drawing once again on Wundt's *Volkerpsychologie* but also on the work of Durkheim. Like Boas, Radcliffe-Brown and Malinowski retained a commitment to science. Indeed, Malinowski was trained in physics as Boas had been. The British social anthropologists likewise emphasized the importance of the description of primitive societies on the basis of first-hand experience. However, where Boas was initially primarily concerned with the collection of artefacts and myths and the reconstruction of the history of these phenomena, Radcliffe-Brown and Malinowski gave more attention to the study of the everyday behaviour of the people they studied.

Malinowski was one of the first anthropologists to adopt intensive fieldwork methods, not only learning the language of the Trobriand Islanders but also gaining data through what we would today call participant observation (though his personal diaries reveal that his adoption of this method was more limited than at one time thought) (Malinowski 1967). In part the British anthropological focus on the study of behaviour arose from the fact that the cultural descriptions they sought to produce were framed by the idea that societies were systems among whose elements synchronic, functional relations could be discovered. Radcliffe-Brown believed that societies maintained themselves in equilibrium, and that each of their elements made a distinctive contribution to serving system needs. Malinowski sought to explain the features of societies in terms of their function in serving the bio-psychological needs of individual members. He treated societies as more loosely structured than Radcliffe-Brown; and where the latter regarded social norms as the key factor in explaining behaviour, Malinowski focused on how individuals use social rules to achieve their ends, and indeed deviate from those norms where it serves their purposes. While Radcliffe-Brown believed that it was possible to identify laws governing the structure and change of social systems, and advocated a comparative sociology in pursuit of this goal (see, for example, Radcliffe-Brown 1952), Malinowski's orientation was more idiographic, though still committed to a science of social life.[25]

How influential the developments in anthropology were for Chicago sociology is a matter of debate. But it is worth noting that the Chicago department was a joint sociology and anthropology department until 1929, two of its members being students of Boas.

And there is no doubt that many Chicago sociologists were familiar with developments in that field.

CONCLUSION

In this chapter I have sketched the wealth of ideas about the relationship between the methodologies of the natural and social sciences to be found in philosophy, and in the emergent social sciences in the nineteenth century. These ideas were well known among US social scientists. Many had studied in Europe, and especially in Germany. Boundaries between disciplines were not as strong then as they are today, and there was much interdisciplinary influence. As I noted a moment ago, sociology and anthropology shared the same department at Chicago until well into the century. Faris (1937) reports the close relationship among the psychology, philosophy, and sociology departments there. The historical school of economics and its debate with Menger are given a prominent place by Albion Small in his book *Origins of Sociology*, and were given similar coverage in his courses. As Bulmer has shown, relations between members of the various social science departments at Chicago were very close indeed in the 1920s and 1930s. He quotes Blumer:

> There was a considerable amount of crossing over from one
> discipline to another by both faculty people and students so
> that I had a feeling that when one comes to identify what
> might be regarded as the sources of stimulation of the period,
> one has to recognize that this stimulating milieu ... was by no
> means confined to sociology – it was in a wider context there.
> (Interview with Blumer by James Carey, 22 May 1972;
> quoted in Bulmer 1984:192)

The developments in philosophy and in the social sciences outlined in this chapter form the back-drop, then, to the Chicago sociology of the 1920s and 1930s. However, the intellectual life of the United States was also pervaded at this time by the influence of an indigenous philosophical current: pragmatism.

Chapter Two

PRAGMATISM

The most important philosophical influence on the development of Chicago sociology, and on Blumer's methodological ideas, was pragmatism. It was from pragmatism that Blumer and other Chicagoans derived many of their ideas about the character of human social life, and some of their methodological ideas too. In the list of writers to whom Blumer ascribes the development of symbolic interactionism (Blumer 1969a:1), pragmatists abound: most notably James, Dewey, Mead, and Cooley. Even late on in his life, Blumer still thought of himself as a pragmatist (Verhoeven 1980:9).

Before he arrived at Chicago, Blumer had come into contact at Missouri with an influential student of Dewey, Charles Ellwood. Ellwood was a sociologist, and his views could certainly be included under the heading of symbolic interactionism (see, for example, Ellwood 1933).[1] Of course, when he arrived at Chicago as a graduate student in 1927, Blumer came into an environment dominated by pragmatism. The philosophy department at Chicago had been a major centre in the development of pragmatist ideas, under Dewey's leadership, and its influence had been felt throughout the university. Blumer was supervised by Ellsworth Faris, a social psychologist who had studied with Dewey and Mead. The head of department at that time was Robert Park, who had been an enthusiastic student of both Dewey and James. In addition to this, along with many other students from the sociology department, Blumer attended the lectures on advanced social psychology given by George Herbert Mead. Later, he became Mead's research assistant, and completed the teaching of Mead's social psychology course when Mead became terminally ill.

In short, then, Blumer was exposed early in his intellectual career to the direct and indirect influence of pragmatist philosophers. But, over and above these local influences, it would be difficult to exaggerate the impact of pragmatist philosophy, particularly that of William James and John Dewey, on the intellectual life of the United States in the early decades of the twentieth century. James was one of the most widely known philosophers of his time, not only through his books but also through the many addresses he gave to professional and lay audiences. At this point in its development in the United States, philosophy had not yet been fully professionalized as a distinct academic discipline, not even at Harvard where James taught; and this was reflected in James's orientation and influence (Kuklick 1977).

Like James, Dewey was also enormously influential outside as well as within philosophy. This was no accident; even more than James he believed that knowledge must not be separated from practical affairs, that it gained its only justification from its contribution to the resolution of human problems. Both writers expended much effort in broadcasting their views to the public, with considerable effect.

As a philosophical movement, pragmatism was indigenous to the United States, but it drew many ideas from elsewhere. Hegelianism, historicism, and neo-Kantianism were particularly influential, but so also was British empiricism and even the positivism of Mach and Pearson. Whereas both the nature and origins of pragmatism are matters of dispute, it is generally agreed that its central ideas were developed by Charles Sanders Peirce (pronounced 'Purse'), William James, and John Dewey.

Let me begin by trying to sketch the general shape of pragmatism as a set of philosophical ideas, with the proviso that in various respects this sketch misrepresents individual pragmatists, among whom there were serious disagreements. Pragmatism is a combination of two main tendencies. On the one hand, there is the belief that experience is the starting point and the terminus for all knowledge. Most pragmatists believed that we cannot know anything beyond our experience; an idea that I referred to in the previous chapter as 'phenomenalism', and which was shared with many positivists and with Kant and the neo-Kantians.[2] Furthermore, like the historicists, the pragmatists viewed experience not as a sequence of isolated sensations but as a world of interrelated phenomena that we take for granted in everyday life. It is a shared world too, not something internal and subjective.

The other component of pragmatism is the idea that humanity must be understood as part of the natural world, and that this includes what was taken to be the most distinctively human phenomenon: rational thought. The pragmatists believed that philosophical problems can often be resolved by examining the function of thinking in humanity's adjustment to its environment; in other words by studying its function in nature. This idea derived in part from the influence of Darwin, though not all pragmatists accepted Darwin's account of evolution.

A basic ingredient of pragmatism was the psychology of the Scottish philosopher Alexander Bain, and in particular his conception of belief as a predisposition to act.[3] From the pragmatist point of view, beliefs are rules or habits implying likely courses of action under particular circumstances. As participants in everyday life, we act on the basis of a whole set of beliefs about the world that are taken for granted. Cognition – including its most developed forms, science and philosophy – arises from some interruption in the flow of action, and is concerned with resolving problems and thereby facilitating the successful resumption of courses of action. Thus, doubt arises in the context of action and existing belief, and relates to some particular feature of the world. Doubt about the existence of the world or about the very possibility of knowledge, and philosophical problems resulting from such scepticism, simply do not arise in everyday life or, for that matter, in science. As a result, they are not a legitimate matter of concern from the pragmatist point of view.

Philosophy and science develop from problems in life, then; and they are, or should be, directed towards the solution of those problems. Philosophical disagreements that make no difference to how we would act are meaningless. Like the positivists, many pragmatists took science as the archetypal form of knowledge, viewing human knowledge developmentally, as evolving to facilitate the progressive mutual adjustment of humanity and its environment. They were influenced here by Hegel, Darwin, and Spencer.

The traditional account of the origins of pragmatism is that some of its core ideas were developed by Peirce in the 1870s, in association with William James and other members of the 'Metaphysical Club' at Harvard University (Fisch 1986). Subsequently, Peirce, James, and others developed different versions of pragmatism, so much so that Peirce later coined the term 'pragmaticism' to distinguish his own views from those of others (particularly James), declaring this term to be 'ugly enough to be safe from kidnappers'.

CHARLES SANDERS PEIRCE

Peirce developed a very distinctive and complex philosophical viewpoint, drawing on many different philosophical traditions, as well as on his experience as a scientist and logician. He reacted both against the Cartesian view that knowledge can be founded on clear ideas whose truth is intuitively certain, and against the British empiricist claim that it should be based solely on sense data. While he recognized that in developing our understanding of the world we rely on that which is given to our senses, he pointed out that even for us to be able to think about such givens we must transform them into a picture of the world ordered by necessary relations. In his terms, 'firstness', the empirically given, cannot be grasped cognitively in itself. In becoming aware of it we transform it into a 'second', and in recognizing it we turn it into a 'third', an object defined in terms of certain patterns of expected behaviour. An important feature of Peirce's thought is his emphasis on the reality of universals (thirdness), both in the form of scientific laws and as everyday beliefs taking the character of habits of human behaviour.

For Peirce there was no solid foundation for our knowledge of the world. We must begin from within commonsense, we cannot avoid assumptions:

> As against Descartes, Peirce never tired of claiming that doubts based upon the logical possibility of error are not genuine doubts, and that legitimate inquiry cannot take place in the absence of genuine doubts. ... Where inquiry begins on the assumption that a proposition is doubtful if it is logically possible that it is false, then inquiry can be successful only if it terminates in the establishment of propositions so true that it is logically impossible that they be false. ... But, for Peirce, such a view of inquiry is self-defeating and effectively renders the attainment of knowledge impossible because there simply are no propositions so true that it is logically impossible for them to be false.
>
> (Almeder 1980:5-6)

Here Peirce drew on the Scottish commonsense philosophy of writers like Thomas Reid. Peirce argued that we cannot be absolutely certain of any of our knowledge,[4] but he also insisted that we cannot and do not find all of it doubtful simultaneously. We treat most of it as true until further notice; and rightly so. Peirce did not regard commonsense as arbitrary. Rather, it was the product of evolution. Evolution had, in his view, given us an intuitive tendency to produce sound hypotheses (Rescher 1978). Our ideas are corrected over time by experience. Those that work, in the sense of facilitating successful action, are retained, while those that do not are discarded. Peirce referred to his own position as 'critical commonsensism', representing an acceptance of the validity of much commonsense knowledge, but also a willingness to subject it to assessment when it became doubtful (Almeder 1980:80-97).

This process of self-correction of experience is most obvious and efficient in the case of science. And, indeed, Peirce defines truth as that opinion towards which scientific inquiry will converge in the long run; though he also retains the idea that this opinion would correspond with how the world actually is. As we shall see, subsequent pragmatists tended to abandon this correspondence element of Peirce's conception of truth. It is in this sense that Peirce remained a realist where other pragmatists were phenomenalists. At the same time, Peirce was also an idealist: while he argued that the knowledge held by an individual or finite group of people refers to something independent of itself, he seems to have believed that that independent world was composed of ideas not of matter (materialism) or of some neutral stuff (neutral monism).

Peirce regarded science as a natural outgrowth of human life. Indeed, in places he conceives of inquiry in physiological terms, as a development of the instincts for feeding and breeding (Feibleman 1960: 52-3). Doubt, the starting-point for inquiry,

> is an uneasy and irritating state which signifies the disruption of habits and paralyzes practical action, but which at the same time stimulates us to the kind of action which will bring the irritation to an end, as when the irritation of a nerve stimulates a reflex action to remove that irritation.
>
> (Skagestad 1981:31))

Inquiry is directed towards fixing belief: towards finding a stable resolution to the doubt that stimulated it.

Peirce reviews several methods of fixing belief: the methods of tenacity (sticking to a belief through thick and thin), of authority (the enforcement of beliefs within a society), of the *a priori* (reliance on arguments from first principles), and of science. He argues that science is the most effective, in the sense of producing stable belief in the long run, and that it should be adopted, even in philosophy.[5]

Peirce portrays scientific inquiry as marked by three phases. The first phase, following the identification of a genuine problem or doubt, is the generation of hypothetical explanations for the problematic phenomenon. This he calls 'abduction'. The next phase is deduction, the logical derivation of empirical implications from that hypothesis. The final stage is induction, the testing of these implications through the collection of data about new cases. In this form he advocates what has come to be called the 'hypothetico-deductive method'.

The most influential of Peirce's ideas, the one that gave pragmatism its name, is the pragmatic maxim. This was proposed as a device for clarifying the meaning of intellectual concepts, and exposing empty metaphysical ideas. It was the heart of his attempt to apply the method of science to philosophy. Peirce defines the pragmatic maxim in various ways, but the following is the version that probably captures his intentions best:

> In order to ascertain the meaning of an intellectual conception one should consider what practical consequences might conceivably result by necessity from the truth of that conception and the sum of these consequences will constitute the entire meaning of the concept.
>
> (Peirce 1934: vol. V, para. 9)

He argues that where the properties to which concepts refer do not differ in their perceptible effects, the concepts do not differ in meaning. Peirce provides as an example of definition by the pragmatic maxim the definition of relative hardness of materials in terms of their capacity to scratch one another: to say that something is hard is to say that if we attempt to scratch it by most other substances it will not be scratched.[6]

The pragmatic maxim was interpreted in a rather different way by William James. He placed it in a philosophical context that was centred not on experimental science, but on the psychology and ethics of everyday human life.

WILLIAM JAMES

William James began his career as a psychologist, concerned with the growing body of physiological research and its implications for human psychology. He was thoroughly familiar with German developments in these fields and with the philosophical controversies to which they had given rise.[7] His driving concern was the conflict between the deterministic and reductionist conception of human life to be found in the physiological and psychological literature and philosophical views that treated consciousness as a realm in its own right and human behaviour as the product of free will. James wished to abandon metaphysical dispute in favour of psychological inquiry, but he was not prepared to accept reductionism or even the psycho-physical parallelism of Wundt.

James agreed with the idealists and the neo-Kantians that the structure we find in experience is the product of the mind's structuring activity; but he argued that mind is not located in some transcendental realm, it is part of nature. Conscious experience is just as much a natural feature of the world as are physiological processes, and like them it is a product of evolution. However, it is not fixed and determined in character. He rejected any attempt to reduce human life to a pattern of sensations caused by deterministic processes. He viewed experience as partly determined and partly self-determining. What is consistent in human behaviour is the product of habits that may be reshaped at any time.

One of the key elements of James's psychology is the idea that experience is not a string of distinct sensations associated together, but is a stream that is characterized by continuity, diversity, and vagueness.[8] We experience not isolated sense data, as the positivists claimed, but a continuity of indeterminate extension. James insisted that experience is always richer than our conceptions of it; and he discounted logic, conceived as a realm of timeless thought, in favour of life, the here and now of decision and action.

> James . . . believed that the nature and scope of our feelings escape the grasp of our thought – at least in its formal patterns – that our thought ranges beyond the boundaries of what we say, and that both feelings and thoughts are incompletely or inadequately conveyed in language.
>
> (Jones 1985: 47-8)

For James the world is richer than science and rationality allow.

One of the most controversial aspects of James's thought is his treatment of the concept of truth. We saw that Peirce retained a concept of truth as correspondence between beliefs and reality as an ideal towards which scientific opinion progressively approximates, although he insists that we can never be sure that our beliefs are true. James largely abandons any element of correspondence and simultaneously moves the discussion out of the sphere of science, in which Peirce primarily locates it, into the field of everyday human behaviour. According to him, it is in that context that we must examine the function of human thought; and its function is not to copy reality but to satisfy the individual's needs and interests, to enable the achievement of satisfactory relations with her or his environment. He argues that we should not suppose that there is a single, true account of the world. Thus, our identifications of objects are always for particular purposes; no property is essential to a type of thing.

James claims that, as a matter of fact, when we judge ideas to be true or false we do not decide this merely on the basis of factual evidence but in wider terms. We take account of the likely consequences for our well-being of believing the idea to be true. Indeed, in certain circumstances we are justified in believing things for which we have little strict evidence. Thus, he argued that the truth of religious beliefs should be decided by the consequences of such belief, not on the basis of whether those beliefs 'correspond' to reality. This is not a matter of believing what serves our purposes on a particular occasion. Rather, we accept as true those ideas that work for us in a broad sense and in the long run. For James, truth is what it has proved to be generally expedient to believe.

Within this context, James regarded introspection, which was still the dominant research technique in psychology at the time, as no more unreliable than other methods, though neither was it infallible. Its products were to be judged in the same way as any other knowledge claims: according to their implications for everyday life.

For James, the pragmatic method was a device for deciding which ideas are worth taking seriously and which can be rejected. Those that make no difference to how we live our lives are metaphysical and can be dismissed. An example that James uses is the question of whether or not the world reveals God's design. He claims that we would not act differently whichever of these two beliefs we adopted.

By contrast, whether we believe in free will or determinism would make a big difference to how we act, and so this is a meaningful issue. And belief in free will is vindicated because it is essential to well-being.

Sometimes, James posits a world independent of our experience that produces, or at least places limits on, that experience. For example, he argues that while truths are inventions they are not arbitrary, because to be true they must somehow take account of reality. But he dismisses the possibility of our gaining knowledge of this reality. All distinctions – including those between real and fictional, true and false, existent and non-existent, mental and physical – occur within experience; they do not, because they cannot, relate experience to something outside of itself.

James's ideas shaped those of Dewey and Mead, particularly in portraying mind as a part of nature and beliefs as instruments for the achievement of human ends. However, much more strongly than James, these authors locate inquiry in the context of human society as a collectivity facing problems that must be overcome for its improvement. Furthermore, as for Peirce, science was for them the pre-eminent source of knowledge, though it was not fundamentally distinct in character from the more mundane problem-solving to be found in everyday life, and it was to be directed towards the solution of social problems.

JOHN DEWEY

Dewey was a Hegelian at the beginning of his intellectual career, attracted to that philosophy because of its capacity to overcome the dualisms traditional in western philosophy and theology: between mind and matter, subject and object. Antipathy to such dualisms persisted with his shift to a pragmatic or instrumentalist philosophy, under the influence of James, Peirce, and, his colleague at Michigan and Chicago, George Mead.

Dewey viewed human life as part of nature, but rejected mechanistic or materialistic accounts of it. One of his most influential early articles was a critique of the stimulus–response model of behaviour. For him the act was the basic unit of psychology, and an act was an organic unit, not a mere concatenation of stimulus and response. The starting point for analysis of action was the orientation of the organism and its receptivity to certain stimuli.

Dewey pointed out that it is only by virtue of this receptivity that an object becomes a stimulus. Moreover, the process of action involves the co-ordination of activity; even the perception of the stimulus is directed towards the achievement of the goal that governs the act. Like most other pragmatists, Dewey refused to make any attempt to address the issue of what is beyond experience. Primordially, cognition begins not from a world of objects but from a sense of a whole within which various discriminations can be made. Objects as stable and meaningful phenomena are constituted by observation and thought. This is not to say that they arise out of nothing, but it is to claim that the way they appear to us is in large part the product of our perceptual and cognitive activities, conscious and subconscious. And we can know nothing of objects independently of such activities – indeed as such they would not be objects: objects are always objects for some organism.

Like Peirce, Dewey sees inquiry as arising from problems occurring in the course of action and being directed towards the solution of those problems. However, given his phenomenalism, he rejects the idea that claims are true when they correspond to reality. As does James, he focuses on how the concept of truth is used and defines it in terms of its function. The truth of a claim is judged according to whether it helps in solving our problems. Dewey argues that the relationship between a warranted assertion and the original problematic situation is analogous to that between a key and a lock. In short, the justification of knowledge and of methods of inquiry lies in the facilitation of successful action in the world.

A central issue for Dewey was the relationship between science and life. He regarded the disparity between the development of scientific knowledge on the one hand and the state of thinking about values and moral beliefs on the other as scandalous. For him, human intelligence, of which science was the most developed form, is a product of evolution that functions to allow humanity to gain increasing control over its environment. He held that the idea that philosophy and science are contemplative in character was not only wrong but represented an obstacle to human progress. Dewey, like James, attacked this 'spectator' theory of knowledge, arguing that knowledge is an instrument used by humans to solve problems and achieve their goals, and it is only in these terms that it has value.

Dewey advocated, and sought to put into effect, the application of the scientific method of inquiry to the organization of social life, particularly in the area of education. He was responsible for the establishment of an experimental school at the University of Chicago, and he played a leading role in the spread of progressive educational ideas in the early decades of this century. Dewey interpreted policies in education and other areas as hypotheses whose validity could be tested by putting them into practice, monitoring their effects, and modifying them on the basis of the results until they proved to be effective solutions to social problems.

In his influential book *Experience and Nature*, Dewey advocated the application to philosophy of what he calls the 'empirical' or 'denotative' method. Dewey defined this method as follows: 'to settle any discussion, to still any doubt, to answer any question, we must go to some thing pointed to, denoted, and find our answer in that thing' (Dewey 1925:10). He claims that this is a doctrine of humility, but also of direction: 'it tells us to open the eyes and ears of the mind, to be sensitive to all the varied phases of life and history' (Dewey 1925:12). This method is not empirical in the narrow sense intended by positivists: the experience to which appeal is made is closer to Dilthey's life experience. Experience is the world we find ourselves in, composed of people, actions, tools, institutions, and so on, not a set of fundamental sense-data. This is not, of course, to say that the objects which our experiences refer to necessarily have the character our experience suggests. But even if they do not, Dewey insists, our experience of them was real none the less. Experiences are things we have, not things we know; even though one of the things we have is knowledge. Doubts about the validity of specific elements of this knowledge arise, but we do not have doubts about the very possibility of knowledge as such. The experience of having knowledge is given; it cannot be thought away. Hume sought to do this, but he could not live on that basis outside his study; or, strictly speaking, even within it. For all practical purposes, even Hume did not doubt that he had experience of a world in which he and others moved and acted.

It is important to note that on this interpretation experience is not subjective. The distinction between what is subjective and what objective is made within experience. In this sense the debates between phenomenalists and realists, idealists and materialists are misconceived, according to Dewey. Our world, our experience, is neither primordially objective nor subjective, neither psychic nor physical. We may distinguish between objectivity and subjectivity, and between psychic and physical elements, but such distinctions are the products of cognitive operations upon our experience, not of something lying behind it.[9]

For Dewey, then, the method to be applied in philosophy and the social sciences is that used by natural scientists. This method:

places before others a map of the road that has been travelled; they may accordingly, if they will, retravel the road to inspect the landscape for themselves. Thus the findings of one may be rectified and extended by the findings of others, with as much assurance as is humanly possible of confirmation, extension and rectification. The adoption of empirical, or denotative, method would thus procure for philosophic reflection something of that cooperative tendency toward consensus which marks inquiry in the natural sciences. The scientific investigator convinces others not by the plausibility of his definitions and the cogency of his dialectic, but by placing before them the specified course of experiences of searchings, doings and findings in consequence of which certain things have been found. His appeal is for others to traverse a similar course, so as to see how what they find corresponds with his report.

(Dewey 1925:35-6)

In *Experience and Nature* Dewey's account of scientific method has an inductivist cast, inquiry involves sensitive and intensive observation of phenomena. Elsewhere, though, Dewey places much more stress on experimental method. In *The Quest for Certainty*, he contrasts ancient science, concerned with the observation of the qualities of phenomena as they appear to the senses and the interpretation of these phenomena in terms of fixed and immutable forms, with modern science's use of experimental modification of phenomena to discover the quantitative relations that produce them. He remarks that '[science's] aim is to discover the conditions and consequences of [the *happening* of experienced things]. And this discovery can take place only by modifying the given qualitites in such ways that *relations* become manifest' (Dewey 1929:104). Such modification may involve direct manipulation or, as in the case of astronomy, change in the conditions of observation through the use of instruments. Dewey declares that 'the progress of inquiry is identical with advance in the invention and construction of physical instrumentalities for producing, registering and measuring changes' (Dewey 1929:84). In his later work *Logic: the Theory of Inquiry*, he developed this hypothetico-deductive conception of science, drawing on the work of Peirce.

When Dewey arrived at Chicago from the University of Michigan, he brought two of his colleagues with him. One of these was George Herbert Mead. Dewey's ideas had been developed in close collaboration with Mead, and this continued in their time at Chicago. Although sharing the same fundamental philosophical attitudes, however, the work of Dewey and Mead developed different focuses. Mead became a leading figure in the development of social psychology; and, in many respects, it was out of his social psychology that his wider philosophy grew.

GEORGE HERBERT MEAD

Mead studied physiological psychology and philosophy in Leipzig and Berlin, coming under the influence of Wundt and later of Dilthey. He never provided a book-length account of his views. Although he published a considerable number of articles, much of our knowledge of his ideas comes from the volumes of lecture notes published after his death.[10]

Mead sets out to offer an account 'that is descriptive of the world so far as it comes within the range of our thought' to identify 'the essential characters of the world as they enter into our experience' (Mead 1938:626). In my terms he adopted a phenomenalist position, rejecting realism (in the form of both materialism and absolute idealism) on the grounds that it posits a world beyond and independent of our experience about which we can know nothing. At the same time, Mead criticized the attempts of positivists to discount the world of everyday experience in favour of supposedly more fundamental and immediate givens. For him human experience is the world that we take for granted in our practical activities, what he referred to as 'the world that is there'. That world is objective; in other words, it is shared. Parts (and only parts) of it become subjective when a problem arises preventing us achieving our goals. The problem is overcome by reconstructing relevant parts of our knowledge in such a way as to facilitate the achievement of our goal. Once that is done, our knowledge becomes objective again.

Like other pragmatists, Mead also adopted a naturalistic view of the human mind, treating it as the product of humanity's progressive adjustment to its environment. Furthermore, he does not regard that environment as something fixed and independent of human beings: it is defined by human needs and concerns, and changed by the various ways of meeting our needs and satisfying our concerns that we develop. So, human experience and its environment constitute a reality that changes over time: it is not given independent of us nor is it fixed in character.

This creation and modification of an environment in the course of adjustment to meet needs is not unique to humanity. According to Mead, it is characteristic of all animal life. Mead became an early advocate, along with Dewey, of the functionalism suggested by James in his *Principles of Psychology* (James 1890). This represented a rejection of the concern of Wundt and other psychophysicists with the introspection of mental contents, in favour of a focus on acts, both mental and behavioural.[11] From the functionalist point of view, the act, conceived as an organic process, is basic to psychology. Like Dewey, Mead rejected the simple model of animal behaviour in which an environmental stimulus calls forth a response from the organism. What is perceived and responded to is conditioned by the act in which the animal is engaged.

While Mead viewed human behaviour in the context of nature, and thus as analogous to the behaviour of other animals in many respects, he was primarily concerned with the distinctive features of human behaviour. He took consciousness and rationality as marking off human beings from other animals. But, in line with functionalist psychology, human consciousness was to be understood as having evolved in order to facilitate action. Mead extended this point of view by treating action as social, as involving multiple participants. This focused attention on the question of how individuals co-ordinate their behaviour to engage in such joint acts. Such co-ordination is not, of course, distinctive to humanity. Some insect species display astonishing feats of social organization, and many types of animals collaborate in catching food, rearing their young, and so on. Mead argues, however, that the co-ordination of human activities often takes place in a quite different way from that in which it is achieved in other forms of life. It relies on the use of symbols, and especially language. As we shall see, his ideas about the emergence of language and its role in social life were central to his philosophy.

Mead saw human language as arising out of what he referred to as 'the conversation of gestures' among animals, whereby the initial stages of an act serve as a stimulus calling out a response from others. The snarl of one dog may elicit a snarl or flight on the part of another. Mead argues that such gestures do not simply express emotion, as Darwin had claimed, but are the primary means of communication in animals and are essential to the co-ordination of action among them. Gestures have meanings: they predict likely future behaviour. However, animals are not aware of those meanings. Mead argues that 'awareness or consciousness is not necessary to the presence of meaning in the process of social experience' (Mead 1934:77). Even among humans interaction can be meaningful without the participants being conscious of the meanings involved: 'meaning is visible in the overt behaviour of animals (including humans) whenever gestures serve as predictive stimuli that convey reliable information about the actions that are likely to follow' (Baldwin 1986:74).

What is distinctive about human communication, Mead claims, is the use of significant symbols, symbols that are employed to convey meaning with conscious intent. Of particular significance here is the fact that vocalizations can be heard by the speaker as well as the hearer. As a result, the speaker may experience the same covert response to the gesture as do others. To the extent that a vocalization produces functionally identical responses in speaker and hearer, it is a significant symbol, a universal that can be used for intentional communication.

Mead believed it to be particularly significant that in humans the capacity for language is combined with increased inhibition of response made possible by the human nervous system: the ability to suspend and thus to modify responses to stimuli. Phylogenetically, Mead traces this capacity back to the shift to an upright posture, and the consequent ability of humans to use their hands to manipulate physical objects. He distinguishes three phases of the human act: perception, manipulation (the contact experience), and consummation (the achievement of the goal to which the act was directed). The act can be suspended and reoriented on the basis of what is discovered in the manipulatory phase. Instead of being completed automatically once begun, possible responses to stimuli *and the reactions of others to these* can be played out in the imagination, and courses of action assessed and reconstructed.

The emergence of significant symbols and the inhibition of response are critical for the development of the self and thereby of mind. For Mead, the human sense of self is not a product of physiology alone, it is a social product. It is only as a result of the distinctive form of communication with others made possible by significant symbols that we begin to distinguish between self and non-self. In doing this, we view ourselves as an object by 'taking the role of the other': by adopting the perspectives of others performing other phases of joint acts in which we are all participating. What Mead means by this is not some process of telepathy whereby we enter the mind of another, nor even a form of introspection where we imagine what some unique individual other may be feeling. What is 'taken' is a universal, a publicly available, and therefore in Mead's terms an 'objective', perspective. And it is a perspective that is integral to a system of co-ordinated action.

Ontogenetically, Mead traces the development of the ability to take the role of the other through play and games. He suggests that this development of a 'self' arises initially through children's play, where the child tries out different roles and sees the acts in which he or she is engaged from different points of view. This capacity is developed further through games where roles are defined in terms of consensual rules that represent, in Mead's terms, a 'generalized other'. Here the variety of different perspectives with which the child is familiar come to be integrated to one degree or another in a single general other.

Mead argues that this creation of a group perspective from the various perspectives appropriate to particular roles is essential for the co-ordination of action. More than this, though, it is the basis for cognition, which Mead conceptualizes as a covert dialogue between what he calls the 'I' and the 'Me'. The I and the Me are phases of the self. The Me contains society, it is an organized set of attitudes, including the generalized other (though it also includes diversity and conflict). The I, on the other hand, is the response of the organism to the attitudes of others or to that of the group. Where the Me is conventional and habitual, the I introduces novelty and creativity.

As we have seen, Mead does not regard mind, or consciousness of meaning, as the basis for all communication and co-ordination of action. Indeed, much human action is carried out without such awareness: 'It needs to be emphasised that most of the time we live in a world that is simply there and to which we are so adjusted that no thinking is involved' (Mead 1934:135). Much action is subconscious. Reflective consciousness arises when an act is checked, where contact experiences do not match our expectations. Where a problem emerges the individual sets about resolving it by evaluating the initial expectations and the contact experiences to find some way of bringing them into harmony, to find a course of action that will consummate the act. Philosophy and science are the highest examples of such conscious reflection. While they are concerned with the pursuit of knowledge, their function is to provide resources for problem-solving in everyday life through the clarification of means and ends and the relationships between them (see Mead 1964:xxiii-xxiv).

Reflective consciousness introduces an element of emergence or creativity into the process of action. However, while Mead viewed mind as a distinctively human phenomenon, it was still part of nature. Indeed, Mead sees the whole of the universe as characterized by emergence rather than by rigid determinism. Within time 'what is taking place conditions that which is arising' but does not 'determine in its full reality that which emerges' (Mead 1932:16). This is because of what he calls 'sociality', the capacity of phenomena to be several things at once. The elements of nature are able to participate simultaneously in different systems. These systems are objective perspectives.[12] For example, 'a stone is simultaneously in chemical, thermal, gravitational, visual and perhaps child's play systems' (Campbell 1985:96). The appearance of human minds capable of occupying their own systems as well as those of others is 'only the culmination of that sociality which is found throughout the universe' (Mead 1932:86).

Most of Mead's work was concerned with developing the various aspects of his social psychology. Even his rare discussions of scientific method are set within this context: in many ways they are contributions to the social psychology of science rather than to scientific methodology. He says very little about the implications of his social psychology for the process of inquiry in the human sciences.[13]

Mead was not the only one to use pragmatism as a basis for the development of social theory. Another important figure who drew on pragmatism and was important for the development of Chicago sociology was Charles Cooley. Indeed, Cooley was much better known and more influential during his lifetime than was Mead.

CHARLES HORTON COOLEY

Cooley was employed at the University of Michigan as a sociologist.[14] By current standards, however, his work is as much philosophical and psychological as sociological, and he also made an important contribution to the institutional economics movement. Coser notes that he was 'more influenced by historians, psychologists, philosophers and literary men than by sociologists' (Coser 1971:322). Cooley regarded his own work as a 'sociological pragmatism' (quoted in Jandy 1942:110) and he was much influenced by William James: 'Cooley's major theoretical reference point was the work of William James. ... It was Cooley, along with Mead, who harvested the fruits of James's innovations in philosophy and psychology' (Parsons in Reiss (ed.) 1968:59; quoted in Coser 1971).

However, it would be misleading to regard Cooley as a pragmatist in any simple sense. He was a highly individualistic thinker, who had only limited contact with other academics. The most important influences on his thinking occurred through the books that he read. He was stimulated to embark on sociology by reading Spencer, though he did not accept Spencer's views. Emerson was perhaps the most lasting influence on him; and through Emerson, as well as directly, Goethe. Indeed, at one point Cooley describes Goethe as 'the perfect sociologist' (cited in Mead 1930:693). This link with German Romanticism was important for Cooley's thinking.

Cooley refused to distinguish between individual and society because for him they were mutually defining: 'A separate individual is an abstraction unknown to experience and so likewise is society when regarded as something apart from individuals' (Cooley 1922:36). For Cooley society was mental, it exists as 'the contact and reciprocal influence' of ideas (Cooley 1922:119). Thus, 'the imaginations which people have of one another are the *solid facts* of society, and ... to observe and interpret these must be a chief aim of sociology' (Cooley 1922:121).

Cooley regarded society as based upon sympathy, on the ability of each of us to share our thoughts with others through communication. Social experience involves imaginative not material contacts. My sympathies reflect my social participation, my mind is a microcosm of the groups to which I belong. Our very sense of self, of individuality, depends on social participation, and especially on language. Cooley encapsulated this in the concept of the 'looking glass self'. Summed up in Bierstedt's words, this implies that 'I am not what I think I am; I am not what you think I am; I am what I think you think I am' (Bierstedt 1981:98). On this view, the self involves three components: the imagination of our appearance to the other person, the imagination of our judgement of that appearance, and some sort of self-feeling such as pride or mortification (Cooley 1922:184). In this way one's sense of self depends on the looking glass, on the other person in whom one sees oneself reflected; and sense of self can therefore change over time and across situations. However, Cooley gave particular emphasis to primary groups in shaping selves.

For Cooley, 'sympathetic introspection' is the essential methodological basis for sociology. More than Mead and other pragmatists, Cooley draws a sharp line between our understanding of material things and of human phenomena. While he accepts that all knowledge requires sense activity, he argues that in dealing with physical things sense is sufficient, whereas in understanding people's behaviour sensations are only signs standing for the inner, complex experience of others. As signs, sensations set in motion a process of thought and sentiment that is similar to that in the person whose behaviour we are trying to understand. Whereas Mead sees understanding as based on universals, the same responses being elicited in all, Cooley sees it as a much more uncertain and subjective process:

> The question of more or less subjectivity, as among different kinds of knowledge, I take to be one of more or less agreement in the elementary perceptions. If the phenomena can be observed and described in such a way as to command the assent of all intelligent men, without regard to theory or to bias of any sort, then the factual basis of knowledge acquires that independence of particular minds that we call objectivity. A yardstick is objective because it provides an undisputed method of reaching agreement as to certain spatial relations. ... Strictly speaking, there are no yardsticks in social knowledge, no elementary perceptions of distinctively social facts that are so alike in all men, and can be so precisely communicated, that they supply an unquestionable means of description and measurement. ... [For example,] the distinctively social

phenomena connected with marriage are inward and mental, such as the affection and desire of the parties, pecuniary considerations, their plans for setting up a household, and so on. These ... can be known and communicated, but not with such precise agreement among observers as to make decisive measurement possible.

(Cooley 1926:67)

Cooley does not rule out the use of statistical method, which he takes to represent the methods of the natural sciences. He regards it as a useful complement to sympathetic understanding. But sociology cannot be turned into a natural science:

The social processes of actual life can be embraced only by a mind working at large, participating through intellect and sympathy with many currents of human force, and bringing them to an imaginative synthesis. This can hardly be done with much precision, nor done at all except by infusing technical methods with a total and creative spirit.

(Cooley 1926:78)

The possibility of understanding, and even prediction, is given by the fact that we are part of what we are studying, but their achievement also requires an element of 'genius':

The human mind participates in social processes in a way that it does not in any other processes. It is itself a sample, a phase, of those processes, and is capable, under favourable circumstances, of so far identifying itself with the general movement of a group as to achieve a remarkably just anticipation of what the group will do. Prediction of this sort is largely intuitive rather than intellectual; it is like that of the man with a genius for business as contrasted with that of the statistician; it is not science, but it is the very process by which many of the great generalizations of science have first been perceived.

(Cooley 1926: 78)

Cooley's notion of sympathetic introspection draws on the ideas of the Romantics and is similar to the concept of *Verstehen* found among the historicists. He also emphasized the importance of familiarity with the processes being observed, a theme that is central to Blumer's naturalistic method:

> Predictions of any sort ... are most likely to be sound when they
> are made by those who have the most precise familiarity with
> the observable processes, and it is the increase of this
> familiarity on the part of social observers, along with their
> greater insight into principles, that should make them better
> guessers of what is to happen than they have been in the past.
>
> (Cooley 1926:78-9)

CONCLUSION

I have presented pragmatism as a loosely associated set of ideas
centred on two key elements: a phenomenalism that treats the whole
of our experience as constituting the world, or at least as all that can
be known of the world; and a naturalism that views humanity,
including rational thinking, as part of nature, and seeks to interpret
cognitive activities in terms of their function in human life processes.
The various representatives of pragmatism I have discussed differ in
how they interpret and apply these two basic ideas, but they also
share a broad perspective on human behaviour and how we should
set about understanding it.

It is important to remember that although Peirce is now probably
the most renowned pragmatist, at least among philosophers, this was
not the case in the early decades of this century. Most of his writings
were inaccessible then, and as a result were little known and hardly
understood. Ironically, given that he seems to have invented the
term, his views are probably furthest from what 'pragmatism' is now
taken to represent. James and Dewey, by contrast, were very well
known, and their works were widely published and acclaimed; if not
always understood in the way that they wished. Their ideas were
influential for several generations of American scholars, in many
fields. And, indeed, over and above this, as we saw, several of the
Chicago sociologists had direct contacts with one or both of these
thinkers. As such their ideas represent an important part of the
intellectual resources on which the Chicagoans drew in developing
their approach to sociology.

Much the same must be said of Cooley. His books rapidly gained
the reputation of seminal contributions to American sociology, and
the kinship of his ideas with those of the pragmatist philosophers
no doubt aided their reception. Moreover, much more than the

writings of James and Dewey, they were directed towards the specific subject-matter of the emerging social sciences.

Although he wrote many articles outlining his ideas (see Reck 1964), Mead, like Peirce, never produced the extended accounts of his ideas that James, Dewey, and Cooley provided. As a result, he did not achieve a similar level of influence in his lifetime. However, unlike Peirce, Mead taught in a university most of his adult life and could thereby communicate his ideas to students. Indeed, his lectures were popular and drew large numbers of students, among them many sociologists. Blumer came into direct contact with Mead at Chicago, as well as with others who had been strongly influenced by him, notably Faris. There is no doubt that this shaped in a profound way his thinking about the nature of social life and how it should be studied. However, Blumer was not a Meadian in the sense of contributing to the development of Mead's philosophy. His project was different, and while he drew on Mead's work, he did so for particular purposes and against the background of other sources of ideas. Most important of all, though, his ideas were grounded in the sociological research that was going on around him in the Chicago department and in which he was involved. It is to a discussion of this that I now turn.

Chapter Three

CHICAGO SOCIOLOGY

In previous chapters I have examined the philosophical background to the methodological ideas prevalent among Chicago sociologists in the 1920s and 1930s. I want now to look at Chicago sociology itself. This was the immediate context in which Blumer worked. It set the framework for his conception of the purposes and nature of sociology. In fact, it seems to me that though Blumer read widely in the philosophical literature, and while many of his arguments have precursors in that literature, Chicago sociology and its fortunes in this period were the most important influences upon him.

When Blumer arrived at the University of Chicago in the early 1920s, its department of sociology was pre-eminent in the United States, maintaining that status until at least the mid-1930s. Other social science departments at Chicago were also important centres in their fields (Bulmer 1984). It was a time of expansion and high intellectual excitement.

The University of Chicago had been established in 1892 by William Rainey Harper, using money from Rockefeller and other wealthy patrons. Harper succeeded in attracting prominent figures from other universities to most of the new departments at Chicago. From the beginning, the new university was in the front rank. One of the people Harper recruited was Albion Small, who became head of what was initially called the Department of Social Science and Anthropology.

The main stimulus to the development of sociology in the United States in the late nineteenth century was the social reform movement and the liberal theology and social philosophy associated with it. They arose in the face of the social problems created by rapid industrial expansion, rampant capitalistic enterprise, urbanization, and population increase. Oberschall notes that at a time when universities were being established and expanded on a massive scale:

> the novel and amorphous discipline of sociology received the backing ... of groups in favour of reconstruction: the protestant clergy (especially its social gospel wing); the municipal reformers; the various groups and organizations active in the areas of philanthropy, charities and correction, social settlement and social work; and the backers of other Progressive causes, all of whom were seeking an academic foothold and a scientific justification.
>
> (Oberschall 1972:187-8)

At Chicago and elsewhere, there was a growing emphasis in the early decades of the century on the scientific study of social life (Fuhrman 1978). It came to be argued that only by fundamental research designed to discover the laws of social change could effective social policies be developed (see Faris 1967; Bulmer 1984; Harvey 1987). Important here were the views of Albion Small and especially of William I. Thomas. Although Small had created the sociology department and set the tone within it, he did not dominate it. He cultivated an eclectic attitude towards current American and European approaches to sociology (Faris 1967:128).[1] He also encouraged members of his department to begin research on the city of Chicago, a line of development initiated by Henderson and Thomas, and pursued vigorously by Park and Burgess and their students in the 1920s and 1930s.

WILLIAM I. THOMAS: STUDYING THE SUBJECTIVE AND THE OBJECTIVE

Thomas was largely responsible for providing the theoretical foundations for subsequent empirical research within the Chicago department.[2] He was widely read in the humanities and had studied in Germany, particularly in the emerging fields of *Volkerpsychologie* and ethnology. He was also familiar with the stirrings of US anthropology in the work of Boas. Indeed, Thomas considered himself an anthropologist in the early part of his career (Diner 1975:527). Central to his work was the concept of social control. He argued that the increasing rapidity of social change forced the need for deliberate social control by intellectual elites. He drew on the evolutionary ideas of Spencer, but tempered these with an emphasis on the creativity of individuals. This emphasis was highlighted in his concept of 'the definition of the situation', summed up in his maxim: 'If men define situations as real, they are real in their consequences' (Thomas and Thomas 1928:572). For Thomas, as for Mead, human action always contained the possibility of novelty:

> the definition of the situation is a necessary preliminary to any act of the will, for in given conditions and with a given set of attitudes an indefinite plurality of actions is possible, and one definite action can appear only if these conditions are selected, interpreted, and combined in a determined way and if a certain systematization of these attitudes is reached, so that one of them becomes predominant and subordinates the others. It happens, indeed, that a certain value imposes itself immediately and unreflectively and leads at once to action, or that an attitude as soon as it appears excludes the others and expresses itself unhesitatingly in an active process. In these cases, whose most radical examples are found in reflex and instinctive actions, the definition is already given to the individual by external conditions or by his own tendencies. But usually there is a process of reflection, after which either a ready social definition is applied or a new personal definition is worked out.
>
> (Thomas and Znaniecki 1927:68-9)

With this emphasis on definitions of the situation, Thomas challenged the instinct theory that was influential in psychology when he began his career. He developed a more social psychological approach to motivation based on what he called 'the four wishes': for new experience, security, response, and recognition.

An important aspect of Thomas's thought was the distinction between values and attitudes, values being (objective) features of society to which people adopt (subjective) attitudes. Thomas argued that human behaviour is always the product of both values and attitudes. This distinction between objective and subjective factors in the generation of human action suggests that his implicit epistemological assumptions were realist, in contrast to the phenomenalism of Mead and other pragmatists:

> We must put ourselves in the position of the subject who tries to find his way in this world, and we must remember, first of all, that the environment by which he is influenced and to

which he adapts himself is his world, not the objective world of science. ... The individual subject reacts only to his experience, and his experience is not everything that an absolutely objective observer might find in the portion of the world within the individual's reach, but only what the individual himself finds.

(Thomas and Znaniecki 1918-20/1927:1846-7)

On the basis of this largely implicit – and non-materialistic – realism, Thomas made the study of both objective and subjective aspects of social reality a central requirement in Chicago sociology. From this point of view it was essential to learn to see the world from the perspectives of those under study, but at the same time this subjective point of view was to be located within an objective, scientific account of the world.

Thomas's methodological views are exemplified in his best-known work, *The Polish Peasant in Europe and America,* written with Florian Znaniecki (Thomas and Znaniecki 1918-20). One of the central purposes of the study was to identify the causal processes underlying the adjustment of Polish immigrants to life in the United States. Thomas argued that in their initial years of settlement the Polish immigrant community experienced social disorganization; and this was the explanation, he felt, for the high rates of crime for which they had become notorious. Thomas was particularly concerned with how groups overcame disorganization and readjusted to new environments (Carey 1975).

From his conception of the nature of human social life, Thomas drew conclusions for methodology that represented a 'synthesis of the anthropologist's or ethnographer's participant observations, the case study method of the social worker, and the content analysis procedures of the traditional humanistic disciplines' (Janowitz in Thomas 1966:xxii-xxiii). At the same time, Thomas and Znaniecki also saw their work as an application of the methods of natural science to the study of the social world:

The marvellous results attained by a rational technique in the sphere of material reality invite us to apply some analogous procedure to social reality. Our success in controlling nature gives us confidence that we shall eventually be able to control the social world in the same measure. Our actual inefficiency in this line is due, not to any fundamental limitation of our reason, but simply to the historical fact that the objective attitude toward social reality is a recent acquisition.

(Thomas and Znaniecki 1927:1)

This quotation echoes Comte, and foreshadows the views of later sociological positivists like Lundberg. And, indeed, like the positivists, Thomas and Znaniecki's goal was the identification of sociological laws that captured processes of social change. However, by contrast with most positivists, they believed that personal documents, and life history material in particular, were best suited to this task because they facilitated the detailed description of social adjustment, and the subjective and objective factors involved in that process. In a famous passage Thomas and Znaniecki claim that the life history is the most perfect kind of data:

> even when we are searching for abstract laws life-records of concrete personalities have a marked superiority over any other kind of materials. We are safe in saying that personal life-records, as complete as possible, constitute the perfect type of sociological material.

(Thomas and Znaniecki 1927: 1832-3)

The methodological approach adopted in *The Polish Peasant* was inductive. A vast body of materials was collected from which the authors claimed to infer their conclusions: 'The analysis of the attitudes and characters given in notes to particular letters and in introductions to particular series contains nothing not essentially contained in the materials themselves' (Thomas and Znaniecki 1927:76). This process of induction included the search for negative cases:

> while it is only natural that a scientist in order to form a hypothesis and to give it some amount of probability has to search first of all for such experiences as may corroborate it, his hypothesis cannot be considered fully tested until he has made subsequently a systematic search for such experiences as may contradict it, and proved those contradictions to be only seeming, explicable by the interference of definite factors.

(Thomas and Znaniecki 1927:65)

However, searches for negative instances are rarely explicit in *The Polish Peasant*. Indeed, the relationship between the data and the theoretical analysis was often remote (Blumer 1939).

The Polish Peasant became an influential example of the case-study method and of the use of personal documents. In the 1920s many were searching for a scientific approach to the study of the social world which took account of what they believed to be its distinctive features, notably the role of subjective factors in human behaviour. In addition, the Methodological Note which opened the volume (in its 1927 edition) set out a number of views that were to prove influential for later Chicagoans. Faris claims that this Note weakened the influence of instinct theory and 'helped to give sociologists the courage, in defiance of the growing vogue of behaviouristic psychology, to find a place for subjective aspects of human life' (Faris 1967:18) And, certainly, the Methodological Note was a rich source of ideas, not always well-integrated, from which a variety of conclusions about method could be, and were, drawn. It not only stimulated the development of the qualitative case-study work for which Chicago is renowned but also the developing field of attitude measurement.

It would be difficult to exaggerate the influence of *The Polish Peasant* on US sociology. Its impact is symbolized by the fact that in 1937, almost twenty years after its original publication, when members of the American Sociological Society were asked to nominate the most influential sociological monograph, this book was the majority choice.[3] On the basis of this survey, Herbert Blumer was asked by the Social Science Research Council to carry out an appraisal of the book (Blumer 1939). In this appraisal, while critical of the study in some fundamental respects, Blumer endorses both the importance of understanding the attitudes or perspectives of people in explaining their actions, and the value of personal documents in achieving such understanding. It is also here that he first presents explicitly the dilemma he sees facing sociology: between understanding the subjective elements of action and applying the canons of scientific research (see Chapter 6).

Despite *The Polish Peasant*'s great influence, it is striking that the main source of data used by Thomas and Znaniecki – personal letters – was rarely used by other Chicago studies, and is very rarely used today. However, this study did stimulate the Chicagoans' use of life history materials, and their heavy reliance on written documents. The format of *The Polish Peasant* also differs somewhat from later Chicago work and from current ethnography. As the authors remark, it is 'largely documentary' in character (Thomas and Znaniecki 1927:viii). Much of the 2,224 pages of the book are occupied by several collections of letters and one substantial life history. The authors' contribution consists largely of introductions, conclusions and footnote annotations. Only one section of the book (the first half of volume 2 of the 1927 edition) approximates the format of most later Chicago studies and the pattern of ethnographic accounts as we know them today: a narrative illustrated by data inserted at relevant points; though even here it is whole documents, rather than extracts from them, that are quoted.

In what is effectively a follow-up to *The Polish Peasant*, Thomas, Park, and Miller (Park and Miller 1921) employ a wider range, but smaller amount, of documentary data: extracts from published and unpublished autobiographies, newspaper and magazine articles, published letters, academic articles and books, government publications, as well as one or two previously unpublished personal letters. The backgrounds of immigrants from a wide range of societies are described; their experiences are documented and the demoralization that often occurs reported; typologies of immigrants and of immigrant institutions are presented; and a review of immigrant communities and their influence on the adjustment of individual immigrants is provided. This book is much closer in form to later Chicago studies, consisting of a narrative structured in terms of a set of theoretical ideas about social organization and disorganization, and illustrated by data documents. It seems likely that this book, as much as *The Polish Peasant*, formed the model for subsequent Chicago research.

ROBERT PARK AND CASE STUDY RESEARCH AT CHICAGO

The most significant growth in empirical research at Chicago dates from the growing influence of Robert Park following the dismissal of Thomas in 1918.[4] Park was an ex-newspaper reporter and editor who had been trained in philosophy, coming into contact with both American pragmatists and German neo-Kantians. After studying German and philosophy at Michigan, where he developed a passion for Goethe's *Faust* as well as taking some courses with John Dewey, Park worked on newspapers in various cities, coming to advocate what he called 'scientific' or 'depth' reporting: the description of local events in a way that pointed up major social trends. This was the 'big news' that he later required his students at Chicago to capture. Subsequently becoming disillusioned with the world of newspapers, he decided to return to university, studying with William James at Harvard, and then in Germany under Simmel and Windelband. It was under the supervision of Windelband that he submitted his doctoral dissertation entitled *The Crowd and the Public* (Park 1904). It drew not only on the crowd theory of LeBon and Tarde, but also on Simmel and Durkheim; and it formed the basis for his subsequent writings on collective behaviour. On his return to the United States Park worked as secretary to Booker T. Washington at Tuskegee. Washington was head of a teaching college for black students and an influential promoter of black education. William Thomas attended a conference at Tuskegee, met Park, and invited him to become professorial fellow in the Chicago department.

In his introduction to what became known as the 'green bible' of Chicago sociology, the text that Park and his colleague Ernest Burgess wrote for their students, Park argued that up to the first decade of the century sociology had remained in a speculative stage, but that there were growing signs of its transformation into a scientific discipline concerned with empirical research (Park and Burgess 1969: ch. 1). He also drew on Windelband's distinction between nomothetic and idiographic disciplines, arguing that sociology was a nomothetic science, and therefore had as its aim the development of sociological laws: 'History ... seeks to reproduce and interpret concrete events as they actually occurred in time and space. Sociology, on the other hand, seeks to arrive at natural laws and generalizations in regard of human nature and society, irrespective of time and place' (Park and Burgess 1921:11). For Park, as for Thomas, these sociological laws were 'laws of becoming', not static laws of the kind sought by natural law theorists and many positivists.[5] However, such laws were not thought to lead to complete determinism. Park stressed the constant possibility of change:

> he approached the study of social structures with the assump-
> tion that their persistence was problematic, that one must acc-
> ount for stability by looking for patterns within change. Park
> once remarked to his class that society could be visualized as
> like a table, which was only a complex of atoms in motion; on a
> larger scale, society too was a complex of small scale processes,

which through their patterned sequence and interaction held it together through the changes forced on it by history.

(Matthews 1977:134)

While viewing science as a nomothetic discipline, Park recognized that in practice the distinction between what sociologists and historians do is not clear-cut. Sociology originated in history and anthropology, and historical and anthropological work often shades into sociology. Indeed, Matthews claims that Park's sociological approach was dualistic, seeking to combine the nomothetic and idiographic in the form of social ecology and social psychology:

> The existence of two analyzable 'orders' of social forces in the real world, the ecological order of unwilled, symbiotic interaction and the moral order of conscious meaning and willed institutions, which affected each other, meant that the student of society must employ both the analysis of consciousness and of external competitive forces. He must both explain social phenomena, in the sense of discovering the causal forces which mold them, and make them intelligible, in the sense of revealing their function for and conscious meaning to the people who live them.

(Matthews 1977:133-4)

Like Thomas, then, Park emphasized the importance of studying both objective and subjective factors affecting human behaviour.

Park's views paralleled those of Thomas in another respect too. The social world, both objective and subjective, was taken to be external to and independent of the investigator. It was a world waiting to be explored, and personal documents, such as life histories, were conceived as a direct means of access to it:

> Life histories ... nearly always illuminate some aspect of social and moral life which we may have known hitherto only indirectly, through the medium of statistics or formal statements. In one case, we are like a man in the dark looking at the outside of the house and trying to guess what is going on within. In the other, we are like a man who opens the door and walks in, and has visible before him what previously he had merely guessed at.

(Park 1929:47)

There is an implicit, and rather naive, realism here which, I shall suggest, had important consequences for the attitude to methodology adopted by the Chicagoans.[6]

In terms of social theory, Park's approach to sociology was strongly influenced by his period of study with Simmel. Park was not the first to introduce Simmel into Chicago sociology: Albion Small had translated a series of extracts from Simmel's writings for the *American Journal of Sociology* in the early 1900s. However, Park took much more from Simmel than had Small. In an unpublished autobiographical statement written in 1929 he reports: 'It was from Simmel that I finally gained a point of view for the study of the newspaper and society' (quoted in Levine 1971:1). Park drew from Simmel a concern with the forms of social interaction and with their emergence, as well as particular concepts such as 'social distance' and 'marginality'. Equally important may have been Simmel's urbane perspective on the city as a setting in which different social worlds could flourish in freedom, and which were to be studied as natural products, not subjected to either veneration or approbation.[7]

> Following Simmel, Park sees collectivities not as substantive entities but as networks of interaction. Crowds are made up of persons interacting through milling, sects through interstimulation of unrest, racial groups through the communication of shared grievances, publics through the circulation of news. Through their various processes of communication, collectivities attain some consensus regarding values and goals. Concerted action is thus the dynamic aspect of moral order and social control.
>
> (Levine 1971:liii)

For Park the study of collective behaviour was not a sociological specialism, it was the core of his social theory: he viewed social forms as arising out of collective action and as continually subject to possible transformation by it.

However, Park was eclectic in his use of Simmel. He linked the latter's concern with social forms to the idea that social control is the central problem of society, and thus to the work of Spencer, Durkheim, Sumner, and Thomas. Also, by contrast with Simmel, Park was as much concerned with the *content* of interactions as with their form. In their research, Park's students focused on concrete collectivities, looking at how they came into being, persisted, and changed, rather than treating them as instances of analytically abstracted types of social interaction.[8] This focus on the particular and concrete may well have been inherited from William James.

From Park's realist perspective, then, there was a concrete world beyond the doors of the study and the library that required investigation. This is summed up in a much cited quotation:

> You have been told to go grubbing in the library, thereby accumulating a mass of notes and a liberal coating of grime. You have been told to choose problems wherever you can find musty stacks of routine records based on trivial schedules prepared by tired bureaucrats and filled out by reluctant applicants for aid or fussy do-gooders or indifferent clerks. This is called 'getting your hands dirty in real research'. Those who thus counsel you are wise and honorable; the reasons they offer are of great value. But one thing more is needful: first-hand observation. Go and sit in the lounges of the luxury hotels and on the doorsteps of the flophouses; sit on the Gold Coast settees and on the slum shakedowns; sit in the Orchestra Hall and in the Star and Garter Burlesk. In short, gentlemen (*sic*), go get the seats of your pants dirty in real research.
>
> (quoted in McKinney 1966:71)

However, I shall suggest later that this emphasis on first-hand observation as a source of data did not in general lead to studies of the kind that we would today call 'participant observation'.

Park was committed to the science of sociology (as proclaimed in the title of the green bible) and he saw empirical research as central to that science. He argued that cities, and the city of Chicago in particular, were the sociologist's equivalent of the psychological laboratory.[9] As a newspaper reporter he had spent much time exploring cities, and writing feature articles about what he discovered for the Sunday editions.

> I found that the Sunday paper was willing to publish anything as long as it concerned the local community and was interesting. I wrote about all sorts of things and became in this way intimately acquainted with many different aspects of city life. I expect that I have actually covered more ground, tramping about in cities in different parts of the world, than any other living man.
>
> (Park 1950:viii)

Park applied much the same approach to Chicago, becoming thoroughly familiar with its different localities and insisting that his students do the same. Often he would take them on tours of relevant areas and introduce them to contacts. As we have seen, Park stressed the value of first-hand experience as against book knowledge, a contrast that was based on William James's distinction between 'acquaintance with' and 'knowledge about'. And, like James, Park felt that analysis could never exhaust experience:

It has been the dream of philosophers that theoretical and abstract science could and some day would succeed in putting into formulae and into general terms all that was significant in the concrete facts of life. It has been the tragic mistake of the so-called intellectuals, who have gained their knowledge from textbooks rather than from observation and research, to assume that science had already realized its dream. But there is no indication that science has begun to exhaust the sources or significance of concrete experience. The infinite variety of external nature and the inexhaustible wealth of personal experience have thus far defied, and no doubt will continue to defy, the industry of scientific classification, while, on the other hand, the discoveries of science are constantly making accessible to us new and larger areas of experience.

(Park and Burgess 1921:15)

There are echoes here not just of James but also of the Romantics and the historicists.

Of particular importance for Park was the fact that in modern societies experience is differentiated. He stressed that we must come to see things through other people's eyes if we are to learn about the world. Park reports the great influence that an article by William James, entitled 'On a certain blindness in human beings', had on him. James had read it to the class when Park was a student. In this article, James stresses the communality of all human beings, and indeed of all nature. At the same time, he recognizes that:

Each is bound to feel intensely the importance of his own duties and the significance of the situations that call these forth. But this feeling is in each of us a vital secret, for sympathy with which we vainly look to others. The others are too much absorbed in their own vital secrets to take an interest in ours. Hence the stupidity and injustice of our opinions, so far as they deal with the significance of alien lives.

(James 1899:113)

Unless we are prepared to try to understand others' 'secrets' we will not be able to understand their lives. Park comments on James's article:

The universe was not for him a closed system and every individual man, having his own peculiar experience, had some insight into the world that no other mind could have. The real world was the experience of actual men and women and not abbreviated and shorthand descriptions of it that we call knowledge.

(Park in Baker 1973:255)

Like James, then, Park stressed the variety and value of human experience. More than James, though, perhaps as a result of the influence of Dewey and Mead, he saw this experience as a social phenomenon. An important task of sociological research for Park was to gather, preserve, and represent the experiences of participants in city life.

What Park advocated, however, was not simply the collection of facts, even of facts about people's experience. He criticized earlier social investigations modelled on Booth's study of London, such as the Pittsburgh survey (Bulmer 1984:66-7), for lacking the necessary theoretical analysis. In several articles, notably 'The City: suggestions for the investigation of human behavior in urban areas' (Park 1952), Park elaborated a theoretical framework for the pursuit of research on Chicago by his students. He argued that the city should be viewed in much the same way that ecologists study plants and animals. He viewed Chicago, and large cities in general, as displaying a variety of natural areas, each located in a particular part of the city, and having a characteristic culture. These areas tended to retain their character and position despite changes in the population that occupied them, such as changes in ethnic composition. Park advocated the investigation of these natural areas and of the cultures associated with them, not simply as a descriptive exercise but rather as a series of case studies exemplifying basic sociological processes.

However, although Park made considerable use of the concepts of ecology, this theoretical framework was only loosely formulated. Matthews comments that even Park's later essays:

tend to offer a relatively modest use of specifically ecological concepts to provide a very loose and general theoretical crust over a mass of data and interpretation from political economy and contemporary applied work in urban geography, land values, and descriptive sociology, the latter often the work of Park's own students. ... Park's loose usage (of terms like 'succession' and 'natural area') often remained at the level of dramatic metaphor rather than closely articulated theory.

(Matthews 1977:237)

The Chicago studies were not designed to test this theoretical framework, at least not in a direct way. Rather, that framework served as a map whose details were to be filled in by empirical research.[10]

While sociological research at Chicago was often focused on what were publicly recognized as social problems – race riots, crime, delinquency, and so on – Chicago sociologists were not simply social reformers for whom social research was a means to an end. Not only were they strongly committed to a science of social life, but they often expressed a genuine delight in the diversity and 'colour' of city life. In many ways their work was a celebration of the city. In Matza's (1969) terms, they adopted an 'appreciative' stance. And, to some degree, this urbane view of the world represented a challenge to reformism. It was associated with a belief in the capacity of people, even those believed to be most deprived and backward, to organize their own lives.

Like Thomas, Park believed that the increased pace of social change that the United States was witnessing required increased social control. However, he was more pessimistic than Thomas about the possibility of this, and did not see it as arising from intellectual or political elites. It had to come from mass communication among a democratic public (see Fisher and Strauss 1978a). Among some Chicago sociologists at least, including Park, there was a distaste for 'do-gooding' and for those who wished to solve social problems by organizing people's lives for them, especially if this was done without first finding out how people lived and why they acted as they did (Matthews 1977; Bulmer 1984; Harvey 1987).[11]

While Park stressed the value of first-hand knowledge – that of both informants and the researcher – attitudes to methodology in the Chicago department were catholic. Students were also encouraged to use official documents, including statistical data, as well as to develop spot maps detailing the distribution of various types of social phenomena across the city. And following the arrival of Ogburn in 1927, statistical research gained a high profile in the department.

The central concerns of the Chicago department were the pursuit of research and the training of graduate students. These two activities were carried on simultaneously: the students were treated as fellow researchers, and expected to produce valuable research findings. The level of commitment expected, and given, was high. In the 1920s and 1930s Chicago sociology faculty and students produced a large number of monographs presenting the fruits of their research; most, though not all, of it carried out in the city of Chicago (Anderson 1923; Thrasher 1927; Mowrer 1927; Cavan 1928; Wirth 1928; Landesco 1929; Zorbaugh 1929; Shaw 1930; Shaw and Mackay 1931; Frazier 1931; Cressey 1932; Young 1932; Reckless 1933; Hayner 1936).

EXAMPLES OF CHICAGO CASE STUDIES

A characteristic example of the Chicago research of the 1920s and 1930s is Zorbaugh's *The Gold Coast and the Slum* (Zorbaugh 1929). Effectively this book is an account of a journey through Chicago's North Side, revealing the contrasting social worlds to be found there. There is the 'Goldcoast', abutting the banks of Lake Michigan, where the 'high society' of Chicago is to be found, and Zorbaugh provides an analysis of the 'status games' played by its inhabitants. There is the rooming-house area, characterized by mobility, isolation, loneliness, and suicide. Towertown is the bohemian quarter of Chicago, adjoining the red light district of cabarets and dance halls where bootlegged liquor is sold. Finally, there is the slum, successively occupied by waves of European immigrants from different countries, and later by Southern blacks. The rooming-house district and slum, in particular, are areas where the traditional mores and controls have broken down, and where the inhabitants adjust to their circumstances in ways that cut them off still further from, and bring them into conflict with, the rest of society. These are the major sites of social disorganization.

In presenting sketches of the different social worlds bordering on one another in this area of Chicago, Zorbaugh draws explicitly on various kinds of data: public records and statistics; interviews with people who know the areas well; relevant published accounts such as books and magazine articles, fictional and biographical; public reports; social work case records; extracts from diaries and calendars; and life history documents provided by inhabitants. However, reading this book against the background of familiarity with contemporary ethnographic accounts, one is struck by two features. First, the minor role played by what have become the staples of ethnographic methodology today: semi-structured interviewing and participant observation. The second notable feature, of rather more importance, is the relative lack of attention paid to methodological issues.[12] These features are general to Chicago research, and I shall discuss each of them in turn.

Types of data used

Chicago research of the 1920s and 1930s is often regarded as providing the original model for modern participant observation studies. This is misleading. Like most Chicago studies, *The Goldcoast and the Slum* relies heavily on documents that were already published or that were available from agencies of various kinds. Although ethnographers today make some use of such documents, they rarely do so on the same scale.[13] Zorbaugh also employs personal documents elicited from inhabitants of the different areas. For the most part these seem to have been obtained in written form. This again contrasts with contemporary ethnography, where the elicitation of written documents from participants is unusual, except in the form of diaries. Furthermore, while Zorbaugh probably collected much information through informal conversations with inhabitants, these are rarely reported as data. In fact, the only interview data explicitly presented in Zorbaugh's book arises from his discussions with a Chicago local historian. This also illustrates the fact that, where interviews are used by Chicagoans, they are as often with experts of one kind or another as with participants.

The term 'participant observation' was not used by the Chicagoans, and when it was introduced in 1924 it had a different meaning from that common today. It referred to someone who was already part of the situation being studied whom the researcher employed to obtain descriptions of events (Lindeman 1924). This method, and the more modern version of the researcher herself or himself adopting the role of an observational participant, seem to have had only a marginal role in Chicago research. While Zorbaugh no doubt spent a considerable amount of time on the streets of the North Side, his observations are rarely explicitly reported as data. Furthermore, there is little evidence that he negotiated access to any of the institutions or groups he mentions, or even infiltrated them, to observe social interaction there more closely.

There are few explicit examples of participant observation in the Chicago studies. Only in the work of Cressey and Anderson does something like modern participant observation seem to have played an important role.

Cressey (1983) notes that, in eliciting documents or carrying out interviews, the role adopted by Chicagoans was generally that of what he calls 'the sociological stranger'. Here the researcher presents herself or himself as a professional, analogous or even equivalent to a doctor or social worker, an 'expert' requiring information and perhaps also offering help. Cressey's own work on taxi dance halls was an exception to this tendency, making considerable use of informal conversations with taxi dancers and their patrons, and carried out by Cressey and others masquerading as dancers or patrons.[14] Even here, though, while Cressey begins his book with a description of 'a night at a taxi dance hall', most of the evidence explicitly employed in the book is the traditional 'documentary' data used by Chicago studies. And the informal participation in the halls seems to have been used primarily to get access to the accounts of participants, rather than to provide the basis for the observer's own descriptions.

Another example of Chicago research approximating to, but not quite matching, modern participant observation is Nels Anderson's study *The Hobo*. In her book *Scientific Social Surveys and Research* Pauline Young, a fellow Chicago graduate, describes Anderson as:

> an intimate participant observer of the life of the hobo on the road, in the 'jungle', in lodging houses, at Hobohemia, at work and at Hobo College in Chicago. He identified himself with the life of the hobo for an extended period and gained insight into the inner life which would have been almost impossible had he not been able to eliminate social and mental distances through intimate participation.
>
> (Young 1939:203)

Anderson accepts the description, but qualifies it:

> I think that at that time that neither she nor I had ever heard

the term 'participant observation', yet at Chicago that type of research was gaining a vogue. While this method was faithfully followed in my work, it was not in the usual sense of the term. I did not descend into the pit, assume a role there, and later ascend to brush off the dust. I was in the process of moving out of the hobo world.

(Anderson 1975:xiii)

Indeed, it seems that the fact that Anderson lived in the hobo area of Chicago while collecting the data for his study was the result of a mistake, not part of the research design: 'Because of my failure to put a higher estimate of the cost of living in my proposal for the study I was forced to take a room in a working man's hotel in Hobohemia where I slept and worked' (Anderson 1983:403).

Anderson's father had been a migratory worker, and Anderson himself had adopted a similar life before being persuaded by an employer to resume his education, and subsequently coming to Chicago to study sociology. Much of the account of Hobohemia and the life of the hobo that Anderson provides takes the form of generalized description that is clearly based on his own past experience and knowledge. The data that are provided, however, as with other Chicago studies, mostly take the form of extracts from written documents or interviews with hobos themselves and others involved with their lives, as well as public documents of various kinds. Furthermore, the two or three examples of data Anderson cites that are the product of his participant observation are presented as documents, and are treated no differently from documents of other kinds.

The data cited by the early Chicagoans, then, are predominantly the accounts of others, both experts and participants, usually in written form, extant and elicited: there is little emphasis on descriptions produced by researchers themselves in the role of participant observers.

Neglect of methodological issues

What is also surprising about the Chicago research is the relative absence of methodological discussion about the use of different kinds of data and the problems of interpreting them. Many types of data are presented in the same form as 'documents'. This emphasis on documentation probably arose from two models: historical research and natural science. In his *Origins of Sociology*, Albion Small underlines the importance of documentation in the work of Ranke and the historical school, and Thomas probably acquired a similar orientation through his training in the humanities. In her book *Field Studies in Sociology*, one of the earliest research methods texts, designed as a codification of good Chicago practice, Vivien Palmer mentions the historical model but also stresses the analogy with natural science. She remarks: 'Undoubtedly one mark of the development of sociology as a science will be the compilation of generally understood research documents which approximate scientific records in exactness and conciseness' (Palmer 1928:193). Indeed, Palmer argues that, because of the exploratory nature of sociological research, documentation should be more detailed than it is in the physical sciences. She outlines the following prerequisites of a document:

1) Uniformity, in order that the documents can be compared quickly and accurately, and in order that they may be readily classified.

2) The statement of facts concerning the informant and the conditions under which the document was secured in order that anyone can critically evaluate it.

3) A full, accurate account of the findings.

4) The investigator's own criticism of the document.

(Palmer 1928:193)

It is ironic, then, that in general the Chicagoans provide little information about how their research was carried out or about the data used. Zorbaugh gives virtually no information. Anderson simply lists the documents, giving a brief description of each. Cressey wrote an informative article about his research methods, but it was not published at the time (Cressey 1983). As Platt comments: 'when we look at the Chicago studies, it seems clear that: ... it was regarded as relatively unimportant who obtained the material, whether it was originally oral or written, and whether it reported specific incidents or generalizations'. What seems to have been taken as of overriding significance is that the documents have 'objective existence' in written form (Platt 1987:3). She continues:

Descriptions such as 'manuscript' or 'record of an investigator',

> with no indication of how the record or manuscript was obtained, recur in footnotes. . . . [Furthermore,] 'Document' can include anything from a quotation from an academic source to an extract from participant observation field notes.
>
> (Platt 1987:3)

Another respect in which the Chicagoans' use of data departs from the requirements laid down by Palmer concerns the researcher's methodological assessment of documents. She emphasizes this, appealing to the model of criticism laid down by the historians Langlois and Seignobos (1898). However, the Chicago studies rarely provide any explicit methodological assessment of the data used. The mode of presentation employed is realistic, or naturalistic, description. The process by which the account has been constructed remains largely hidden.[15]

A partial exception is Shaw's life history of Stanley, a 'jack roller' or mugger. He reports that his book (Shaw 1930) was the product of six years' involvement with Stanley, the latter being one of a large sample of 'repeated male offenders' on parole from correctional institutions that Shaw became involved with in his role as a residential settlement house worker. Shaw provides considerable background information about Stanley, derived from social work, medical, legal, and police records as well as 'a rather intensive study of his behaviour and social background and ... a somewhat intensive program of social treatment' (Shaw 1930:1). The life history was produced through an initial, stenographically recorded interview in which the main points in Stanley's career as a delinquent were identified, and then several drafts written by Stanley, stimulated by examples of the level of detail required provided by Shaw on the basis of material supplied in interview. In addition, factual claims made in the autobiography were checked where possible against official records. Shaw assures his readers that 'aside from a number of corrections in punctuation, the story is presented precisely as it was written by the boy' (Shaw 1930: 47).

Also included in *The Jack Roller* is an assessment of its methodological status by Burgess. This reflects the latter's concern to develop case study method as a scientific approach to the study of the social world. Burgess emphasizes that case study and statistical methods have different but complementary features, and he seeks to counter the criticisms that were often directed at case studies: that they were subjective and unrepresentative.

For the most part within Chicago, however, limited attention seems to have been given to methodology. This may have stemmed, in part, from Park's realism, his assumption that the social world was simply out there, waiting to be discovered.[16] What was required was to go out into the world and capitalize on others' and one's own experience. Matthews (1977:179) reports that Park's implicit definition of science 'seems to have been adequate explanation of external reality through direct observation and then classification within a set of interrelated concepts' and the adequacy of explanation 'would be measured subjectively, not through a very explicit and precise method of inference and verification'. And he quotes Park as follows:

> The question of methods of investigation is important, but it is distinctly secondary. I think we should assume that we can study anything in regard to which we need knowledge. It is important that we employ the best methods such as they are. ... If we succeed in getting a more accurate, objective, intelligible statement about the matter than anyone else, we may count the results of our investigations as science. Science is not a ceremonial matter, as some reverent souls seem to think.
>
> (Park quoted in Matthews 1977:179)

This attitude probably reflects Park's view of the role of the sociologist as 'merely a more accurate, responsible, and scientific reporter' (quoted in Bulmer 1984:91).

BLUMER'S EMPIRICAL WORK

One of the most substantial pieces of research carried out by the Chicagoans, now largely forgotten, is the study of the effects of films on audiences, and especially on young people, carried out by Herbert Blumer and Philip Hauser.

Blumer had been educated at the University of Missouri, where he subsequently became an instructor in sociology from 1922 to 1925. Simultaneously, he played professional football, notably for the Chicago Cardinals. He enrolled as a graduate student in the Department of Sociology at Chicago when he was on leave from Missouri, after resisting pressure to resign following Ku Klux Klan criticism of a lecture he had given. At Chicago he was supervised by

Ellsworth Faris and also worked with Robert Park. His PhD research was concerned with the methodological foundations of social psychology and was completed in 1928. In the same year, the Motion Picture Research Council invited a group of psychologists, sociologists, and educators to discuss research into the effects of films on children. Blumer was among those invited.

At this time the movies were a relatively new and extremely popular form of entertainment, and there was much public discussion about their effects on the younger generation. One of the most popular genres was the gangster film, and there was particular concern about whether such films caused delinquency, and crime generally. Funds were raised, a committee established, and a series of research projects initiated. Blumer was involved in the production of two books in the series sponsored by the funds, one written with Philip Hauser on *Movies, Delinquency and Crime*, the other, by Blumer alone, entitled *Movies and Conduct* (Blumer and Hauser 1933; Blumer 1933). Some other Chicago sociologists, notably Cressey and Thrasher, were also involved in this series of publications.

In the first of these two books, Blumer and Hauser were specifically concerned with the extent to which the movies encouraged delinquency and crime. They note that a wide range of factors are probably involved in the generation of delinquent and criminal acts. The question was whether the viewing of motion pictures contributed to this process, and if so what role it played. The main data used were life histories and short essays focused on the experience of movies written by inmates of various penal institutions, ex-convicts, and schoolchildren. These data sources were supplemented by interview and questionnaire responses.

The authors focus their attention on those cases where, on the basis of informants' accounts, films did seem to have played a role in generating delinquency or crime. They investigated the variety of ways in which this can occur: through giving an appetite for an expensive life-style, providing a legitimating model for deviant behaviour, or in furnishing techniques for pursuing criminal activities. Blumer and Hauser's conclusion is that films can be a powerful influence on children, but that they 'may exert influences in diametrically opposed directions .... Movies may create attitudes favorable to crime and the criminal or unfavorable to them' (Blumer and Hauser 1933:201). They suggest that:

two conditions determine the nature and direction of the

effects of motion pictures on the behavior of a given person: first, the diversity and wide range of themes depicted on the screen; and second, the social milieu, the attitudes and interests of the observer.

(Blumer and Hauser 1933: 201-2).

The authors claim that the influence of films is particularly strong in socially disorganized areas, where sources of social control such as the family, school, and church are weak: 'The child in the high-rate delinquency area tends to be sensitized and the child in the low-rate delinquency area immunized to delinquent and criminal attitudes depicted on the screen' (Blumer and Hauser 1933:202).

In his other book on the effects of films, *Movies and Conduct,* Blumer adopts a wider focus and uses a broader range of data. He examines the use of the experience of films in children's play, the imitation of characters in films by adolescents, the effects of films on day-dreaming, and the impact of films on perceptions of other ethnic groups, on ideas about the relations between the sexes and between children and parents, and on children's ambitions. The data used in the first study were supplemented with further life histories, interviews, and questionnaire responses, this time primarily from college and high school students. In addition, use was made of observers' reports of conversations about films and of children's play.

Blumer shows that in a substantial proportion of cases films did seem to influence children's behaviour, though he makes clear that the long-term effects of this influence are difficult to assess. He notes that the impact of films may be particularly great on adolescents because they are in the process of adapting to membership of the adult world. Once again, he argues that the influence of films may run counter to that of other educational institutions, and that the influence is likely to be particularly great in 'disorganized city areas' (Blumer 1933: 198). Blumer believes that the effect of films is likely to be the acquisition of 'a disconnected assemblage of ideas, feelings, vagaries and impulses' (Blumer 1933: 199), rather than a clear and consistent message. And he shows that the same film can be interpreted quite differently, and can therefore have diverse effects. The responses of the audience members will depend on their prior attitudes and backgrounds, and on the role of the groups to which they belong in discussing and making sense of what has been seen.

Blumer presents his research on the effects of films as

exploratory. He set out to find out whether, and if so how, films affect people's lives. In the process the concept of 'movie effects' was developed and refined by examining the different ways in which films can influence people. Also, theoretical ideas about the conditions under which films may have maximum impact were stimulated, drawing on ideas common among Chicago sociologists and derived largely from Thomas. However, there was no direct attempt to test ideas about the effects of films. In an interview with Jennifer Platt many years later, Blumer himself describes the study as 'exceedingly underdeveloped', it was not 'a definitive analytical effort in the sense of separating out the motion picture influence as over against other kinds of influence' (Platt 1982: lines 41 and 47-9).

The data used in this research were mainly qualitative in character, and took the form, for the most part, of people's accounts of how they had been affected by films. The data were mostly elicited by the researchers, usually in written form, and were generally relatively unstructured in character; though Blumer does provide counts of the different types of response where he judges this to be appropriate. Most of the data used for illustrative purposes come from the written life histories.

Blumer's research on the movies stands very much in the tradition of the Chicago research of the 1920s and 1930s. Its emphasis is on the need to capture the attitudes or perspectives which mediate the effects of objective factors, in this case of films. It also displays the characteristic Chicago concern with how people adapt in different ways to the same type of stimulus, and with the role of social organization and disorganization in this. Its heavy reliance on elicited written documents and its limited use of participant observation also matches other Chicago studies. Furthermore, once again there is relatively little information about how the research was done, and explicit methodological assessment of data is rare.

This research on the cinema was the major empirical research project that Blumer worked on. His later writings, apart from those devoted to metatheory and methodology, were, for the most part, theoretical discussions not tied directly to specific empirical research.[17]

CONCLUSION

There is a tendency in the sociological literature to see Chicago sociology as predominantly symbolic interactionist and qualitative in character. While these descriptions capture some aspects of the Chicago studies, they neglect the theoretical and methodological diversity within the department, and the eclectic attitude adopted towards theory and methodology of most of those associated with it (Bulmer 1984; Harvey 1987).

Although symbolic interactionism was not recognized as a distinctive tradition at this time, and was not the only theoretical current flowing through the Chicago department, the ideas represented by that term were an important component of the thinking of Chicago sociologists. They tended to be identified with social psychology *per se*, and social psychology was given a prominent role. Matthews (1977:98) reports Park declaring that 'all sociology is social psychology'. However, this is not to say that Chicago social psychology was distinctively Meadian in character; in fact it seems to have been a blend of ideas derived from James, Dewey, Cooley, Mead, and Thomas. Furthermore, initially, to the extent that Chicago social psychology was regarded as a theoretical paradigm to be contrasted with others, the contrast was with instinct theory and other forms of biological reductionism (varieties of materialism) and with the experimental introspectionist psychology of Wundt and others. Initially, Chicago social psychology was allied with behaviourism in its opposition to these trends. It was only later, with the growing influence of behaviourism, that Chicago-style social psychology came to be regarded as anti-behaviourist. Blumer's invention of the term 'symbolic interactionism' in 1937 probably reflects this changing situation.

The idea that the Chicagoans were committed to qualitative sociology is probably even more misleading. Certainly, many Chicago studies made only limited use of quantitative data, and even less use of statistical analysis, but quantitative and qualitative data were generally regarded by Chicagoans as complementary (Harvey 1987). The work of some of the Chicagoans, such as Burgess and Shaw, exemplified this. Park was somewhat distrustful of statistical techniques, but nevertheless he encouraged students to use quantitative data where available and relevant; and even to develop measurement scales, as in the case of Bogardus's social distance scale (Bogardus 1933). Moreover, even before the arrival of Ogburn in 1929, Burgess had already developed and applied basic statistical techniques in the analysis of the geographical distribution of various kinds of social phenomena in the city of Chicago, as well as in preliminary attempts to identify the causes of delinquency and to develop attitude scales for the prediction of parole violators. Ogburn was brought to Chicago on the basis of general agreement that the department needed strengthening in the statistical area so that it did not lag behind other centres. Once there, he provided a competing pole of attraction to Park, strongly influencing many graduate students, notably Stouffer and Hauser.[18]

The growth of quantitative research in the department following Ogburn's arrival led to an explicit methodological conflict about the relative merits of case study and statistical methods. This was part of a wider debate in US sociology in the 1920s and early 1930s. A growing number of sociologists advocated statistics as the key to scientific progress in sociology, notably Giddings, Chapin, Ogburn, Lundberg, and Stouffer. Furthermore, some adopted an explicitly positivistic attitude condemning case study work as pseudo-scientific, or at best pre-scientific (Lundberg 1929). It is in the context of this emerging debate, examined in the next chapter, that Blumer's methodological writings arose.

Chapter Four

CASE STUDY VERSUS STATISTICS: THE RISE OF SOCIOLOGICAL POSITIVISM

From the 1920s onwards, there was increasing debate within US sociology about the role of what were then regarded as the two main social research methods: case study and statistics. As we saw, this debate took place both within the Chicago department and outside. At times it became intense. For some the issue involved, in today's parlance, a choice between competing paradigms, only one of which was scientific. For others, it was a matter of different methods with characteristic strengths and weaknesses that suited different research problems. There is no doubt, however, that by the 1950s, broadly speaking, quantitative methods, in the form of survey research, had become the dominant sociological approach and that case study had become a minority practice (Platt 1986).

The meanings of the terms 'statistical method', 'survey research', and 'case study' were not well defined in the debates that took place, in part because the ideas and techniques referred to were in the process of development. The term 'social survey' underwent a quite dramatic change of meaning over the course of the first half of the present century. At the beginning it referred to a descriptive study of an area geared to the identification, diagnosis, and remedying of social problems, with Booth's study of London representing an influential model. By the 1940s, however, the term had largely acquired the principal meaning it has today: a study relying on the analysis of interview or questionnaire responses from a large number of people. The meaning of 'statistics' has been more stable, but remains ambiguous. It can refer to information in numerical form, such as the numbers of people convicted of various crimes or the average income of families in a given area. Equally, though, it may refer to the range of techniques, descriptive and inferential, that have been developed to deal with such data. Finally, it can refer to the discipline that is concerned with developing such techniques and the mathematical theories underlying them.

Within US sociology, as elsewhere, statistical method developed initially around the collection and interpretation of official statistics of various kinds.[1] Much of Ogburn's research, for example, was concerned with the analysis of available demographic, economic, and political data. Burgess's quantitative work in the 1920s and 1930s, arising out of his interest in the early social surveys, was centred on the use and improvement of census data. These data provided the basis for the identification of natural areas in Chicago.

The concept of the case study seems to have arisen from a number of sources: the clinical methods of doctors; the case-work technique being developed by social workers; the methods of historians and anthropologists, plus the qualitative descriptions provided by primarily quantitative researchers like LePlay; and in the case of Park at least, the techniques of newspaper reporters and novelists were influential. The diversity of models perhaps explains the variety of conception and practice to be found among advocates of case study.

In essence, the term 'case study' referred to the collection and presentation of detailed, relatively unstructured information from a range of sources about a particular individual, group, or institution, usually including the accounts of subjects themselves.[2] The Chicago studies I discussed in the previous chapter, both community studies and life histories, were generally regarded as falling into this category, even though they sometimes made use of statistical data.

Advocates of case study pointed out that such studies produced much more detailed information about a case than that available about each instance in a statistical aggregate. This was essential, they suggested, for us to understand human behaviour. Understanding a human activity requires that we look at its development over time *and* at its environment, at the configuration of social factors that make up the situation in which it occurs, and the way in which these factors interact. It was argued that the case study was ideally suited to facilitate this understanding; as, for example, in the study of delinquency:

> The detailed case, particularly the life-history document, reveals the process or sequence of events in which the individual factors and the particular social environment to which the

child has been responsive have united in conditioning the
habits, attitudes, personality, and behavior trends.

(Shaw 1931:150)

It was also claimed that, whereas the statistical method might be able
to deal with situations where behaviour had become routinized, so
that it was essentially standardized and repetitive, that method was
not adequate to deal with creativity and innovation. Cooley, for
example, remarks that:

> no exact science could have foreseen the sudden rise of the
> automobile industry and the genius of Henry Ford, although
> now that this industry is developed and institutionalized we
> may perhaps calculate with some precision what it will bring
> forth in the near future.

(Cooley 1926: 75)

Another important argument in support of the case study was
that, unlike the statistical method, it was able to document the
subjective side of action, which many, and not just Chicagoans,
regarded as essential to the explanation of human behaviour. In an
influential paper on 'Case study and statistics', Burgess suggests that
'quantitative methods deal in the main with the cruder, more
external aspects of human behavior, and ... some other more
sympathetic and discerning method is necessary to probe beneath
the surface and to depict and analyze the inner life of the person'
(Burgess 1927:112). To underline the point he asks:

> How can attitudes, the basic subject matter of human nature
> and society, be stated numerically? How can the so-called
> intangible facts of life, its qualitative aspects, be apprehended
> by so crude an instrument as statistics? What figures will
> measure the degree of affection between husband and wife, or
> the nature and intensity of a father's pride in his children, or
> qualities of personality like charm, loyalty, and leadership?

(Burgess 1927:111-12)[3]

Thrasher provides a concrete illustration, and summation, of
these arguments in favour of case study:

> To study a delinquent as a mere individual ..., as if he could
> have developed in a social vacuum, is to get a very imperfect
> picture of him. The delinquent must be studied as a person ....
> His sentiments and attitudes ... are most intimately related to

94

the social complexes or configurations which have co-operated with other factors to create his personality. ... What is defined by the gang as devilish good sport and adventure ... may be defined by the larger society as serious delinquency. There are two distinct social worlds here that must be considered if any real insight into the problem is to be achieved. The real meaning of the delinquent or his behavior, therefore, can only be understood in its *gestalt* or its social configuration.

(Thrasher 1927b:143; quoted in Burgess 1927:116-17)

As we saw, in general the Chicagoans did not reject statistics, and made some use of statistical analysis even in the 1920s. Indeed, Burgess argued that the two methods were complementary. Statistical method provided the basis for the identification of typical cases to be studied in depth, and for subsequent generalization of findings. This approach was applied by Burgess in his own work, and by his student Clifford Shaw. Furthermore, most advocates of statistical method did not deny the value of case studies. Giddings (1924), an early champion of the use of statistics in sociology, distinguishes between statistical and case-study methods on the basis that the former are concerned with the distribution of a particular trait, or a small number of traits, in a population, whereas the case study is concerned with the whole variety of traits to be found in a particular instance. He emphasizes the role of historical criticism in the case study, though also the advantages of applying quantification and statistical analysis here too. Giddings argues that both methods are important, and that both are scientific. These views, that the difference between the two methods is a matter of focus, and that case study should itself become statistical, were to prove influential (Cavan, Hauser, and Stouffer 1930; Stouffer and Lazarsfeld 1937; Lazarsfeld and Robinson 1940).

In general, however, whatever value they ascribed to case study in its existing form, the advocates of statistical method regarded the latter as the ideal basis for the study of the social world. For them, quantification was an essential requirement of science. Ogburn, for example, declares that 'a body of knowledge ought not to be called a science until it can be measured', and while he notes that 'not all measurement is statistics', he none the less insists that 'Of all the methods in sociology, statistics has the highest scientific value' (Ogburn 1927:379 and 380). In supporting this point of view, he declares that in the future every sociologist will be a statistician and that the field of statistics will disappear because 'it will be almost universal, not only in sociology and economics, but perhaps in social psychology and politics too' (Ogburn 1930:6). Ogburn drew a sharp distinction between 'knowledge' and 'understanding':

> Knowledge and understanding are at opposite ends of a continuous distribution. ... The tests of knowledge are reliability and accuracy, not understanding .... A person, untrained scientifically, may live for a long time among other people and come to have a pretty good understanding of them; yet he would scarcely be called a scientist. His understanding would not be of that accurate, systematic, transferable kind called science.
>
> (Ogburn 1932:5)

Ogburn argued that not all of the topics dealt with by sociology were currently amenable to a statistical approach, but that in those where this had been applied 'we certainly know much more about the structure and functioning of society' (Ogburn 1927:390).[4]

In the 1930s and 1940s, some of the advocates of statistical method came to adopt an even more extreme position than Ogburn. They argued that it should be applied across the board to all areas of sociology, and that failure to do so simply represented the attachment of sociologists to outdated philosophies.

THE ARGUMENTS OF THE SOCIOLOGICAL POSITIVISTS

An important stimulus to the growing influence of quantitative methods in sociology from the 1930s onwards was the rise to prominence of positivist ideas in physics, philosophy, and psychology.

In physics Einstein's special theory of relativity had a tremendous impact, not only on physicists' views of the universe, but also on their ideas about their own subject. Einstein's theory overturned elements of Newtonianism, such as the concepts of absolute space and time, that had been taken for granted by many as proven beyond doubt. A common response was to reject theoretical concepts that refer to unobservables, and to attempt to restrict physics to the description of observables.[5] In Chapter 1 I noted the beginnings of this trend in the ideas of Mach, Pearson, and others. In the 1920s these ideas were developed by the Vienna and Berlin circles of physicists and

philosophers to produce what has come to be known as logical positivism. For these positivists, like Hume, there were only two kinds of meaningful statement: those that are true by definition, in which were included mathematics and logic; and those that are open to scientific test. And, in the most radical form of this view, for a statement to be open to test it had to refer only to observables, in the sense either of perceptual givens or phenomena subject to intersubjective agreement. Any statements that were neither true by definition nor open to test were dismissed as meaningless.

In the United States a similar development occurred in the form of Bridgman's operationism. This emerged explicitly as an attempt to prevent physicists ever again being placed in the distressing situation of being shown to have taken metaphysics for reality: 'if experience is always described in terms of experience, there must always be a correspondence between experience and our descrip- tion of it, and we need never be embarrassed, as we were in attempt- ing to find in nature the prototype of Newton's absolute time' (Bridgman 1928:16-17). Operationists argued that as far as possible scientists must limit themselves to the study of observable features of the world, features about whose morphology all observers can agree. Concepts must be defined in terms of the operations that will allow anyone to observe the same thing. In the 1930s operationism was adopted by a number of psychologists and sociologists as the bas- is for a scientific approach to the human sciences (Benjamin 1955).

In psychology the largely independent (Smith 1986) emergence of behaviourism had similar methodological consequences. Behaviourism arose from studies of animal behaviour. In that field considerable use had originally been made of interpretations of animal thinking and experience, but this practice came under increasing attack as hypothetical and intuitive (Mackenzie 1977). Greater emphasis was placed on the description of behaviour and of the stimuli to which the animal was assumed to be responding. The success of behaviourism at this time was also in part a response to the apparently inconclusive results of psychophysical research on humans, that relied on introspection.

One of the first to apply behaviourist ideas to the study of human behaviour was Max Meyer at the University of Missouri, whose ideas impressed the young Blumer (Blumer 1977). However, the beginnings of the behaviourist movement are usually traced to the publication in 1913 of John Watson's article 'Psychology as a behaviorist views it' (Watson 1913). Watson argued that mentalistic concepts and introspection must be abandoned in favour of observation of an organism's responses to controlled, physical stimuli. References to subjective states that could not be translated into descriptions of behaviour should be eliminated. Analysis should consist only of a description of the behaviour observed, without any attempt to infer what is going on in the 'mind'. Human thought was simply 'subvocal speech', a series of muscle movements. Watson was an instructor in the psychology department at the University of Chicago and a colleague of Mead, though Mead distanced his own 'social behaviourism' from Watson's approach.

Behaviourism, operationism and/or logical positivism were adopted, in one form or another, by several influential sociologists in the inter-war period, such as Stuart Chapin, Luther Bernard, Read Bain, and in particular George Lundberg. I shall focus primarily on the writings of Lundberg, since he presented his views most explicitly and comprehensively and because Blumer engaged in several dialogues with him.[6]

Lundberg explicitly states his adherence to positivism, and Karl Pearson seems to have been a particularly important influence on him.[7] However, he also drew on pragmatism. At one point he remarks: 'I have never had occasion to differ with George Herbert Mead' (Lundberg 1954:183), and he lauds Mead and his student Charles Morris as the source of 'the objective approach to language'. This, he claims, 'has definitely destroyed the necessity of a separate realm of the mental as a category in sociological explanation. All the phenomena of mind can be studied as language behavior by the same general methods which we use in studying other behavior' (Lundberg 1939a:49).

This reveals an important degree of overlap between some interpretations of pragmatism and positivism. As I noted in Chapter 2, the pragmatic maxim is similar in some respects to operational definition and to the verifiability principle of the logical positivists. Within logical positivism there was conflict between those who saw scientific tests as appealing to sense impressions (for instance, Carnap) and those who interpreted them in terms of intersubjective agreement (for example, Neurath), with the latter eventually prevailing. Mead's conception of the symbol as universal, as calling out the same response in all, is close to the idea that intersubjective agreement is the basis for meaning and truth.[8]

Like many pragmatists and positivists, including even Thomas and Znaniecki, Lundberg locates his methodological prescriptions within a socio-historical framework that portrays humanity as evolving in the forms of its adjustment to its environment, with science as the most advanced stage of this adjustment:

> of the various methods which man has employed in his age-long struggle to adjust himself to his environment, there is one method which has proved itself incomparably superior to all others in the results it has achieved. That method is the scientific method. The implication seems clear that a method which has proved itself so effective in one field of human adjustment should be employed also in those fields where man's adjustment and control is relatively imperfect, namely, in his social relations.
>
> (Lundberg 1929:23)

Lundberg's response to his own question 'Can science save us?' was a resounding 'Yes' (Lundberg 1947 and 1949). While Ogburn, for example, regarded some areas of sociological investigation as not at present amenable to quantitative method, Lundberg denies that there are any limits to its application. He rejects the various arguments used to support such limitations: that the social world is too complex, that it includes subjective elements and so on (Lundberg 1929).[9] He does so on phenomenalist grounds. In his view all phenomena, whether atoms or attitudes, are merely elements of our experience, and for that reason have the same fundamental character. The only important difference between them is the extent to which they are shared and thus objective. His phenomenalism is strikingly illustrated in the following:

> In any valid epistemological or scientific sense we must say that the substitution of a Copernican for the Ptolemaic theory of the universe represented a major change in the universe. To say that it was not the universe but our conception of it which changed is merely a verbal trick designed to lead the unwary into the philosophical quagmires of Platonic realism, for obviously the only universe with which science can deal is 'our conception' of it.
>
> (Lundberg 1933:309)

All phenomena, whether categorized as physical or mental, are human responses. They are the only world we can and need to know.[10]

In Lundberg's view, then, arguments about the distinctive character of social phenomena involve an appeal to metaphysical assumptions about essences that has no place in science.[11] Discussing what had become a standard example used to illustrate the difference between human behaviour and that of physical phenomena (MacIver and Page 1949:628), Lundberg argues that

> The 'essential' difference from the point of view of causation between the paper flying before the wind and the man before a crowd disappears if in each case *all the influences* of which the 'flying' is the resultant are in each case accounted for by methods subject to corroboration, of the type recognized in the natural sciences. Among these influences, in the case of the man, the natural science sociologist would, as a matter of course, include *all* his mental states, his cultural background, and his appreciation of the significance of the crowd's pursuit, to the extent that they are observable in the scientific sense (a problem of technology). The mental appreciation of significance, if it exists and is an influence in determining the man's flight, exists in the form of language symbols, which the man can communicate to himself and to us and which, therefore, are observable and subject to check. In short, all the influences the 'moral' scientist would seek out, except those which the 'moral' scientist professes to secure through occult and uncheckable processes, are included also by the natural science sociologist.

> (Lundberg 1955:199)

Lundberg argues that the apparent complexity and elusiveness of social phenomena derive from the currently inadequate development of social science methodology. He claims that advances in physical science have stemmed chiefly from refinement of observational technique.[12]

The major obstacle facing the application of quantitative method in sociology, from Lundberg's point of view, then, is the commitment of sociologists to theological and metaphysical ideas about the social world:

The principal obstacle to a fully positivistic sociology, in every respect compatible with the other sciences, is an adherence to certain verbal patterns which, through long habituation, we have come to mistake as being inherent in societal phenomena. It is quite common for researchers in sociology to be told that however rigorously they have applied the rules of scientific method, their results unfortunately do not square with 'the very nature of the thing' studied, that its 'true or real content' has been missed, and so forth. From the point of view I am attacking, the mere objectivity of findings in the sense of corroboration by other workers is not enough. The findings must also, and primarily, square with some objective reality which is declared to 'exist' independently of anybody's observations or corroborations. One is reminded of a learned gentleman named Sachs who in 1850 took the astronomers severely to task for their presumption in claiming they had discovered the planet Uranus. 'How do they know', he said, 'that the star they call Uranus *is* Uranus?' Today, people want to know how we can be sure that the phenomenon measured by the Chapin scale '*really is*' socio-economic status.

(Lundberg 1939a:49-50)

The first priority for Lundberg, if sociology is to progress, is to discard these metaphysical prejudices, and to apply what he takes to be the method of natural science. He regards science as broadly the same in whatever field it is applied. He quotes Karl Pearson:

The scientific method is one and the same in all branches and that method is the method of all logically trained minds. ... The unity of all science consists in its method, not in its material alone. The man who classifies facts of any kind whatever, who sees their mutual relation and describes their sequences, is applying the scientific method and is a man of science. The facts may belong to the past history of mankind, to the social statistics of our great cities, to the atmosphere of the most distant stars, to the digestive organs of a worm or to the life of a scarcely visible bacillus. It is not the facts themselves which make science, but the method by which they are dealt with.

(Pearson 1911:10-12; quoted in Lundberg 1929:3)

Like Pearson, Lundberg rejects the concept of causation as 'animistic' and 'theological' (Lundberg 1939b/1964:260). The goal of sociology is to find the laws of social phenomena just as the physicist seeks to identify those of physical phenomena, but in neither case are these laws defined in terms of causality or necessity. Instead, they are conceived as summaries of our experience of regularities among phenomena:

> [A law is] the résumé or brief expression of the relationships and sequences of certain groups of ... perceptions and conceptions, and exists only when formulated by man. ... Law in the scientific sense is thus essentially a product of the human mind and has no meaning apart from men. It owes its existence to the creative power of his intellect. ... The reason we find in natural phenomena is surely put there by the only reason of which we have any experience, namely the human reason ... the logic man finds in the universe is but the reflection of his own reasoning faculty.
>
> (Pearson 1911: 82,86,87,91; quoted in Lundberg 1929:6)

With Dodd (Dodd 1942:822-3) Lundberg argues that statements of probability must replace claims about causality.[13] On this basis it becomes necessary to collect data from a large number of cases and to apply statistical analysis.

Another key scientific principle for Lundberg is the application of methods that allow observers to agree on facts. The correctness of our knowledge is simply 'the similarity of our perceptions when compared with other people's' (Lundberg 1929:26-7). It is in terms of this definition of truth that operationism, behaviourism, and quantification gain their importance. It is only by specifying the operations by which we observe phenomena in terms of features that are evident to anyone with normal human perceptual capacities that such agreement can be produced. Sociology must rely on descriptions of phenomena that are 'the same to all normally constituted minds' (Lundberg 1929:8). Lundberg advocates operational definition, then, as a way of facilitating the process of objective empirical research, eliminating mere verbiage and replacing reliance on intuition with standardized observation. There is nothing beyond operations, they define the whole meaning of a concept (Lundberg 1955): 'the definition of a phenomenon and its measurement is in science the same operation; that it consists of agreeing upon sufficiently definite symbols with which to designate *that which* evokes a certain type of human response' (Lundberg 1938:199).

Similarly, quantification is necessary because it increases the precision with which agreement about the differences between phenomena can be achieved: 'Only when the quantitative stage is reached do our generalizations begin to partake of the nature of exact science' (Lundberg 1929:19).

Lundberg does not assume that social science methodology should be identical to that of the natural sciences (see Lundberg 1929:viii; Lundberg 1933:299-300). Any method can be used, as long as it provides for intersubjective agreement and gives information on a large number of cases. It is the absence of these factors that is the basis for Lundberg's rejection of case study and life-history materials as 'pseudo-scientific' (Lundberg 1929: 168); as, at best, appropriate only to the initial stages of a science before more rigorous techniques have been developed. Lundberg criticizes *The Polish Peasant* and the work of Thrasher and Anderson on precisely these grounds:

> The scientific value of all these [studies] depends, of course, upon the validity of the subjective interpretations of the authors as well as the extent to which the cases selected are typical. Neither the validity of the sample nor of the interpretations are objectively demonstrable on account of the informality of the method.
>
> (Lundberg 1929:169)

For Lundberg, the issue of the relative value of the case method and statistical method is simply whether we use: 'the informal, qualitative, and subjective method of "commonsense" or ... the systematic, quantitative and objective procedure of statistical method' (Lundberg 1929:176). Bain took a similar view:

> When, if ever, do life histories and diaries become valid data for science? ... Whenever they furnish materials which are clearly enough defined and frequent enough in occurrence so that a number of competent observers, working independently, can arrive at like conclusions both as to the existence and meaning of the defined data. When we apply such a rigid methodological criterion, it is evident that most so-called 'scientific' results from the use of life documents, life stories, interviews, diaries, autobiographies, letters, journals etc., are pure poppy-cock.
>
> (Bain 1929b:155-6)[14]

The sociological positivists criticized case-study research, then, because it failed to provide evidence of intersubjective agreement, and also because the number of cases studied, and the unstandard-ized character of their description made generalization impossible. Underlying this criticism is a denial that case study and statistical research are fundamentally different in character. Lundberg points out that both social workers and social scientists using qualitative data make implicit statistical claims, whether they recognize it or not (Lundberg 1929:21). From this point of view, statistical method is merely a more rigorous version of the case study. Thus, Lundberg rejects the distinction between qualitative and quantitative:

> The current idea seems to be that if one uses pencil and paper, especially squared paper, and if one uses numerical symbols, especially Arabic notation, one is using quantitative methods. If, however, one discusses masses of data with concepts of 'more' or 'less' instead of formal numbers, and if one indulges in the most complicated correlations but without algebraic symbols, then one is *not* using quantitative methods.
> A striking illustration from a recent book by a prominent sociologist will make the point clear. After a discussion of the lamentable limitations of statistical methods, the author appends this remarkable footnote: 'Wherever the statistical method definitely gains the ascendancy, the number of students of a high intellectual level who are attracted to sociology tends to fall off considerably' (Znaniecki 1934:235). In short, this author finally reverts to a statistical proof of the deplorable effects of statistics. It must be clear that the only operations as a result of which one could make [this] statement ... would be (1) to measure the degrees of relative intelligence of students; (2) to measure the quantitative variations in registrations of the better students in different sociology departments; (3) to measure the degree to which quantitative methods dominate the departments; and (4) to correlate the last two factors. ... The measurement of the factors here is a serious and difficult business. The generalization as quoted above was the result of a few strokes of the pen. In short, what the critics of the better quantitative methods seem to prefer is informal, impressionistic, and imaginary statistics supporting their prejudices.
> (Lundberg 1939b/1964:59-60)

104

For Lundberg, then, the difference between quantitative and qualitative data is nothing to do with differences in the nature of the phenomena described; it is simply 'a question of the type of symbols and language which we choose to designate phenomena' (Lundberg 1942:741). He argues that we must choose those that give us objective knowledge.

Initially, like Bain, Lundberg regarded standardized observation schedules as the key to scientific progress in sociology. He suggests that if social workers were to use such schedules this would produce those rigorous data about a large number of cases which are essential for the application of the statistical method (Lundberg 1929). However, in most of his own research he relied on questionnaires, presumably as the only practical alternative for obtaining the kind and amount of data required for statistical analysis.

As with most positivists, Lundberg viewed himself as cutting away pointless metaphysical discussion in sociology, thereby clearing the decks for the pursuit of solid knowledge of the kind produced by the physical sciences. While Lundberg's views were extreme in comparison with those of most US sociologists in the 1930s and 1940s, emphasis on and use of quantitative method increased during this period, stimulated not only by the spread of pragmatist and positivist ideas, but also by the development of scaling and correlational techniques that could be applied to data from social surveys.[15] This trend culminated in studies like *The People's Choice* and *The American Soldier*, which came to exemplify sociological research in the 1950s (Lazarsfeld *et al.* 1948; Stouffer *et al.* 1949). By that time quantitative method was the dominant methodological approach (Lundberg 1955); it had become part of what Mullins calls 'Standard US Sociology' (Mullins 1973).[16]

CRITICS OF THE POSITIVISTS

The influence of the Chicago department declined in the late 1930s and 40s, as other places, like Columbia and Harvard, became important centres for the training of postgraduate students in sociology (Harvey 1987). These other institutions often promulgated rather different methodological approaches from that of Chicago, and this, along with the growing use of quantitative method at Chicago itself, led to a methodological shift towards quantitative techniques within US sociology. However, there were

opponents of positivism and the dominance of quantitative method
outside of Chicago, such as Ellwood, Lynd, MacIver, Sorokin, and
Znaniecki. Indeed, with the exception of Blumer, these authors presented a more vociferous opposition than did the Chicagoans. I shall
illustrate the arguments used through a discussion of an influential
article by MacIver and of Znaniecki's book *The Method of Sociology*.

Like Thomas and Park, MacIver distinguished between objective
and subjective factors, and insisted that both were essential in
sociological explanations:

> Every social phenomenon arises out of and expresses a relation
> or adjustment between an inner and an outer system of reality.
> Each system, the inner and the outer, is complex and coherent
> in itself. The inner is a system of desires and motivations; the
> outer, a system of environmmental factors and social symbols.
> The explanation of every social phenomenon involves a
> discovery of the specific character of the inner system relevant
> to it and of the outer system in which it occurs.
>
> (MacIver 1931:25)

MacIver rejects the idea that sociology can be a natural science
in the sense of being concerned merely with 'objects amenable to
registration by means of instruments, objects divisible into units
capable of summation and other quantitative processes' (MacIver
1931:26). The social sciences suffer from the 'embarrassment' that
they must deal with:

> phenomena which involve a kind of causation unknown in the
> purely physical world, since they are ... brought into being ... by
> that elusive and complex, but undeniable, reality, the mentality
> of man. Not a single object which the social sciences study
> would exist at all were it not for the creative imagination of
> social beings.
>
> (MacIver 1931:26-7)[17]

In the terms I am using in this book, MacIver's position is that of
a realist, not a phenomenalist. And it is primarily because of what
he takes to be the nature of the social world, in other words on
ontological not epistemological grounds, that he criticizes the
application of quantitative method:

> The aim of the sciences of society should not be to dress
> themselves in the garments of their elders and look so like
> them that the guardians of the halls of science will not perceive

the difference. The object of science is to carry the light of understanding, to show us truth. If a piece of research aids us to understand better, more fully, some aspect of this so complex universe of man and nature, then it is worthwhile. If it does not, then no parade of figures will make it anything more than labor lost. Our methods should be adjusted to our materials and not our materials to our methods.

(MacIver 1931:27)

As MacIver points out: 'We do not cut wood with a shears or cloth with a saw'. While there are methods common to all the sciences, each has distinctive ones as well: 'The botanist cannot be content with the methods of the astronomer or the biologist with those of the physicist' (MacIver 1931:28).

MacIver also emphasizes the importance of theoretical reflection, as against what he sees as the obsession of many quantitative researchers with collecting facts. He notes that 'facts do not lie around, like pebbles waiting for the picker':

... the facts come into being only with the work of interpretation, and they grow more numerous and more interesting and more complicated and more ordered and more simple as the interpreter brings his own intelligence into play. They will give him no answers except the answers he himself construes for his own questions. And he cannot ask questions unless he knows what he is in search of.

(MacIver 1931:28-9)

MacIver stresses that he accepts the value of quantitative methods, but that this value is overestimated:

I am not ... arguing against what is called the quantitative method in the social sciences. The further it can go the better, the surer, our knowledge will become. I am arguing against the naive assumptions which accompany a too exclusive confidence in the use of statistics. I am suggesting that the quantitative method can by itself yield us nothing but quantities, and that in the social sciences quantities ... are not the goals, but only the media, of our research. What we are really seeking to understand are systems of relationship, not series of quantities. With the quantitative method must go hand in hand the

107

method of logical analysis and synthesis.

(MacIver 1931:30)

There is a subtle dialectic in MacIver's argument between the suggestion that the methods of the natural sciences are inappropriate to the study of the social world and the charge that the advocates of quantitative method have misunderstood the nature of natural science. Concluding with an emphasis on the latter point, he asks:

> What would we think, to take a crude example (but one very suggestive of the practice of many social researchers), of the meteorologist who sought to discover the relationship between lightning, thunder, and rain-clouds solely by the statistical method; who collected as many instances as possible in which lightning was seen and no thunder heard, in which thunder was heard and no lightning seen, and in which both lightning and thunder were observed but no rain fell; who then computed percentages and let it go at that?

(MacIver 1931:30-1)

Another forthright critic of the increasing emphasis on quantitative method in the 1930s was Florian Znaniecki, who had worked with Thomas on *The Polish Peasant*. He attacked the logic of this approach, labelling it 'enumerative induction'. He argues that this 'originates in the common tendency to reach quickly secure, even though superficial and inexact, generalizations for the purpose of ordinary practical orientation'(Znaniecki 1934:235). Enumerative induction involves trying to discover the characteristics of phenomena belonging to a particular class by studying a number of cases belonging to this class and describing what they have in common. Znaniecki points to a paradox here: if you do not know the essential features of a type of phenomenon you cannot identify instances of it; but if you do know what those features are, you already know what enumerative induction is designed to tell you.[18]

Like MacIver, Znaniecki recognizes that for some purposes the statistical method increases the reliability and precision of knowledge. But he insists that it cannot give us knowledge of the essential characteristics of phenomena, of the characteristics they have as a result of their participation in social or cultural systems. It gives us only tendencies and probabilities, often about what are only superficial features of the phenomena of interest.

The thrust of Znaniecki's critique is that statistical method is not the method of natural science. He argues that natural scientists do not study large numbers of cases and try to derive theories from measurements. Rather, they study a single case or a small number of cases in depth, and develop theories that identify the essential features of each case as an instance of a general class. He illustrates the point in a similar manner to MacIver:

It is as if a physicist, instead of measuring temperature by the expansion of certain bodies, counted the bodies which expand as against those which do not, in order to find out approximately how true is the statement that bodies expand.

(Znaniecki 1934:312)

Znaniecki argues for the application of true natural science method to sociology: 'The method of sociology in spite of the difference in object-matter, must be fundamentally similar to that of the natural sciences.' And for him, the task of science is the search for universal laws, relations of causality or functional dependence, not statistical generalizations. Science studies closed or at least semi-closed systems; it cannot study concrete phenomena in themselves, either individually or in aggregate, since any phenomenon is open to many alternative descriptions. He suggests that 'Whether any given object or agglomeration of objects appears to the scientist as a system (in itself) or as an element (of a larger system) depends on his "point of view", that is on the kind of problems he means to solve' (Znaniecki 1934:12). Here, Znaniecki's views are close to those of the neo-Kantians and the pragmatists, yet without adopting their phenomenalism. He is explicitly realist:

The attitude of the positive scientist, the specialist in any field, is uniformly realistic. He always means to learn as exactly as possible about reality such as it is, independently of him. Whether his object-matter be nature or culture, he eliminates himself entirely, tries to behave not as a human being who wishes reality to accord with his particular prejudices, but as an impersonal 'knower'. If he notices that his experience and activity do affect his data, he treats this as a source of error to be avoided.

(Znaniecki 1934:35)

On the basis of this realism, Znaniecki argues that quantitative method is only to be applied where the phenomena being investigated are quantitative or can be assumed to resemble a quantitative model in all important respects: 'In all sciences which are dealing with reality, quantitative categories have a theoretic significance only if they concern real quantities, objective characteristics of real systems or elements' (Znaniecki 1934:307). And in his view this is not true of much of social life.

In short, then, Znaniecki agrees with the positivists that natural science principles should be applied to the study of human society, and he even accepts Bain's and Lundberg's arguments that the apparent complexity of the social world is a product of our inadequate methodology. However, he disagrees profoundly with them about the nature of the method of the natural sciences. For him this involves the search for the necessary relations that constitute social and cultural systems; and these can only be identified through in-depth investigation of a small number of cases.

Znaniecki also argues that the nature of cultural systems has implications for how we study them. Although they are independent of individual researchers, they are not independent of the people who are involved in them and their cultural knowledge. Cultural phenomena involve what he calls a 'humanistic coefficient'. In studying them, we must approach them in a different way from that in which a natural scientist approaches physical phenomena, since they can only be understood as human products:

> The scientist who wishes to study the poem, the ceremony, the bank, cannot approach any of their elements the way he approaches a stone, or a tree, as a mere thing which is supposed to exist independently of any human being for all human beings to see who have similar sense organs: for if he tried to do so, the reality of the elements would escape him entirely and he would fail to understar d the real role which they play within their respective systems. This role is determined not merely by the characters these elements possess as natural things, but also (and chiefly) by characters which they have acquired in the experience of people during their existence as cultural objects.
>
> (Znaniecki 1934:39-40)

Cultural objects must be studied both by interpreting what people communicate about their experiences with these objects and through observing their 'outward behavior' towards these objects. While this is different from the way the natural scientist approaches physical phenomena, it does not 'preclude the possibility of attaining the same degree of scientific objectivity in both cases':

> In both cases the observer must start with primary sensual data, and in both he must go beyond them, interpret them as significant of a certain objective reality, though a reality in one case is regarded as independent of man, a world of things connected into systems by natural forces, in the other case as existing for man and through him, a world of values connected into systems by active human tendencies. ... The difference between things and cultural values, as far as methods of observation are concerned, means simply that in observing natural things we need to take into account only what these things signify in our experience as we have learned to interpret them (or similar things) in our past, whereas in observing values it is indispensable to notice how other human agents deal with them, and interpret this treatment in the light of instances where we actively shared the experience of these or similar values with other agents.
>
> (Znaniecki 1934:172-4)

Znaniecki's position is a complex one, then. He remarks that he has been

> forced to emphasize ... the primary and essential meaningfulness of social reality, to accept human values and activities as facts, just as human agents themselves accept them, but to study them objectively and with the application of the same formal principles as the physicist and the biologist apply to material nature.
>
> (Znaniecki 1934:viii)

Znaniecki deplores what he sees as the swing from speculative theorizing to 'fact-grubbing', both quantitative and qualitative. He argues that what is required is the systematic development of theory from data.

CONCLUSION

In the debate about case study and statistical methods we can see the emergence of many of the arguments that are used today by advocates of qualitative and quantitative approaches. At the same time, some of the issues stand out more clearly. We can trace, for example, how the question of whether to study a small number of cases in depth or to survey a larger number more superficially came to be conflated with the quite separate issue of quantification. We can also see how the problem of generalization from a sample to a population became mixed up with that of deriving laws from the study of a finite number of cases. Also evident is how quantitative method and natural science subsequently became identified with one another in a way that they were not at the beginning; and how the conception of science as the pursuit of causal laws was abandoned by quantitative researchers and later by qualitative researchers too. Less obvious, but no less interesting, is how advocacy of both methods seems to have been founded on an inductivist conception of science.

The arguments of MacIver and Znaniecki are typical of the kinds of criticism made of positivism and of the application of quantitative method to sociology in the 1930s. Another critic at that time was Herbert Blumer. The character of natural science methodology and its relevance for social research, and the value of statistical and case-study methods, were major themes of his Ph.D. dissertation, produced in 1928. And these issues were also central to his methodological and metatheoretical writings down to the 1970s and 1980s. Furthermore, his writings came to have considerable influence when the quantitative – qualitative debate re-surfaced in the latter half of this period, more so than those of MacIver and Znaniecki. In the next chapter I shall analyse Blumer's critique of the growing influence within US sociology of positivist ideas and quantitative method.

Chapter Five

AGAINST THE TREND: BLUMER'S CRITIQUE OF QUANTITATIVE METHOD

Much of Blumer's methodological writing takes the form of critical assessments of the use of quantitative techniques in sociology, and of the methodological ideas underlying their use. In particular, Blumer criticizes the idea that if social science is to enjoy similar success to the natural sciences, 'it must develop devices which secure objective data suitable for quantitative treatment by the techniques of statistics' (Blumer 1930:1101). I shall begin by looking at Blumer's criticisms of statistical method and quantitative measurement, and then examine the assumptions that underlie these criticisms.

STATISTICAL METHOD

As we have seen, for an increasing number of sociologists in the 1920s, 1930s and 1940s, statistical analysis symbolized scientific method, and sociologists made increasing use of statistical techniques during this period. Lundberg had claimed that 'the method, *par excellence*, of classifying, summarizing, and generalizing, if not the only scientific method of bringing together large quantities of data for generalization, is the statistical method' (Lundberg 1929:179; quoted in Blumer 1930:1102). Many others agreed with this even when they did not share other aspects of his sociological positivism.

In his dissertation and in a review of Lundberg's book published two years later, Blumer presents a number of arguments against this claim (Blumer 1928 and 1930). First, he points out that quantitative method is not equivalent to statistical method, and that 'historically physical science employed quantitative procedure with conspicuous success before statistical thought and technique made their appearance' (Blumer 1930:1103). Second, he denies that statistical method could be the method of science, on the same grounds as Znaniecki (1934): that scientific laws are universal not probabilistic (Blumer 1928:392-4): It should be apparent that the solution of the theoretical problems of social psychology require a type of information which cannot be furnished by a procedure which studies merely the aggregate and secures principles applying only to a certain portion of its members (Blumer 1928:393-4). Blumer was aware of the trend towards statistical explanation in twentieth-century physics, but he argued that this was not a sound basis for its extrapolation to the social sciences. Referring to quantum theory, he remarks that: 'In the experience of physical sciences statistics seem to come in at the point where natural scientific procedure breaks down' (Blumer 1930:1103). Along with many physicists at this time, including Einstein, Blumer rejected the idea that there can be statistical laws. One of the reasons for this was his belief, following Mead (1917), that exceptions to universals are the growth points of science, forcing reconceptualization of theories. From this point of view, acceptance of statistical laws implies a toleration of exceptions and thereby impairs scientific growth. Finally, Blumer questions whether increasing exactness in social science must take the form of mathematical and quantitative expressions. He is presumably thinking here of the capacity of ordinary language to make precise discriminations. He comments that: 'the case-study, interview, and life-history may be valuable because they reveal generalizations which are not statistical; to force them to yield such generalizations may be to destroy their value' (Blumer 1930:1103).

Turning specifically to the application of statistical method to social psychology, Blumer claims that it is of limited value because it can only deal with static situations, not processes developing over time. He declares that the results of applying statistical method to the study of social phenomena have on the whole been 'insignificant and disappointing' because it is associated with a stimulus-response model of human behaviour. This model, he believes, renders 'futile' many attempts to find statistical correlations, because it simply does not match the nature of most human social life. He echoes Cooley's argument that statistical methods are only appropriate where behaviour is routinized.

Blumer also points to the difficulties involved in inferring from knowledge about an aggregate to knowledge about individual members, a problem of particular significance given that he takes social psychology to be concerned with individuals. Furthermore, he emphasizes that statistical analysis can only give us correlations, not causal relations. In an exact reversal of the views of quantitative researchers that the case study is useful only as an initial exploratory technique, Blumer argues that statistical method is useful primarily as:

> [a] preliminary instrument ... suggesting possible significant factors in the complex processes which social psychology is seeking to unravel. ... In suggesting a relation ... it makes it possible to come back to the individual cases within the aggregate and study them in the light of the suggested relation.
>
> (Blumer 1928:395)

In the early part of Blumer's career the statistical techniques used in sociology were generally very simple. By the mid-fifties, when he wrote again at some length about statistical method, the situation had changed dramatically. Much more sophisticated techniques for the analysis of social survey data had been developed, notably in the work of Lazarsfeld and his students. But these developments made little difference to Blumer's attitude. At this time Blumer wrote an article criticizing what he referred to as 'variable analysis', analysis seeking 'to reduce human group life to variables and their relations' (1956:683).

Blumer makes two kinds of criticism of this type of analysis. First, he questions some features of current practice. He argues that very often the variables employed by quantitative researchers have been selected on a theoretically arbitrary basis – for example, because they can be easily measured. Furthermore, he claims that these variables are rarely 'generic': typically, they refer to specific cultural and historical contexts, or they are decomposed into indicators of the same character. As a result of these features variable analysis does not lead to the identification of universal principles of social life but only to correlations among localized factors.

However, Blumer goes beyond criticisms of current practice to deny the applicability of this method to much of social life, in principle:

> the crucial limit to the successful application of variable analysis to human group life is set by the process of interpretation

or definition that goes on in human groups. This process,
which I believe to be the core of human action, gives a
character to human group life that seems to be at variance with
the logical premises of variable analysis.

(Blumer 1956:685)

Blumer argues that those using variable analysis typically neglect the
crucial role that interpretative processes play in the formation of
human behaviour. At best, they seek to include them merely as an
intervening variable. But, Blumer claims, interpretation must not be
treated in this way because 'it is a formative or creative process in its
own right' (Blumer 1956:687). The meanings conferred on objects
vary between people, and over time for the same person. 'This
varying and shifting content offers no basis for making the act of
interpretation into a variable.' And Blumer reports that he can 'see
no answer to [this problem] inside the logical framework of variable
analysis' (Blumer 1956:688).

As in his earlier discussion, Blumer acknowledges that statistical
method might be appropriate where interpretation has become
routinized. But he argues that even here variable analysis can
produce only summaries of patterns of behaviour, and that these
patterns may change at any time as a result of participants
reinterpreting the situations they are in, thereby invalidating the
description. Furthermore, drawing on an idea that was common to
Thomas and Park, Blumer claims that in modern societies more and
more of social life is governed by explicit processes of interpretation
rather than by traditional norms.

Blumer develops another, related, argument against the omnibus
use of variable analysis. He identifies as a 'profound deficiency' of
this approach its 'inevitable tendency to work with truncated factors
and, as a result, to conceal or misrepresent the actual operations in
human group life'. He suggests that this stems from 'the logical need
of variable analysis to work with discrete, clean-cut and unitary
variables' (Blumer 1956:688). Blumer denies that the empirical
reference of a 'true sociological variable' is unitary or distinct.
Rather, it is 'complex and inner-moving':

In variable analysis one is likely to accept the two variables
(independent and dependent) as the simple and unitary items
that they seem to be, and to believe that the relation found
between them is a realistic analysis of the given area of group

116

life. Actually, in group life the relation is far more likely to be between complex, diversified and moving bodies of activity. The operation of one of these complexes on the other, or the interaction between them, is both concealed and misrepresented by the statement of the relation between the two variables. The statement of the variable relation merely asserts a connection between abbreviated terms of reference. It leaves out the actual complexes of activity and the actual processes of interaction in which human group life has its being. We are here faced, it seems to me, by the fact that the very features which give variable analysis its high merit – the qualitative constancy of the variables, their clean-cut simplicity, their ease of manipulation as a sort of free counter, their ability to be brought into decisive relation – are the features that lead variable analysis to gloss over the character of the real operating factors in group life, and the real interaction and relations between such factors.

(Blumer 1956:689)

In summary, Blumer identifies serious problems with statistical method: a failure to produce generic principles; neglect of the creative character of human interaction; and a mistaken treatment of complex and dynamic features of social life as if they were well-defined variables entering into fixed relationships irrespective of context. He suggests that these problems make statistical method ill-suited for much sociological research. While he notes that it can be useful in the study of 'those areas of social life and formation that are not mediated by an interpretative process', and as a means 'of unearthing stabilized patterns which are not likely to be detected through the direct study of the experience of people' (Blumer 1956:689-90), he clearly regards it as inappropriate for studying the bulk of human behaviour.

QUANTITATIVE MEASUREMENT OF SOCIAL PHENOMENA

The other aspect of quantitative method that draws Blumer's fire is the use of measurement techniques in defining and operation-alizing sociological concepts. He begins one of his most influential articles, 'What is wrong with social theory' (Blumer 1954), by noting differences in the nature of theory between 'empirical science' (by which, in this context, he means the biological and physical sciences) and current social science. He notes that social theory is divorced from empirical research: 'its lifeline is primarily exegesis' and when applied to the empirical world it 'orders [that] world into its mold', whereas there should be 'a studious cultivation of empirical facts to see if the theory fits' (Blumer 1954:3-4). Elsewhere, Blumer points out that this divorce between theory and research in sociology: 'throws open theorizing to the legitimate charge of being speculative and research to the likewise legitimate charge of being planless and frequently pointless' (Blumer 1940:708).

With the positivists, then, Blumer rejects speculative theorizing divorced from empirical research. He insists that concepts must always be linked to perception:

> As I see it, most of the improper usage of the concept in science comes when the concept is set apart from the world of experience, when it is divorced from the perception from which it has arisen and into which it ordinarily ties. Detached from the experience which brought it into existence, it is almost certain to become indefinite and metaphysical.
>
> (Blumer 1931:530-1)

From this point of view, concepts are important because they are the points at which theory links to the world (Blumer 1954:4).

Blumer also agrees with the positivists that one reason for the gap between theory and research is the absence of well-defined and precise concepts. When concepts are clear, theoretical statements 'can be brought into close and self-correcting relationships with the empirical world' (Blumer 1954:5). However, most concepts in the social sciences are vague, and this

> means that one cannot indicate in any clear way the features of the thing to which the concept refers; hence, the testing of the concept by empirical observation as well as the revising of the concept as a result of such observation are both made difficult.
>
> (Blumer 1940:707)

Vague concepts allow and encourage speculative theorizing.

However, Blumer is very critical of the remedies to this problem recommended and adopted by quantitative researchers. He argues that the problem remains even after their techniques have been applied. For instance, Blumer points out that despite a considerable amount of work in the fields of attitude research and opinion polling, the concepts of 'attitude' and 'opinion' remain vague and ill-conceived (Blumer 1948 and 1955). Neither concept provides a rigorous basis for identifying instances, nor does it facilitate the cumulation of knowledge about the class of phenomena that it denotes. For instance:

> the current conception of attitude ... does not tell us ... what data to include as part of an attitude and what to reject as not belonging to an attitude. Not knowing what enters into an attitude, we obviously lack guidance in selecting the kinds of data needed to identify or to delimit the attitude. Instead, we have to proceed arbitrarily, either relying on our personal impressions of what to include or else falling back on some technical device, such as a measurement scale.
>
> (Blumer 1955:59)

Blumer distinguishes between more and less extreme versions of the positivist approach to measurement. In its most radical version, concepts are defined in terms of the results produced by procedures designed to yield 'stable and definitive' findings in repeated applications (Blumer 1954:6). Blumer argues that while it is quite possible to produce a measurement scale that provides stable results, to treat those results as standing for nothing beyond the application of that procedure is to deny them conceptual relevance: 'the stable content that is isolated has no nature; that is to say that the operation by means of which one arrives at this content does nothing more than indicate that there is something that is stable' (Blumer 1940:711).

Blumer insists that a concept gets its significance, and its usefulness, from being related to other concepts, but that within the framework of operationism the stable results produced by one operation cannot be related to those produced by another, other than in the form of quantified correlations. At best, this would produce 'an exceedingly odd framework of interrelated symbols':

> These symbols would be nothing like concepts as we are familiar with them, as in present-day social psychology. For the symbolized item would have neither a content capable of being studied nor a nature capable of generic extension; it would never stand for a problem to be investigated nor have any

evolutionary development. To apply such symbols to human conduct as it is being studied by social psychology, one would have to work through concepts such as those we now have. And once this step is taken one is thrown back to the initial problem of the concept.

(Blumer 1940:712)

In short, radical operationism cannot resolve the problem of vague concepts because it offers only correlations between the results of applying different operations, and in themselves these scores tell us nothing about the world:

Until the specific instances of empirical content isolated by a given procedure are brought together in a class with common distinguishing features of content, no concept with theoretic character is formed. One cannot make proposals about the class or abstraction, or relate it to other abstractions.

(Blumer 1954:6)

The less extreme, and more common, form of operationism involves taking existing sociological concepts and operationalizing them in terms of the results of measurement operations. Blumer notes that 'seemingly such a method would yield a precise content, capable of exact test' (Blumer 1940:710). However, he points out that this involves taking a concept that already has a meaning, albeit vague, reducing it to those parts that can be measured, but then reverting to the original wider meaning in the interpretation of the results. He claims that, judging by the results of the application of this strategy, 'what is omitted is the most vital part of the original reference' (Blumer 1940:711): 'I notice that when vague and indefinite concepts are broken down into very precise and definite terms that can be tested empirically, it frequently happens that those simple terms cannot be recombined to produce the original concept' (Blumer 1939:162). As an example, Blumer cites the case of 'intelligence':

the concept of intelligence refers to something that is regarded as present in the empirical world in diverse forms and diverse settings. [It] is seen in empirical life ... in such varied things as the skillful military planning of an army general, the ingenious exploitation of a market situation by a business entrepreneur, effective methods of survival by a disadvantaged slum dweller, the clever meeting of the problems of his world by a peasant or primitive tribesman, the cunning of low-grade delinquent-girl morons in a detention home, and the construction of telling verse by a poet. It should be immediately clear how ridiculous and unwarranted it is to believe that the operationalizing of intelligence through a given intelligence test yields a satisfactory picture of intelligence. To form an empirically satisfactory picture of intelligence, a picture that may be taken as having empirical validation, it is necessary to catch and study intelligence as it is in play in actual empirical life instead of relying on a specialized and usually arbitrary selection of one area of its presumed manifestation.

(Blumer 1969a:31)

Blumer seems to be putting forward two reasons why the meaning that is lost in operational definition may be important. The first is that operational definitions often denote collections of phenomena which do not capture our everyday usage of the concept that they are supposed to be defining. In his discussion of public opinion polls, for example, he claims that what they measure does not match what we typically mean when we use the concept of public opinion. Though he does not explain why, Blumer seems to be insisting here that definitions of sociological concepts must capture the commonsense meanings of those concepts. However, he may have believed that this was necessary because sociological explanations necessarily make reference to the commonsense concepts on which human actions are based, and/or because in applying the results of sociological research to everyday practice we necessarily employ the concepts in terms of which that practice is framed.

The second reason why Blumer believes that operational definition cannot resolve the problem of the concept is a more conventional one. In his article on opinion polling he suggests that what the polls measure is not what a sociological analysis of the concept of public opinion would indicate to be relevant. Here Blumer is appealing to the argument that definitions of scientific concepts must be devised in such a way as to capture those phenomena among which hold the causal or functional relations that science seeks to discover. Those relations and the character of the phenomena that they relate must be *discovered*, they cannot be legislated by definitions. This is an argument to be found in many philosophical assessments of operationism (see, for example, Hempel 1965).

Blumer suggests that quantitative measurement would be appropriate 'if the problems out of which the concepts arose and the items to which they refer were themselves essentially quantitative' (Blumer 1940:711). But he argues that this assumption is simply an act of faith on the part of quantitative researchers, and one that the evidence suggests is not justified.

In addition, Blumer notes that a further problem with quantitative measurement is that it fragments conceptual meaning because different operations are used to measure the same concept in different situations, and the result is that an abstract variable is decomposed into separate concrete concepts:

> indicators are constructed to fit the particular problem on which [the researcher] is working. Thus, certain features are chosen to represent the social integration of cities, but other features are used to represent the social integration of boys' gangs. The indicators chosen to represent morale in a small group of school children are very different from those used to stand for morale in a labor movement. The indicators used in studying attitudes of prejudice show a wide range of variation. It seems clear that indicators are tailored and used to meet the peculiar character of the local problem under study.
>
> (Blumer 1956:684)

Although general terms may be used, because different indicators are used in different locales they provide little basis for a theoretical understanding of the phenomena that the concept denotes.

What Blumer is claiming here, then, is that operationism simply abandons theory rather than uniting it with empirical research, and that it divorces sociological concepts from their commonsense meanings. Even where full-fledged operationism is not adopted, where concepts are retained and measured – rather than defined – by indicators, the gap between concept and indicator remains since the links between the two are weak. Often, too, the variables measured are not generic concepts but localized variables.

In Blumer's view, the source of the gap between theory and empirical research in sociology is not an imperfection of technique, but the inadequacy of theory. Blumer places great emphasis on the value of concepts in introducing new points of view, and their role in 'sensitizing perception' and 'changing perceptual worlds' (Blumer 1931:527) so that we can 'perceive new relations' among phenomena, and he suggests that:

> the milling and halting condition of [sociology] does not come directly from the inadequacy of our techniques, as almost everyone contends, but from the inadequacy of our point of view. The effort to rescue the discipline by increasing occupation with method and by the introduction of precision devices is, I venture to suggest, working along the wrong direction. Perhaps, like other sciences in the past, we await a conceptual framework which will orientate our activities into productive channels.
>
> (Blumer 1931:528)

It is only on the basis of adequate theory, theory that captures the true nature of the social world, that effective techniques can be developed. This view is diametrically opposed to the positivist solution of replacing theory with statements about observable particulars.

However, Blumer goes further than this. In the middle of his article 'What is wrong with social theory?' he makes an even more radical suggestion. He asks whether what he calls 'definitive concepts', concepts that clearly identify relevant instances according to some set of rules, are 'suited to the study of our empirical world'. He notes that to pose this question seems 'to contradict all that I have said ... about the logical need for definitive concepts to overcome the basic source of deficiency in social theory', but he concludes that 'even though the question be heretical, I do not see how it can be avoided' (Blumer 1954:7).

What Blumer is suggesting here is that the inapplicability of definitive concepts may stem not from the theoretical immaturity of social science but from the very nature of the social world (Blumer 1954:7). There are two features of this world that he identifies as obstacles to the formation of definitive concepts. One is that in the social sciences 'many of the primary and basic observations are necessarily a matter of judgment' (Blumer 1940:707). In this respect, like the historicists and Cooley, he contrasts the observation of physical phenomena with that of human phenomena. While Blumer recognizes that the observation of both physical and social phenomena involves inference, he claims that physical objects can be 'translated into a space–time framework or brought inside of what George Mead has called the touch–sight field' (Blumer 1940:714). The observation of many social phenomena, on the other hand, requires

> a judgment based on sensing the social relations of the
> situation in which the behavior occurs and on applying some
> social norm present in the experience of the observer; thus
> one observes an act as being respectful, for example, by
> sensing the social relation between the actor and others set by
> the situation, and by viewing the act from the standpoint of
> rights, obligations, and expectations involved in that situation.
>
> (Blumer 1940:715)

And he adds that in identifying social phenomena we may also rely on noticing gestures that are familiar to us from our own experience. By 'taking the role of the other' we must come to view the situation in the way that participants do. Blumer argues that because we need to use a social, rather than a space–time, framework in observing human behaviour, difficulties arise in 'getting agreement in much of our observation' and in 'bringing our concepts to effective empirical test' (Blumer 1940:716).

The second obstacle to the development of definitive concepts in the social sciences that Blumer identifies is the individual distinctiveness of social phenomena:

> I take it that the empirical world of our discipline is the natural
> social world of every-day experience. In this natural world every
> object of our consideration – whether a person, group,
> institution, practice or what not – has a distinctive, particular
> or unique character and lies in a context of a similar distinctive
> character.
>
> (Blumer 1954: 7)

As a result, in studying social phenomena:

> we do not, and apparently cannot meaningfully, confine our
> consideration of it strictly to what is covered by the abstract
> reference of the concept. We do not cleave aside what gives
> each instance its peculiar character and restrict ourselves to
> what it has in common with the other instances in the class
> covered by the concept. To the contrary, we seem forced to
> reach what is common by accepting and using what is

distinctive to the given empirical instance. In other words, what is common (i.e., what the concept refers to) is expressed in a distinctive manner in each empirical instance and can be got at only by accepting and working through the distinctive expression.

(Blumer 1954:7-8)

In his criticism of the application of quantitative measurement in sociology, then, Blumer employs two different forms of argument. On the one hand, he claims that it does not resolve the problem that it was introduced to deal with: it does not clarify sociological concepts. In part, this is a general argument about the inadequacy of operationism as a philosophy of science, but his arguments about the qualitative character of sociological concepts and the need to preserve commonsense meanings relate to the application of that philosophy to sociology. Blumer's second argument has much more far-reaching implications. Here he questions not just the appropriateness of quantitative measurement but also the use of definitive concepts in sociology. This argument hinges on the claims that the conceptualization of social phenomena involves an ineradicable element of judgement which makes consensus among observers difficult to achieve and that their individually distinctive character rules out the development of concepts defined in terms of the presence of a set of common features. This more radical argument raises questions not just about the applicability of quantitative method in sociology, but about the very possibility of a science of social life. I shall deal with this issue in Chapter 6.

Having looked in some detail at the nature of Blumer's criticisms of quantitative research, I shall now identify what I take to be the distinctive assumptions that underlie them.

THE ASSUMPTIONS UNDERLYING BLUMER'S CRITIQUE

While Blumer shared the positivists' commitment to an empirical science of social life, he differed from them in how he interpreted that commitment. There are at least three areas of disagreement. First, there is the fact that Blumer is prepared to make claims about the nature of human social life. In this sense he is a realist. Second, his view of the nature of the social world is different from the assumptions about that world that the positivists make, despite themselves. Blumer's views are, of course, encapsulated in symbolic interactionism. Finally, whereas the positivists reject our everyday, commonsense experience of the social world as pre-scientific and therefore unsound, Blumer takes it to represent a substantially reliable account of the world, though incomplete and erroneous in details. Following the usage of Peirce, I shall call this his critical commonsensism.

Realism

Much of Blumer's criticism of quantitative method relies on the idea that human social phenomena differ in character from physical objects, and that understanding them requires a different approach, in some respects at least, from that characteristic of the physical sciences. He argues that it is the cardinal feature of science to respect the nature of the phenomena it studies (Blumer 1969a). As we saw, the positivists dismissed such arguments, on the grounds that claims about the nature of reality are meaningless: we can only know phenomena as they appear to us, and we can modify how we experience them by means of the methods that we use to approach them. For us to reach a scientific understanding, those phenomena must take an observable and replicable form. Hence our main concern must be to find ways of making social phenomena observable and replicable. It was for this reason that the positivists advocated methods that produced intersubjective agreement. Blumer responded to this positivistic phenomenalism with what seems to me to have been a largely taken-for-granted realism.

The claim that Blumer was a realist is controversial. Some critics of his work have ascribed the weaknesses they identify to a failure to adopt the realism of Peirce and Mead, suggesting that he was more influenced by the non-realist views of James and Dewey (Lewis 1976; Lewis and Smith 1980). Ironically, other critics have accused Blumer of being a realist in his approach to methodology, rather than a pragmatist like Mead (McPhail and Rexroat 1979). Most significant of all, perhaps, is that Blumer himself denies commitment to realism on a number of occasions, claiming allegiance to pragmatism (Blumer 1969a, 1980a, and 1980b). However, whether or not Blumer was a realist depends, of course, on what we mean by this term. And, unfortunately, not only is it used in different ways by different authors, and often with little clarity, but also it relates to some very difficult philosophical issues (Bhaskar 1978; Papineau

1987). I shall use the term to refer to the belief that our interpretations of the world, even our most basic perceptual judgements, refer to something beyond themselves whose character may be discrepant with what those interpretations imply. From this limited point of view, Blumer is quite clearly a realist. In his reply to McPhail and Rexroat (1979), he presents what he regards as the tenets of Mead's pragmatism:

1 There is a world of reality 'out there' that stands over against human beings and that is capable of resisting actions toward it;

2 This world of reality becomes known to human beings only in the form in which it is perceived by human beings;

3 Thus, this reality changes as human beings develop new perceptions of it; and

4. The resistance of the world to perceptions of it is the test of the validity of the perceptions.

(Blumer 1980a:410)

Broadly speaking, the first, second, and fourth of these assumptions are the core of realism, in the sense in which I am using the term. (The second tenet is important in distinguishing naïve from sophisticated realism.) The third assumption is ambiguous. If what is intended (and use of the word 'thus' implies this) is that our knowledge of the world changes over time, this too would of course be accepted by a sophisticated realist. It is only if the implication of this third assumption is that reality is simply the 'world' that we experience, and therefore changes as our experience changes, that it would mark a departure from realism.[1] Blumer is not clear about which of these interpretations he intends. Part of the problem stems from the fact that he uses the term 'reality' to refer both to our assumptions about what is real and to the world that these assumptions presuppose. Later, I shall suggest that this reflects a problem about the relationship between realism and symbolic interactionism. For the moment, however, I shall assume that even this third assumption is compatible with realism.

As we saw in Chapter 3 the methodological position of Thomas and Park was broadly realist, and to the extent that Blumer's methodological ideas were derived from Chicago sociology, his realism should not be surprising.[2] In an obituary for Ernest Burgess, he described the Chicago research as 'lifting the veils covering what

127

Park used to refer to as the terra incognita of city life' (Blumer 1967a:103). McPhail and Rexroat point out that the metaphors that Blumer uses in his methodological writings reflect realist assumptions. Besides 'lifting the veils that obscure or hide what is going on' (Blumer 1969a:39), even more pervasively, he employs the metaphors of 'unearthing' and 'digging deeper'. All these images fit his portrayal of research as the discovery of reality (Huber 1973a; McPhail and Rexroat 1979).

On the basis of his realism, Blumer emphasizes that all research methods make assumptions about the nature of the world they are designed to investigate. He rejects the positivist idea that it is possible to represent phenomena directly without such assumptions. Furthermore, his critique of quantitative method challenges the assumptions that the positivists actually make about the social world. He claims that they presuppose a world in which social actions are simply automatic responses to external and internal stimuli and are well-defined and stable in character. For much of social life, Blumer insists, this is not true.

Symbolic interactionism

Blumer presents his views about the nature of the social world as elaborations of the ideas of George Herbert Mead and also of Thomas, Dewey, Cooley, and others.[3] He contrasts the symbolic interactionist conception of human action with what he calls the 'stimulus-response' model. The latter portrays human behaviour as resulting from the play of external and internal factors on the individual, much as the direction of movement of a physical object is determined by the various forces operating on it. Blumer believed that this model, in one form or another, had become dominant in the social sciences:

> The prevailing practice of psychology and sociology is to treat social interaction as a neutral medium, as a mere forum for the operation of outside factors. Thus, psychologists are led to account for the behavior of people in interaction by resorting to elements of the psychological equipment of the participants – such elements as motives, feelings, attitudes, or personality organization. Sociologists do the same sort of thing by

resorting to societal factors, such as cultural prescriptions, values, social roles, or structural pressures.

(Blumer 1966a: 538)

Following Mead, Blumer also draws a distinction between the behaviour of animals and that of humans. Animal behaviour consists in the exchange of 'non-significant gestures' or 'non-symbolic interaction'. Humans, by contrast, are able to use 'significant gestures' in symbolic interaction.

This difference in the forms of interaction engaged in by humans and other animals arises from the fact that, unlike animals, humans have selves. The term 'self' does not refer to a psychological or physiological structure. Blumer insists that the self must be conceptualized as a process, it is the reflexive process by which a person is able to treat her/himself as an object. What this means is that through imagination people are able to stand outside of their behaviour and view it from different perspectives. This process creates what we call mind. It transforms human actors' awareness of their surroundings. Rather than these being viewed in terms fixed by biology, people are able to create a world of meaningful objects. Blumer stresses that people live not in a world of pre-constituted objects with intrinsic natures, but in a world of objects created through the process of human perception and cognition:

for Mead objects are human constructs and not self-existing entities with intrinsic natures. Their nature is dependent on the orientation and action of people toward them. ... Readiness to use a chair as something in which to sit gives it the meaning of a chair; to one with no experience with the use of chairs the object would appear with a different meaning, such as a strange weapon. A tree is not the same object to a lumberman, a botanist, or a poet; a star is a different object to a modern astronomer than it was to a sheepherder of antiquity; communism is a different object to a Soviet patriot than it is to a Wall Street broker.

(Blumer 1966a: 539)

The meanings objects have for people, then, are neither universal nor fixed. They are developed in the process of social interaction in particular cultural settings and are therefore variable between, and even within, societies: 'Individuals, also groups, occupying or living in the same spatial location may have ... very different environments;

as we say, people may be living side by side yet be living in different worlds' (Blumer 1969a:11).

In summary, then, symbolic interactionism portrays human beings as living in a world of

> meaningful objects – not in an environment of stimuli or self-constituted entities. This world is socially produced in that the meanings are fabricated through the process of social interaction. Thus, different groups come to develop different worlds – and these worlds change as the objects that compose them change in meaning.
>
> (Blumer 1966a:540)

It is this socially generated ability to view oneself as an object, and to interpret the world in alternative ways, that allows people to modify their interpretations and to choose different courses of action. As a result, human action is quite different from animal behaviour: it is not pre-formed and released by the impact of some external or internal stimulus. Rather, it is constructed through a reflexive process which

> takes the form of the person making indications to himself, that is to say, noting things and determining their significance for his line of action. To indicate something is to stand over against it and to put oneself in the position of acting toward it instead of automatically responding to it. In the face of something which one indicates, one can withhold action toward it, inspect it, judge it, ascertain its meaning, determine its possibilities, and direct one's action with regard to it. With the mechanism of self-interaction the human being ceases to be a responding organism whose behavior is a product of what plays upon him from the outside, the inside, or both.
>
> (Blumer 1966a:536)

As a result of this reflexivity, human behaviour is creative in character. It is not the simple product of internal or external causes, and it is on this basis that Blumer criticizes research on attitudes that treat them as determining behaviour (Blumer 1955).[4]

Blumer recognizes that often human behaviour does not seem to involve much thought and deliberation, it appears to be produced automatically in response to certain situations, and often forms part of large-scale institutional complexes. He refers to such behaviour as 'joint action'. However, he stresses that, though routinized, such behaviour is subject to reconstruction at any time and requires continual interpretation for its sustenance:[5]

> The fitting together of the lines of conduct is done through the dual process of definition and interpretation. This dual process operates both to sustain established patterns of joint conduct and to open them up to transformation. Established patterns of group life exist and persist only through the continued use of the same schemes of interpretation; and such schemes of interpretation are maintained only through their continued confirmation by the defining acts of others. It is highly important to recognize that the established patterns of group life just do not carry on by themselves but are dependent for their continuity on recurrent affirmative definition. Let the interpretations that sustain them be undermined or disrupted by changed definitions from others and the patterns can quickly collapse. ... Redefinition imparts a formative character to human interaction, giving rise at this or that point to new objects, new conceptions, new relations, and new types of behavior. In short, reliance on symbolic interaction makes human group life a developing process instead of a mere issue or product of psychological or social structure.
> (Blumer 1966a:538)

In Blumer's view, not only was the stimulus–response model implicit in the sociological positivism of the 1930s and 1940s, but it has also become dominant subsequently within sociology and social psychology. It is central to much sociological theorizing – Blumer particularly criticizes structural functionalism on these grounds – and to survey research methodology. Blumer argues that this model is inaccurate and that we need to adopt a quite different approach, one that recognizes the creative character of social interaction. It is from his commitment to such an approach that many of his arguments about the inadequacies of quantitative method arise.

Critical commonsensism

The positivists not only rejected appeals to the nature of the social world, they also dismissed commonsense knowledge as pre-scientific and unsound, indeed as one of the obstacles to scientific progress. By contrast, in arguing that the character of the social world is captured better by symbolic interactionism than by the stimulus–response model, Blumer relies on appeals to our commonsense experience of that world. He regards the truth of symbolic interactionism as obvious from our everyday experience: 'The premises of symbolic interactionism are simple. I think they can be readily tested and validated merely by observing what goes on in social life under one's nose' (Blumer 1969a:50). And later in the same article he invites social scientists to 'observe their own social action' to see the truth of the symbolic interactionist view of human action (Blumer 1969a:55).

The argument that our everyday experience of the world should be the starting-point for social scientific inquiry was common to the historicists of the nineteenth century and to pragmatists, especially James. On the one hand, they were opposing the arguments of materialists and empiricists that commonsense be replaced by reliance on scientific knowledge about matter or sense data. On the other, they rejected the efforts of idealists like Hegel to show that commonsense captured only appearance, not the underlying metaphysical reality.

Blumer provides little argumentative support for his reliance on commonsense knowledge, but some support can be found in the writings of pragmatist philosophers. In Chapter 2 we saw how Peirce had argued that all inquiry must work on the basis of commonsense assumptions, that we cannot question all of it since we can appeal to no certainties, neither innate ideas nor sense data. Furthermore, he suggested that there are reasons to believe that much of commonsense knowledge is reliable, since it has been built up in the process of human adaptation to the world. He claims that commonsense assumptions that are not genuinely doubted are propositions that 'lead to modes of activity which are consonant with the course of experience' (Almeder 1980:90): in other words, they allow us to expedite our dealings with the world. This argument is by no means entirely convincing, but it indicates the direction along which a justification for commonsense realism might be sought.

The term '*critical* commonsensism' is appropriate because neither Peirce nor Blumer accepted commonsense at face value: where doubtful, it is to be analysed and checked. Peirce emphasizes the fallibility of all knowledge, including commonsense. We assume that our commonsense assumptions are true, and that assumption is reasonable; but we must recognize that in the future any of them may be found to be false, or we may find it necessary to know more precisely under what limiting conditions they hold. At such times we would need to seek some test of them. Similarly, Blumer emphasizes that, though it is the starting-point, we must not simply accept participants' experience, we can go beyond that to reach a deeper understanding (Blumer 1969a: 39). Indeed, he argues that for the purposes of science, unrefined commonsense knowledge is often inadequate. He comments that '"common-sense", as the term strongly suggests, refers to what is sensed, instead of to what is acutely analyzed'. And while 'common-sense concepts are sufficient for the crude demands of ordinary experience', they are not always satisfactory for scientific purposes (Blumer 1931:523). He draws the following contrast:

> Scientific concepts have a career, changing their meaning from time to time in accordance with the introduction of new experiences and replacing one content with another. Common-sense concepts are more static and more persistent with content unchanged. Since the abstraction covered by the common-sense concept is not made the object of separate study and of experimental testing, there is little occasion for the uncovering of new facts and so for the challenging and revision of the concept.
>
> (Blumer 1931:524)

Blumer notes that scientists relate their concepts together in systems, and suggests that this contrasts with 'the work of technicians, politicians, and statesmen, where concern is with immediate practical problems, where each problem must be given immediate solution, and so essentially separate treatment'. In these circumstances, by contrast with science, 'procedure is opportunistic, knowledge unsystematized, and control uncertain' (Blumer 1931:525).

However, reliance on commonsense, albeit critical reliance, is not unproblematic. I shall discuss two problems here, one relating to critical commonsensism *per se*, the other to the relationship between commonsense realism and symbolic interactionism.

The first issue concerns differences between science and commonsense. Whereas the positivists drew a sharp line between the two, the pragmatists saw science as emerging from commonsense and sharing the same fundamental character. The paradigm case of inquiry used by the pragmatists was an everyday one: we are engaged in action, we encounter an obstacle, and we investigate the situation until we can reconceptualize it in a way that allows us to complete the action and achieve our goals. Indeed, some pragmatists defined truth in terms of the facilitation of practical success. Blumer himself declares that in science 'the success of the activity to which it gives rise becomes the test of the effectiveness of the concept' (Blumer 1931:528). In illustrating his argument, Blumer uses the example of medical diagnosis (p. 529); which, in my view, it fits. However, much science is not so directly addressed to the solution of practical problems.

Although the paradigm of everyday problem-solving is illuminating in many respects, its implications for the nature of science are not clear. Science is institutionalized inquiry, in the sense that while its initial starting-points and ultimate justification may be practical, many of the problems that scientists tackle, and many of their findings, have no direct extra-scientific relevance. And, elsewhere, Blumer emphasizes the autonomy of science: he draws a clear line between it and, for example, political activity (Blumer 1948:548; Blumer 1981: 277, 279-80). But the combination of pragmatism with this conception of science as institutionalized inquiry raises questions:

1 When is scientific as opposed to commonsense inquiry required?
2 What is the relationship between the two? For example, is the difference a matter of degree of rigour, and if so in what respects?
3 How are problems internal to science set and judgements about the validity of hypotheses made? To the extent that scientific problem-setting and solution is autonomous from practical problem solving, the latter cannot act as a criterion of truth. And practical success within science cannot operate as a criterion of truth either because, presumably, truth is the goal of science as institutionalized inquiry. Here the application of the pragmatic definition of truth would lead to circularity.

I do not wish to labour these problems, or to suggest that they are unresolvable. However, they do arise, and they are not addressed by Blumer. And as we shall see, they have implications for the viability of his methodological recommendations.

The other problem I shall mention concerns a potential conflict between realism and critical commonsensism on the one hand and symbolic interactionism on the other. As we saw, a central feature of the latter is the argument that objects do not have any intrinsic meaning – that meaning is conferred on them by us – and that different people, and the same person at different times, may confer different meanings on the same object. In Blumer's terms, people may live in different 'worlds'. But if this is so, it appears to lead to a problem. Must the social scientist regard her or his own commonsense understanding of the social world as an imputation, rather than as reflecting the nature of that world? If so, how can we justify basing scientific inquiry upon it? This is a problem that has been pointed out by some critics of Blumer: McPhail and Rexroat call it an 'ontological paradox' (McPhail and Rexroat 1979).

Blumer did not tackle this problem, even in response to McPhail and Rexroat's critique (Blumer 1980a). I believe that it can be resolved fairly easily, however, once we accept that there can be multiple, non-contradictory descriptive and explanatory claims about any phenomenon. We can describe the same area of our perceptual field as 'a table', 'a collection of atoms', or even as a 'symbol of high social status', without contradicting ourselves. Which of these, or of many other possible descriptions, we select depends on our purposes, not just on whether we believe the description to be true. Similarly, we can explain the same phenomenon as the product of a manufacturing process, of the operation of electro-magnetic force, or of an obsession with upward social mobility. Once again, these explanations are not mutually contradictory. Given this, there is no contradiction between the claim that interpretation is creative and does not simply reflect the nature of the phenomena interpreted on the one hand, and realism, the idea that to be true it must accurately represent those phenomena, on the other.[6]

CONCLUSION

In this chapter I have examined Blumer's critique of the growing use of quantitative method in the social sciences and of the ideas underlying this use. I have also discussed what seem to me to be the three major assumptions on which his critique is founded: realism; symbolic interactionism; and critical commonsensism. It is these assumptions that mark Blumer's position off from that of the sociological positivists and from that of many quantitative researchers. These ideas also form the basis for Blumer's positive recommendations for social research, which I shall examine in Chapter 7. First, though, I want to look at another vitally important aspect of Blumer's approach: his concept of science.

Chapter Six

BLUMER'S CONCEPT OF SCIENCE

In the previous chapter, I examined Blumer's criticisms of quantitative method and of the positivist ideas that were often used to justify it. Despite his differences with the positivists, Blumer shared their goal of creating an empirical science of social life. But, of course, his conception of that science differed sharply from theirs – in large part because of his commitment to realism, symbolic interactionism, and critical commonsensism. However, as we shall see, his views about the nature of and possibilities for social science are equivocal.

There is strong evidence for Blumer's commitment, throughout his career, to the idea of sociology as a science. His dissertation was concerned with outlining what this involved and with investigating the prospects of its achievement. Fifty years later, in a new introduction to his appraisal of *The Polish Peasant*, Blumer focused on the same issue. Furthermore, at various times he indicates acceptance of the natural sciences as a model for social research by appealing to the examples of Galileo, Newton, Pasteur, and, most frequently of all, Darwin (Blumer 1930:1102; 1931 *passim*; 1969a:40).[1]

THE THESIS OF 1928

Blumer's most detailed treatment of the nature of scientific method is to be found in his dissertation (Blumer 1928). He begins from what he calls 'the cry for ... a scientific method' in social psychology. He notes that there is a widespread desire among social psychologists to emulate the physical sciences 'with their notable achievements and their steady and secure advancement' (Blumer 1928:ii). And he is concerned to investigate whether social psychology, conceived as a branch of sociology, can become scientific. He begins by outlining what he takes to be the nature of scientific method, examines in depth the work of the leading writers in social psychology of the day, and then considers various methods that have been recommended in social psychology for the production of scientific results.

Blumer portrays science, by contrast with historical method, as taking what he refers to as 'the continuous heterogeneity' of reality and searching for what is homogeneous, looking for causal relations in which one factor invariably produces another. Here his conception of science draws heavily, and explicitly, on Rickert's account of the generalizing method; though also on a catholic range of other writers, including positivists such as Pearson.[2] He structures his discussion by means of a distinction between the functional and logical aspects of science on the one hand, which are common to all sciences, and the technical aspects that vary between the sciences, on the other.

The *function* of science, Blumer argues, is to transform experience, to identify instrumental relationships among phenomena that will facilitate their control. Science simplifies reality through the isolation of causal relations that permit no exceptions. Such relations are hidden: their isolation necessitates a 'breaking up' of reality into a number of factors so that those that are relevant can be studied and others ignored. The discovery of an exception to a universal law is the starting-point for the process of inquiry. It is a stimulus for the reconstruction of the universal to incorporate the exception. This incorporation takes place through the development of hypotheses that account for the exception as well as the original data, and their testing by experiment.[3]

Blumer lists the *logical* aspects of science as observation, induction, deduction, classification, framing of hypotheses, and experimentation. Of particular importance is experimentation. He uses this term in a general sense to refer to the comparative analysis of cases where the factors of interest vary; not just laboratory experiments but also 'natural experiments', and other forms of systematic comparison. Laboratory experimentation is a *technique* used in certain sciences, and one whose contribution to sociology Blumer sees as limited.[4] What Blumer regards as essential to science are two 'logical' features of experimentation:

One is the simplification of the factors operating in a given

instrumental nexus; the other is the alteration of one of the
factors so as to betray the instrumental connection between
such alteration and the change in other factors. ... The
laboratory situation, of course, lends itself most admirably to
these two accomplishments. Exclusion of extraneous
influences is more readily accomplished; but above all one is
fairly able to control the altering factors. Unfortunately, social
behavior does not lend itself readily to such laboratory
treatment. This, however, does not indicate that experimentation, properly understood, is impossible. If we have recurrent
situations in human behavior in which the factors may be
identified and their course of action *observed* in both their
altering and altered aspects, we have the necessary elements of
experimentation. Certainly, the very process of human
behavior provides the raw material for such a setting. This idea
is contained in the saying, 'Nature performs experiments –
man can observe them'. ... The real problem ... is whether one
can identify or isolate conceptually in a clear-cut fashion the
pertinent factors in human behavior. We take it to be obvious
that this has scarcely been done so far, but the failure may
indicate the use of a false conceptual approach (and a
subsequent 'unknowingness' of the pertinent factors), rather
than an impossibility of identification, intrinsic in the situation.
                                                            (Blumer 1928: 32-4)

While functional and logical aspects are essential to science, its
technical aspects, the particular techniques used, are distinctive to
particular sciences:

A given science, by reason of its distinctness, encounters,
presumably, a peculiar set of problems and a peculiar set of
data. These will have to be grappled with in their peculiarity;
hence the methods employed will take their form and
character from the nature of the problems and the data. These
remarks may sound like needless tautology; yet they become of
guiding significance when one thinks of the modern attempts
to [impose] the techniques of the more exact sciences on the
less successful ones on the claim that they alone are 'scientific'.
                                                            (Blumer 1928:23-4)

Blumer explicitly excludes quantification and measurement from
the functional and logical aspects of science. He emphasizes that

scientific method is not statistical method. Indeed, as we saw in the previous chapter, he believes that the latter can play only a minor role in social science because it is not able to generate universals: 'Natural science gets its laws by starting from intensive studies of individual cases and building up a type; statistics is a means of working with a mass or aggregate – not a means of studying intensively a separate case' (Blumer 1930:1103).

For Blumer, in the 1920s and early 1930s at least, sociology is a nomothetic science, sharing functional and logical features, including the logic of the experiment, with the natural sciences. The task facing sociologists is to develop appropriate techniques to deal with the peculiar character of the phenomena that it studies.

However, although Blumer is clear about the nature of science in his dissertation, at some points he expresses doubts about whether social psychology (and sociology generally) can meet the functional and logical criteria of science, at least in the foreseeable future. These doubts reach a crescendo towards the end of his dissertation in a discussion of the comparative method. He notes that in the social sciences this involves the study of 'instances that have been understood in their unique character' which are then compared in order to 'yield a classification which will in turn lay the basis for the abstraction of common elements' (Blumer 1928:351). He reports that this procedure is constantly being urged upon sociologists. Furthermore,

> it is the procedure which is implicit in the case method, the use of life histories, etc., which aim to secure significant principles of human conduct by collecting individual instances, described in their completeness, comparing these, and isolating out common behavior trends or elements. The sequence of the procedure is essentially: understanding of the individual case – comparison – classification – extraction of the universal.
>
> (Blumer 1928:351)

And basic to the process of understanding the unique case is 'sympathetic introspection' or *Verstehen.*

Blumer notes that reliance on *Verstehen* is not restricted to social science, it is 'a most common procedure in human association'. What is involved is what Mead refers to as 'taking the role of the other'. Blumer argues that in Mead 'considerable obscurity besets this notion' and that Mead 'used it as an explanatory concept without any special endeavour to indicate its exact character' (Blumer 1928:217). Given this, Blumer turns to Cooley for clarific- ation. He argues that introspection in social science differs from its use in everyday life in that there is 'greater care and wisdom in its employment' (Blumer 1928:338). Following Cooley, he specifies this in terms of 'a natural gift of insight' as a required minimum. Also required are: a 'broad knowledge of facts [that] enables one to better discover other facts'; 'social culture', to be gained through 'broad training in the humanities'; and finally 'practice in the use of sympathetic introspection, particularly through imaginative self-identification with *varied* cultural groups', plus patience, firmness, and confidence. Summarizing, 'The formula is essentially to take an individual with a gift of insight and develop widely his knowledge of people; by this means he will become efficient in the understanding of human conduct' (Blumer 1928:340).

However, Blumer underlines the ways in which reliance on sympathetic introspection departs from the requirements of science. He remarks that

> One value of a method in science is that it fosters agreement and the reconciliation of diverse views. Can this be said of the method of sympathetic introspection? If so, how can we account for ... divergent interpretations of the same conduct. ... There is nothing in the discussion of 'sympathetic introspec- tion' by its advocates which shows how this method can lead to the detection of the genuine and the spurious, nor that it easily permits of the verification which marks scientific advance.
>
> (Blumer 1928:340-1)

The understanding of the particular instance 'is gained by rendering it clear and intelligible', but in social psychology this intelligibility 'depends on the judgment, the purpose, and the values of the investigator; it arises from the alignment of things within the nexus of the meanings which are peculiar to him and his time. The meaning of an instance is likely to vary with the interpreter.' Here Blumer addresses the central problem of hermeneutics, noting the truth of the cliché that 'history is always contemporary history' (Blumer 1928:352):

> Different observers might place the behavior in quite a differ- ent setting and in this way interpret it quite differently. An activity need not have a single meaning, but may have an

141

indefinite number of meanings, according to the different settings in which it is placed. This varying character of the instance would seem to coincide with the use of the method of sympathetic introspection.

(Blumer 1928:354)

Blumer notes that 'it is evident from Cooley's remarks that sympathetic introspection derives much of its value from the authority of those who use it' (Blumer 1928:341). And he comments:

It is an acknowledged principle of science that a theory to have value must admit of continual test by the facts or kind of facts from which it arises. The individual element which enters into the use of sympathetic introspection, however, seems to make this impossible.

(Blumer 1928:342)

He concludes: 'it is trite to say that scientific generalizations secure their validity not in the authority of their formulator but in the support of the data' (Blumer 1928:414).

The multiple, competing interpretations produced by *Verstehen* are not the only problem involved in the comparative study of unique cases. Blumer argues that while comparison of unique instances improves understanding of the character of each instance, what similarity such comparison reveals:

is usually limited to a given cultural situation or condition in which a number of instances share. It does not indicate the existence of general principles of human association or conduct, but merely implies that a number of things share in what amounts to ... a unique situation. This isolation of such similarities is scarcely calculated to yield 'laws' or 'generalizations' like those which mark physical science. The fact that the instances show a similarity because of their participation in the cultural nexus is the reason why they illuminate each other. Their comparison leads virtually to a better understanding of the cultural conditions responsible for their similarity; as the instances are being compared a new meaning emerges here, another one there, all working to piece together the cultural circumstances. It is in such a way that the cases throw light upon each other; for with the emergence of every new meaning each case gets a new interpretation and a new significance. The fact that by means of the comparison, new features are added to each case which would otherwise not have been observed and that these new features are similar in a number of instances does not imply that the comparison leads to the isolation of general principles of human conduct.

(Blumer 1928:359-60)

Not only does the application of the comparative method to the study of unique instances involve the problems of dissensus and uncertainty associated with reliance on *Verstehen*, but it also seems unlikely to produce knowledge of the general principles governing human conduct. For both these reasons, this form of the comparative method does not meet the requirements of science.

Blumer contrasts this use of the comparative method with that to be found in what he calls 'scientific analysis'. He argues that natural scientists study cases as exemplars of general classes. The key to scientific analysis is the study first of simple cases clearly belonging to a class, and the use of these to facilitate the understanding of more complex cases later (Blumer 1928:358). He states that 'simplification in natural science has always involved two procedures: (1) the choice of a simple situation or (2) the resolution of a situation into elements or simples' (1928:366). He examines the prospects for the use of each of these strategies in social psychology.

The selection of a simple situation is useful because it facilitates the identification of significant factors and the elimination of irrelevant ones. A simple situation always tends to be a closed system. A number of conditions must be met for a system to be closed:

1 A closed system always implies a system of happenings, that is a series of events which are indefinitely repeatable.
2 In this system, *all the pertinent factors must be identified.*
3 All other factors must be eliminated from consideration, either (a) through their exclusion from the system, or (b) through their uniform stabilization within the system, so that they may not disturb the pertinent factors. It is this elimination which gives the system its closed aspect. If extraneous or undetected factors may come in to influence the course of change, the system ceases to be closed.
4 The *following* of the pertinent factors during the course of change. The pertinent factors must be traceable in this fashion if one hopes to isolate a causal or instrumental relation.

(1928:366)

Blumer underlines the fact that the establishment of these conditions, and thus the study of simple situations, does not necessarily require laboratory experimentation. Closed systems

> may prevail in the ordinary course of events without the necessity of the artificial simplifying conditions of the laboratory. It should be remembered that there are a number of sciences, of which Astronomy is the foremost example, which do not rely upon laboratory procedure in the strict sense of the term, for the simplification of their phenomena.
>
> (Blumer 1928:367)

However, Blumer notes that Znaniecki had attempted to study closed systems in social psychology (Znaniecki 1928), and comments that

> The difficulty of getting a closed system, as it is indicated in the work of this author, might occasion some misgivings as to its possibility in the field of social psychology. If it is impossible, social psychology must resign itself to the complexity of its subject-matter, to the impossibility of strictly natural scientific laws, and must continue to rely upon methods which give only a rough understanding and control of this complexity. But perhaps a closed system, as applied to social behavior, is not impossible; perhaps its failure or absence is merely due to an ignorance of what are the pertinent factors in human behavior. This suggests that perhaps the attainment of the simplified situation represented in the closed system depends on a new conceptual orientation.
>
> (Blumer 1928:368)

Blumer comes to an even less optimistic conclusion in looking at the other strategy of scientific analysis: the attempt to find the simple elements out of which human behaviour is constructed. He reviews work that has sought to find the fundamental motives of human behaviour, arguing that: 'there is nothing in the disciplines dealing with human conduct, particularly nothing in social psychology, which approaches the condition of ultimate elements' (Blumer 1928:390).

Blumer suggests that the failure to apply the comparative method of scientific analysis successfully and the tendency for social psychologists to focus on the unique features of cases and to rely on *Verstehen* may stem from the nature of social phenomena, that they do not have 'the stable character which is essential for classification and comparison' (Blumer 1928:351):

> The success of classification in the natural and biological sciences depends upon the presence of fixed characters in the objects or instances to be classified; characters which can be easily identified by interested observers. It is these characters, of course, which lay the basis for classification. If, however, in the case of historical instances, the 'characters' vary with the current values and meanings, and indeed from individual to individual ..., the way to easy classification and comparison would seem to be blocked.
>
> (Blumer 1928:353)

On this basis, Blumer concludes that the study of unique cases using *Verstehen* may be the only method available in the human sciences, given the nature of social phenomena:

> As used by social psychology [sympathetic introspection] becomes the essential method for the understanding of contemporary problems and life. Wherever any event, individual act, social situation, or cultural phenomenon is to be understood in its full social significance, sympathetic introspection must obviously be employed.
>
> (Blumer 1928:343)

In short, this method is necessary in social psychology 'whatever its shortcomings' (Blumer 1928:344). Furthermore, he points out that

> if the control which is sought by means of ... 'universals' (that is by scientific analysis) can be secured through an insight or intelligent understanding of the particular situation, then the desired ends and the requisite knowledge might be secured without need of general laws.
>
> (Blumer 1928:351)

In other words, while social psychology might not be able to match the logical features of science, it may be able to serve the ultimate function of social science, which in the tradition of Thomas and Park Blumer defines as social control.[5]

Summing up his findings about the application of the scientific method in social psychology, Blumer comments:

> In our journey we have considered both forms of simplification used by natural science – the choice of a simple situation, and

145

the reduction of the complex to ultimate elements – both of which are lacking in the stock of procedures of social psychology. It would seem that investigation (in this discipline) which aimed at the isolation of 'universals' such as characterize natural science would have to rely almost solely upon the classification of the unique or complex given. We have already referred to the difficulties which confront this procedure, and need not refer to them again here. However dismal this may leave the picture with respect to the possibility of introducing a natural scientific technique in social psychology, it is at least worthwhile to realize that this is the situation.

(Blumer 1928:391)

In his dissertation, then, Blumer presents science as the pursuit of universal laws and as requiring the transformation of phenomena into instances of well-defined categories sharing the same features. It involves the study of simple instances, by means of systematic comparison that relies on the logic, if not the procedures, of laboratory experimentation. This provides the basis for later analysis of more complex cases.[6] His review of social psychology suggested that this method had not been successfully applied in that field. He notes that social psychologists have typically sought to compare phenomena that are unique, and have relied on *Verstehen* in describing them. He argues that this research strategy does not meet the requirements of science. However, he also suggests that it may be the only one available in social psychology because of the nature of human social life; and he proposes that it may be possible to use it to serve the same function as science.

Blumer's attitude to the idea of a science of social life in his dissertation is ambivalent, then. On the one hand, he is committed to the pursuit of such a science. On the other, he is rather pessimistic about its achievement, at least in the foreseeable future. This ambivalence persisted, and stands out even more clearly, in his appraisal of *The Polish Peasant*, published in 1939.

APPRAISAL OF *THE POLISH PEASANT*

In Chapter 3 we noted the considerable influence that *The Polish Peasant* had exerted on the development of US sociology. An important aspect of this influence was its role as an exemplar of case-study method. It was perhaps because of his well-known advocacy of case study that Herbert Blumer was selected by the SSRC to assess this study in 1938. His report, and a conference discussion of it in which some eminent sociologists of the day participated (including Thomas, Bain, Stouffer, and Wirth, as well as Blumer himself), was published in the following year (Blumer 1939).

Blumer endorses Thomas and Znaniecki's commitment to the importance of understanding the attitudes underlying people's actions, and the value of personal documents in achieving this understanding. At the same time, though, he is critical of their study on the grounds that they do not establish the theoretical claims that they make:

the important question is whether the materials adequately test the generalizations (regardless of their source) which are being applied ... [and] the answer is very inconclusive. Some interpretations, indeed, are borne out by the content of the documents, and sometimes the interpretations do not seem to be verified adequately; in both instances, of course, the materials are a test. Usually, however, one cannot say that the interpretation is either true or not true, even though it is distinctly plausible.

(Blumer 1939:75)

Blumer also points out that Thomas and Znaniecki do not achieve their goal of producing well-founded sociological laws: 'they have not given any laws of social becoming that stand the test of their own specified requirements, such as that of making a conscientious search for negative instances' (Blumer 1939:18). And he concludes that 'it seems certain that [their] methodological formula is invalid and that the thought of securing "laws of becoming" by it is chimerical' (Blumer 1939:71).

Blumer identifies the source of Thomas and Znaniecki's failure to establish sociological laws in the kind of data that they use:

Perhaps the outstanding obstacle to an unqualified testing of [Thomas and Znaniecki's] theory is that which plagues most of social science, i.e., the absence of definite guides or rules which would enable one to ascertain positively that a given datum is an instance of a given concept and so deserves its application.

(Blumer 1939: 61)

147

The failure of *The Polish Peasant* to meet scientific criteria is not, then, a defect specific to their study. Rather, it is a sign of a problem that faces all sociological – indeed, all social scientific – work.

Up to this point Blumer's appraisal of *The Polish Peasant* is similar in substance to that of Lundberg and Bain. However, Blumer goes on to argue that, despite their deficiencies from a scientific point of view, Thomas and Znaniecki's data and interpretations are 'genuinely revealing'. He suggests in one case that: 'even if the authors' interpretation were not true ... it would be generally true, and would be true in other particular cases' (Blumer 1939:50). And he generalizes this conclusion, remarking that, while the 'separate document cannot very well stand evaluation according to the criteria of representativeness, adequacy and reliability', human documents are none the less 'indispensable' and 'may be of enormous value' (Blumer 1939:80). On this basis he proposes that much of Thomas and Znaniecki's documentary material does serve as an 'inductive foundation' for their theoretical interpretations (Blumer 1939:53).

Some clarification of this apparently paradoxical position is provided in the course of the conference discussion. Blumer defends his position as follows:

> I am skeptical of our being able to develop any very exact laws which involve this factor of subjective human experience, but I do not see anything nihilistic in this position because it is possible to develop a body of very useful knowledge in the form of generalizations even though they are not exact, or invariant, enough to be called laws. Further, one can formulate two or three competing propositions applicable to the same given field and make some distinction between them in terms of how suitable they are.
>
> This is a matter of judgment, but it isn't wholly an arbitrary matter, because I distinctly feel that one who has an intimate familiarity with the people and the type of experience with which he is dealing will make propositions which will seem more reasonable than would be true of propositions proposed by someone who lacks such knowledge.
>
> (Blumer 1939:149-50)

In an article written around the same time Blumer drew the same distinction between the testing of theoretical claims in natural science and what is possible in sociology:

In view of the nature of our problems, our observations, and
our data in social psychology, I expect that for a long time
generalizations and propositions will not be capable of the
effective validation that is familiar to us in the instance of
natural science. Instead they will have to be assessed in
terms of their reasonableness, their plausibility, and their
illumination.

(Blumer 1940:719)

And, in fact, at one point in his appraisal of *The Polish Peasant*, he
remarks that 'perhaps this is all that one can expect or should expect
in the interpretative analysis of human documentary material'
(Blumer 1939:75).

Blumer makes clear that the assessment of generalizations in
sociology relies in part on the experience and 'authority' of the
researcher, and also on the background knowledge of the reader:

Let's say you read the theoretical statements of Thomas and
Znaniecki and the materials to which the authors specifically
relate these theoretical remarks. You then make the judgment
as to how reasonable it is. If it seems to be a reasonable
interpretation, you accept it. That raises the question, what is a
reasonable interpretation? Well, it seems to me that there is a
kind of triadic relationship there. A reasonable interpretation
is largely dependent upon the ability of the person who makes
the generalization. I should expect a person like Mr Thomas
who has had much intimate contact with human beings, who
has studied them extensively, who has marked ability in
understanding human nature, on the whole to make a
reasonable interpretation. Furthermore, there is a body of
material there; you can read that. It is human material; you can
assume the role of the person whose account it is and thus
arrive at some idea of how reasonable the interpretation is.

Then, too, you bring your own background of experience. If
you are a person who has had a lot of contact with human
beings and understands human nature well, and particularly if
you already have a knowledge of the particular people with
which the authors are dealing, you are in a better position to
judge the reasonableness of the interpretation. Thus, the
judgment of the reasonableness of an interpetation is based
upon the background of the reader's own experience and also

149

upon the authority of the person who makes the
interpretation.

(Blumer 1939:146-7)

Here, then, Blumer seems to be arguing that sociology cannot meet
the requirements of science, but that this does not rule out the
possibility of sound understanding of human behaviour through
reliance on *Verstehen.*

As I noted earlier, it is in his appraisal of *The Polish Peasant* that
Blumer first explicitly states the dilemma that he sees facing the
social sciences, though it is implicit throughout his dissertation. The
dilemma arises from the commitment to science, conceived in terms
of the hypothetico-deductive method, on the one hand, and to
symbolic interactionism on the other. The latter demands that if we
are to understand human behaviour we must take account of
subjective as well as objective factors. However, at present at least,
Blumer argues, there seems to be no way of documenting subjective
factors that meets the requirements of science:

> My own feeling is that this work of Thomas and Znaniecki
> presents a dilemma as far as social research goes. My judgment
> is that it conclusively shows the need of recognizing and
> considering the subjective factor in human experience. It is
> also true, however, that the effort to study this factor by the use
> of human documents is attended by enormous difficulty,
> primarily in that the documents do not seem to be an effective
> test of the theoretical ideas one may develop regarding human
> or group behavior. So the dilemma presents itself in this form:
> on one hand, an inescapable need of including the subjective
> element of human experience, but, on the other hand, an
> enormous, and so far, unsurmounted, difficulty in securing
> devices that will catch this element of human experience in the
> way that is customary for usable data in ordinary scientific
> procedure in other fields.

(Blumer 1939:111)

Blumer's appraisal of *The Polish Peasant* was reissued in 1979, and
he wrote an introduction for this new edition. In it he repeated his
praise of the study for containing 'a theoretical scheme of the nature
of human group life that is comprehensive, elaborate, logical, and
very clear' (Blumer 1979a:vii). He also repeats his endorsement of
its methodological stance that both objective and subjective factors

must be included in explanations of human behaviour and of Thomas and Znaniecki's use of human documents. Blumer summarizes the argument of his appraisal in four points, the last of which is presented as follows:

> despite the failure of the human documents to meet the test of scientific criteria (representativeness of data, adequacy of data, reliability of data, and decisiveness of data) the documentary data did clarify and give support to theoretical assertions and, reciprocally, the theoretical assertions illuminated and clarified the data; this set an anomalous relation between theory and data in the use of human documents.
>
> (Blumer 1979:xii)

Here again we have Blumer's ambiguous attitude towards Thomas and Znaniecki's study, stimulated by recognition of the dilemma facing social research. On the one hand, this study does not meet scientific criteria and therefore the findings are not established; on the other, the findings are convincing and the data support them. Blumer claims, not entirely legitimately, that the participants in the conference 'agreed that I had established the four points' (Blumer 1979:xii), and he comments that: 'the conference never succeeded in resolving the dilemma' and that 'it has not been resolved at all during the intervening time' (Blumer 1979:xxxi).

In the remainder of the introduction Blumer discusses each of what he takes to be the criteria to be met by a scientific instrument: representativeness, adequacy, reliability, and decisive validation. He considers why these criteria are not applicable to, or cannot be met by, human documents. He argues that representativeness is inappropriate to the study of documents, and that instead one should select those people for study who are involved in the social activities being researched and who are good observers. As regards adequacy he comments: 'the problem of adequacy of data in the case of human documents is not to be met by the conventional routes of getting an adequate measurement of the variables that are used. Instead, a broad, flexible, and redirecting inquiry is needed' (Blumer 1979:xxxiv). He argues that reliability should be interpreted in terms of the extent to which a variety of documents support the same conclusions producing 'a transcending affirmation' (Blumer 1979:xxxv). He even suggests that it might not matter if the documents were fictitious:

The question may be asked, if the scholarly value of human accounts depends on how accurately they depict the kinds of human experiences being studied, what difference does it make whether the accounts are fictitious or actual happenings? I ask the question not to justify fiction but to pose a very important problem. The problem seems to be less a matter of the honesty of the informant and more a matter of accurate perceptiveness. This puts the problem in a markedly different light from that in which it is usually seen. It is clearly an unresolved methodological problem.

(Blumer 1979:xxxv)[7]

As regards testability, Blumer suggests that many attempts to make human documents test hypotheses undermine their value. However, there are means by which the likelihood of firm and decisive data from human documents can be attained. In particular, we should use documents that come from knowledgeable individuals, or we should ask such individuals to assess the documents we are using. And he comments that 'to ascertain who is knowledgeable and to gain, where needed, their cooperation are separate but manageable problems' (Blumer 1979:xxxvii).

In Blumer's treatment of these issues it is not clear whether he is still working with his original definition of science and suggesting that the sort of analysis that is possible in sociology lies outside its boundaries, or whether he is proposing a redefinition of the concept of science to include sociological analysis. However, it seems likely that, at least later on in his career, the second of these options was his preference. Elsewhere Blumer points out that we do not have fixed and certain knowledge about the nature of scientific method. He argues that there is no consensus among social scientists about the nature of scientific method as used by natural scientists:

There is disagreement as to the logical steps in scientific procedure; there is difference as to the extent and form in which scientific procedure is said to be quantitative or experimental in a strict controlled sense; there is disagreement as to whether scientific method can be reduced to special procedures such as 'operationalism'; there is conspicuous variation in the 'type of world' presupposed by the nature of

152

scientific study – whether it is configurational or an
aggregation of disparate units.

(Blumer 1966c:v)

And he argues that this dissensus is not limited to social scientists:

The history of the portrayals of scientific method over the past
two centuries by natural scientists and sophisticated interpreters shows a comparable picture of differences, change,
shifts, and new versions. The nature of scientific method has
not been, and is not now, a fixed, established datum.

(Blumer 1966c:v)

CONCLUSION

Blumer starts from a conception of science modelled on
experimental method, though not requiring physical control of
variables. In his dissertation, he assesses the prospects of applying
this method in social psychology, and comes to the conclusion that
it has not yet been done successfully, and that there are reasons why
it may not be possible. In 1939, in his appraisal of *The Polish Peasant*,
he points out that Thomas and Znaniecki do not succeed in
establishing their conclusions in a scientific manner. And he
concludes that whereas in the natural sciences theories can be
validated by specific items of data, in the social sciences, at present
anyway, one must rely on judgement based on experience of human
social life. However, he believes that in this way we can judge the
validity of different descriptions and explanations reasonably
accurately, both as researchers and as readers of research reports.
Moreover, as readers, where we do not have relevant experience
ourselves, we can judge accounts on the basis of the degree of
relevant experience of those who provided the accounts (what he
refers to as the 'authority' of the researcher). As a result, Blumer
suggests that the most effective way of improving the validity of social
scientific research is not, as the positivists believed, by the
standardization of method, but through the enrichment of the
experience of researchers:

[There is a] need for an enrichening of experience which will
make it possible for observers to form more dependable
judgments in those observations which give us our trouble. I
don't think that there is any short-cut way of arriving at the

formation of such judgments; it has to be done in the slow and tedious manner of developing a rich and intimate familiarity with the kind of conduct that is being studied and in employing whatever relevant imagination observers may fortunately possess.

(Blumer 1940:718-19)

This expansion of experience is a key feature of what Blumer calls naturalistic research, the kind of research that he sees as the most productive, at least in the current situation of the social sciences. He also implies that we need to reconceptualize science to include research employing naturalistic method. In the next chapter I shall look in detail at the nature of that method.

Chapter Seven

BLUMER'S ALTERNATIVE: NATURALISTIC RESEARCH

From one point of view the nature of naturalistic research is straightforward: it is the case-study research of Chicago sociology. Thus, Blumer cites *The Polish Peasant* as an exemplar of naturalistic research (Blumer 1979a). However, this is not as helpful as it might be since, as I noted in Chapter 3, the Chicagoans were not very explicit about methodology. Furthermore, Blumer himself provides only one account of what he is recommending, and even that is little more than a sketch (Blumer 1969a). In fact, as late as 1979, Blumer stated that the methodology of naturalistic research 'has not been worked out at all' (Blumer 1979a:xxxiv). In this chapter I shall try to work it out as best I can, looking first at Blumer's own description of naturalistic method, and then at some other accounts of the logic of qualitative analysis that may be taken as developments of it.

BLUMER'S DESCRIPTION OF NATURALISTIC METHOD

The defining feature of 'naturalistic research', according to Blumer, is that it respects the nature of the social world. At the level of method, this involves the investigation of 'a given area of happening in terms of its natural or actual character, as opposed to the observation of a surrogate or substitute form' (Blumer 1979:xxiv). Blumer contrasts naturalistic research with a number of other strategies: with laboratory experiments; with studies that are concerned only with products, not with processes; with research that starts with 'a constructed model of what is to be studied [making] ... contact with the actual world through deductions from the model'; with investigations which seek to reconstruct a picture of what happened and then proceed to study that reconstruction; and with studies 'such as survey research, which aim to provide an idea of how people *might* act as opposed to how they have acted or are acting' or which 'seek to measure attitudes or personality traits' (Blumer 1979:xxiv). Blumer's conception of naturalistic research seems to be based, then, on several dimensions of contrast with what he viewed as the dominant tradition of research in sociology. It involves:

1 investigation in 'real world' settings rather than in settings created specially for the purposes of the research;
2 the study of social processes with minimal intervention by the researcher instead of the physical control of variables that is essential to laboratory experimentation;
3 flexible data-collection strategies in which decisions about what data to collect and how are made over the course of the research, as against the pre-structuring of data collection that is characteristic of survey research;
4 investigation of actual processes of social interaction followed over their course, rather than reliance on interviews or questionnaires designed to document types of attitude or personality;
5 research that involves the construction, and continual reconstruction, of a model of the process under study, versus research that sets out to test a set of pre-defined hypotheses.

David Matza provides a more extended discussion of the philosophy – or, more accurately, the anti-philosophy – of naturalism. He points out that, rather confusingly, the term 'naturalism' is often used to refer to the application of the methods of the natural sciences to the study of the social world. However, he argues that this definition of the term confuses means with goals. The overriding commitment of naturalism, he claims, is 'to the phenomena and their nature' (Matza 1969:3). Furthermore, such a commitment:

> stands against all forms of philosophical generalization. Its loyalty is *to the world*, with whatever measure of variety or universality happen to inhere in [that world]. Naturalism does not and cannot commit itself to eternal preconceptions regarding the nature of phenomena. Consequently, it does not and cannot commit itself to any single preferred method for engaging and scrutinizing phenomena. It stands for observation or engagement of course for that is implicit in fidelity to

the natural world. But naturalistic observation may also include experience and introspection, the methods traditionally associated with subjectivism.

(Matza 1969:5)

Central to naturalism is the desire to represent the world as it is, in all its complexity and changeability, and to avoid imposing artificial structures. This is very similar, of course, to the attitude of Dilthey, with his attempt to detect structures within experience, but it also recalls the earlier arguments of Bacon and Newton against deductive forms of reasoning and the use of hypotheses. The suggestion is of some form of inductivism.

For the naturalist, then, the starting-point must be the nature of the phenomena under study, and methods must be devised that are appropriate to that nature, not imported from other sciences. They must capture and preserve the intrinsic character of those phenomena, though Matza suggests that *any* representation involves some level of distortion.[1]

Blumer identifies two phases of naturalistic research which he calls 'exploration' and 'inspection'.

Exploration

The purpose of exploration is *not* to construct rigorously defined theories or to test hypotheses. It is to

move toward a clearer understanding of how one's problem is to be posed, to learn what are the appropriate data, to develop ideas of what are significant lines of relation, and to evolve one's conceptual tools in the light of what one is learning about the area of life.

(Blumer 1969a:40)

The goal is to produce detailed descriptions of events and patterns of activity in the sphere chosen for study:

to develop and fill out as comprehensive and accurate a picture of the area of study as conditions allow. The picture should enable the scholar to feel at home in the area, to talk from a basis of fact and not from speculation.

(Blumer 1969a: 42)

In the exploratory stage of research, then, the sociologist seeks to build up her/his acquaintance with the area of the world to be studied, thereby breaking down any erroneous preconceptions. This requires 'free exploration in the area, getting close to the people involved in it, seeing a variety of situations they meet, noting their conversations, and watching their life as it flows along' (Blumer 1969a: 37). What is particularly important here is that researchers adopt an open-minded and flexible attitude to what they see and hear:

> Exploration is by definition a flexible procedure in which the scholar shifts from one to another line of inquiry, adopts new points of observation as his study progresses, moves in new directions previously unthought of, and changes his recognition of what are relevant data as he acquires more information and better understanding.
>
> (Blumer 1969a:40)

Exploration may employ the use of a wide range of research strategies, indeed any ethical technique that offers further understanding is appropriate including: observation, interviewing, life histories, the study of official and personal documents, and even 'making counts of an item if this appears to be worthwhile' (Blumer 1969a:41). However, Blumer lays particular emphasis on one method:

> One should sedulously seek participants in the sphere of life who are acute observers and who are well-informed. One such person is worth a hundred others who are merely unobservant participants. A small number of such individuals, brought together as a discussion or resource group, is more valuable many times over than any representative sample. Such a group, discussing collectively their sphere of life and probing into it as they meet one another's disagreements, will do more to lift the veils covering the sphere of life than any other device that I know of.
>
> (Blumer 1969a: 41)

Exploration – open-minded, flexible observation of the area under study using any methods that seem appropriate, and producing detailed descriptions of that area – is the first element of naturalistic research. Blumer argues that sometimes this strategy is sufficient to answer the questions posed:

It should be pointed out that the mere descriptive information unearthed through exploratory research may serve, in itself, to provide the answers to theoretical questions that the scholar may have in mind. ... One of the interesting values of exploratory study is that the fuller descriptive account that it yields will frequently give an adequate explanation of what was problematic without the need of invoking any theory or proposing any analytical scheme.

(Blumer 1969a:42)

However, usually exploration must be complemented by a more analytic form of inquiry, which Blumer calls 'inspection'.

Inspection

Blumer argues that scientific analysis requires two things: 'clear, discriminating analytical elements and the isolation of relations between these elements' (Blumer 1969a: 43). Inspection is designed to achieve both these goals, though he gives particular attention to the role of inspection in clarifying concepts.

As we saw in Chapters 5 and 6, there are features of the human social world that Blumer believes make the development of definitive concepts difficult, if not impossible. However, his conclusion is not that we must be satisfied with vague concepts. He argues that concepts in the social sciences play a very important role in 'sensitizing' us to important aspects of the social world, and that this sensitizing function is of great importance in the social sciences. He draws the contrast between 'definitive' and 'sensitizing' concepts as follows:

A definitive concept refers precisely to what is common to a class of objects, by the aid of a clear definition in terms of attributes or fixed bench marks. This definition, or the bench marks, serve as a means of clearly identifying the individual instance of the class and the make-up of that instance that is covered by the concept. A sensitizing concept lacks such specification of attributes or bench marks and consequently it does not enable the user to move directly to the instance and its relevant content. Instead, it gives the user a general sense of reference and guidance in approaching empirical instances.

159

Whereas definitive concepts provide prescriptions of what to see, sensitizing concepts merely suggest directions along which to look.

(Blumer 1954:7)

Blumer does not regard sensitizing concepts as given and fixed in meaning. They can be refined and developed, and it is through inspection that this is achieved. He describes inspection as 'an intensive focused examination' of the empirical content of the concepts used in the analysis, and of the relations among these concepts. It involves subjecting the empirical instances covered by the concept to 'careful flexible scrutiny ... in the context of the empirical area in which they take place'. This inspection is carried out 'with an eye to disengaging the generic nature' of the concept. This requires approaching the concept (or 'analytical element') and its instances in different ways: 'viewing it from different angles, asking many different questions of it, and returning to its scrutiny from the standpoint of such questions'. Blumer uses the analogy of trying to identify the character of a strange physical object:

We may pick it up, look at it closely, turn it over as we view it, look at it from this or that angle, raise questions as to what it might be, go back and handle it in the light of our questions, try it out, and test it in one way or another. ... Such inspection is not preset, routinized, or prescribed: it only becomes such when we already know what [the object] is and can thus resort to a specific test, as in the case of a technician. Instead, inspection is flexible, imaginative, creative, and free to take new directions.

(Blumer 1969a:44)

In inspecting social phenomena, then:

One goes to the empirical instances of the analytical element, views them in their different concrete settings, looks at them from different positions, asks questions of them with regard to their generic character, goes back and re-examines them, compares them with one another, and in this manner sifts out the nature of the analytical element that the empirical instances represent.

(Blumer 1969a:44-5)

Blumer regards inspection of this kind as an essential feature of sociological inquiry:

160

I know of no other way to determine the nature of an
analytical element that one proposes to use in the
analysis of a given empirical area of social life and still
be sure that the analytical element is both germane and
valid for such use.

(Blumer 1969a:45)

Through this process of inspection, Blumer claims, the validity of
sensitizing concepts is assessed and improved. By means of careful
study of empirical instances to which the concept refers, relevant
features of those instances 'not ... covered adequately by what the
concept asserts and implies' may be discovered, leading to revision
of the concept (Blumer 1954:8).

Blumer also sees inspection as involving the development and
testing of theories, it is directed 'at unearthing generic relations ...
and at formulating theoretical propositions' (Blumer 1969a:42-3).
Blumer does not provide an extended discussion of what this
involves, but in an article summarizing Blumer's conception of
naturalistic research, one of his students, Lonnie Athens (1984),
provides some detail, drawing on Blumer's lectures at the University
of California, Berkeley. According to Athens, he sees 'the formation
of theoretical propositions through the linking together of
sensitizing concepts' as requiring an approach that is very similar to
that involved in the development of such concepts:

First, the researcher examines various empirical instances of
the *relationship* between empirical instances of his or her
rudimentary ideas. Next, the researcher compares various
actual instances of the relationship between the rudimentary
ideas and, on the basis of these comparisons, isolates some of
the possible characteristics of their relationship. Finally, once
some of the possible characteristics of their relationship have
been isolated, the researcher then compares further actual
instances of this relationship against the emerging [concept of
the] relationship in order to further develop and refine it.
When the examination of further instances of the relationship
do not produce any more significant modifications in it, then
the relationship may be considered precisely isolated, or as
Blumer puts it, 'pinned down'. The researcher repeats this
process until all the possible relationships suggested between

the rudimentary theoretical ideas during exploration have been isolated.

(Athens 1984: 248)

The development of sensitizing concepts, and their integration into theoretical propositions, through exploration and inspection, is the heart of Blumer's conception of naturalistic research. And he emphasizes that this is a rather different approach from that presented in most methodology texts, where the emphasis is on the hypothetico-deductive method (Blumer 1969a:45).[2]

Equally important, the products of naturalistic research are different from those of much conventional social research. Whereas the latter is concerned with the identification of causal, or at least correlational, relationships among a set of abstract variables, naturalistic research aims at a description of processes of social interaction in their context. We can get a sense of this contrast in product from Blumer's critique of variable analysis:

A variable relation states (for example) that reasonably staunch Erie County Republicans become confirmed in their attachment to their candidate as a result of listening to the campaign materials of the rival party. This bare and interesting finding gives us no picture of them as human beings in their particular world. We do not know the run of their experiences which induced an organization of their sentiments and views, nor do we know what this organization is, we do not know the social atmosphere or codes in their social circles; we do not know the reinforcements and rationalizations that come from their fellows; we do not know the defining process in their circles; we do not know the pressures, the incitants, and the models that came from their niches in the social structure; we do not know how their ethical sensitivities are organized and what they would tolerate in the way of shocking behaviour on the part of their candidate. In short, we do not have the picture to size up and understand what their confirmed attachment to a political candidate means in terms of their experience and their social context.

(Blumer 1956:685)

Naturalistic research is designed to provide precisely what variable analysis fails to offer. Blumer insists that any explanation for patterns of human behaviour must trace out the meanings involved: how they form part of the interactional context, how they change over time, and how they feed into the process of action formation. Without this, he implies, we have no explanation, we have only a truncated and distorted picture of the social world.

Blumer's account of the kind of approach that he recommends as an alternative to that centred on quantitative method is only an outline. Furthermore, he does not provide any examples of studies that have employed this approach, apart from *The Polish Peasant* and other Chicago studies. However, there are other accounts of qualitative method that represent developments of this approach, albeit in different directions, and which are more detailed and provide explicit examples. In the remainder of this chapter I want to look at three rather different examples: analytic induction, grounded theorizing, and the pattern model of explanation. I have selected these because in my judgement they represent the main ways in which qualitative researchers have conceptualized the logic of sociological analysis.

ANALYTIC INDUCTION

In Chapter 4 I discussed Florian Znaniecki's critique of statistical method. Here I want to look in more detail at the alternative that he proposes, what he calls 'analytic induction'. Znaniecki's writings clearly had an important influence on Blumer, and analytic induction was subsequently developed and applied by one of Blumer's students, Alfred Lindesmith, and by one of his students, Donald Cressey.

Znaniecki's argument for analytic induction involves the following steps:

1 all concrete objects are descriptively inexhaustible, so selective description of their characteristics is essential;
2 the criteria for this selection are provided by the participation of these objects in semi-closed systems of various kinds, and the sociologist is interested in social, and more generally, cultural systems;
3 the essential characteristics of the class or classes of phenomena involved in a particular closed system can be identified neither by deductive processes (through identifying

the class *a priori*), nor by enumerative induction (studying the superficial characteristics of objects belonging to a pre-defined class). They can only be discovered by analytic induction. This involves in-depth study of one or a small number of cases, and identification of the functional relationships among the characteristics of each case.

Znaniecki starts from the position that pure research, which he conceives as research concerned with producing theoretical laws, is the 'necessary foundation of all useful legislative and efficient social reform' (Znaniecki 1928:307). The goal of sociology is to identify laws which state that 'whenever and wherever a certain cause A occurs, a certain effect B must inevitably follow unless interfered with by some other definite effect D of some other equally definite cause C' (Znaniecki 1928: 309). Sociologists must not be satisfied with showing that particular social phenomena are a product of 'a number of "cooperating factors" or "contributing causes", the relative importance of which may vary from case to case and the precise effect of any one of which separately remains underdetermined and changing' (Znaniecki 1928: 309). Here Znaniecki is contrasting what he regards as the essence of science – the search for universal laws – with the concern of practitioners of statistical method with assessing the relative contributions to an effect of multiple factors.

Znaniecki traces analytic induction back through Galileo to Aristotle and Plato. He also believes that it is the method used by contemporary scientists. He claims that physicists, chemists, and biologists made progress 'not by agglomerating large masses of superficial observations, but by inducing laws from a deep analysis of experimentally isolated instances' (Znaniecki 1934: 237). What is involved in analytic induction is separating 'the essential from the accidental ... to obtain generalizations which will prove applicable to all similar objects and happenings whenever and wherever they occur' (Znaniecki 1928: 307).

Znaniecki emphasizes that sociological researchers must beware of taking over the categories or views of legislators or social reformers. He argues that in the area of crime, for example:

> Society in generalizing certain acts and applying to them a
> certain category of punishment is exclusively interested in such
> features of these acts as have a practical bearing upon some

classes of values which it recognizes as important, e.g., private property, sexual mores, religion, governmental institutions, life and health of group members. But it is by no means certain that these features are always the most significant theoretically, that they are the ones which will help us most in describing and explaining such acts.

(Znaniecki 1928: 308)

For this reason, Znaniecki rejects the idea that we must define the phenomenon in which we have an interest in advance. Rather, we discover its character in the process of the research. Indeed, such discovery is the goal of the research since the character of the phenomenon is defined by the law-like relations in which it is involved. For this reason a sociologist who uses a term:

must always be ready to qualify it, to exclude from the sphere of its application data which he began by including in it, or to extend its application to data which at first he did not think of taking into account, or even to reject it – all depending on the results of his analytic studies. And in any case he must be sure that his final use of the term be very different from its popular use; if it is not, there is a strong presumption that his research has been as superficial as common-sense reflection.[3]

(Znaniecki 1934:240)

Analytic induction, then, studies a small number of cases in depth in order to discover the nature of the phenomena under investigation:

Emphasis must be put not on the quantity of cases, but on the thorough acquaintance with each case under observation. In physics or chemistry two or three well-conducted experiments are sufficient to establish a causal law. In sociology, taking into account the greater complexity of data and the increased difficulty of observation, from a dozen to a score of instances methodically studied and compared should answer the same purpose.

(Znaniecki 1928: 316)

The process of investigation must be guided by developing theoretical ideas: 'every individual case should be treated as a particular instance either confirming some general causal law already known or leading to the discovery of a new law' (Znaniecki 1928: 316).

The method most commonly employed by natural scientists in identifying laws is of course the experiment, but Znaniecki argues that the nature of social facts precludes the use of this method by sociologists. However, he claims that the logic of the experiment can be used in sociology:

> The logic of the experiment consists in simplifying the conditions in which certain facts occur; the scientist builds a definite and limited system of objects cut off from irrelevant external influences, and investigates the changes which are going on in this system, trying to determine their causal relations. The sociologist can do something similar with less difficulty, for he does not need to build closed systems artificially; he finds them ready-made in social life. Man in his individual and collective behavior is continually constructing and reconstructing limited systems of objects which he intentionally tries to keep undisturbed by external influences. All the scientist needs to do is to determine by exact observation and analysis what these systems are, and to study by comparative method the processes which occur within them.
>
> (Znaniecki 1928: 311)

Znaniecki does not provide any clear and detailed examples of analytic induction in practice, but Lindesmith and Cressey do.[4] While Lindesmith denies any influence from Znaniecki, he adopts very similar views about the process of inquiry. Lindesmith investigated the causal process involved in people becoming addicted to opiates (Lindesmith 1937 and 1968). He presents the method he employs in this research as simply the method of science; citing Mead (1917) and Ritchie (1923) as sources. This method is concerned with capturing universal causal laws – in other words, with identifying the necessary and sufficient conditions under which opiate addiction occurs. He contrasts this approach with statistical method on the grounds that the latter is concerned only with probabilities. Lindesmith declares that the validity of a theory does not depend on the number of cases studied: indeed, a single case could be sufficient. He also notes that, while his research was not experimental in form, it used the logic of the experiment: 'it ... does not involve the multiplication of instances but the search for and examination of crucial cases' (Lindesmith 1937: 8).

There are some minor differences between Lindesmith and Znaniecki. For example, Lindesmith emphasizes the need to search for negative cases:

> Because the verification of a scientific theory consists primarily in the failure to prove that it is wrong, it is most effectively tested by the close examination of precisely those areas in which it seems weakest or of the instances which appear to contradict it.
>
> (Lindesmith 1968: 20)

However, while the search for negative instances is not something that Znaniecki makes central, it is compatible with his position.

Lindesmith's attitude to statistical method is ambivalent. In places he seems to regard it as a self-justifying alternative paradigm:

> The methodological orientation of this study is deterministic rather than statistical. Applied to the study of narcotics addiction, each of these orientations has its own characteristic goals, methodological assumptions and analytic procedures, and neither can be judged by the standards of the other.
>
> (Lindesmith 1968:3)

Yet, elsewhere, he makes clear that he has a low regard for the value of statistical analysis, arguing for example that it leads to an arbitrary choice of theory:

> It is ... possible to formulate a series of theories, each of them applicable to some addicts in some place at some time, and none of them applicable to all addicts anywhere. Under such circumstances no grounds exist for saying any such theory is wrong, that one is right and the others wrong, or one is any better than another. Acceptance of one above the others becomes a matter of personal taste or professional prejudice.
>
> (Lindesmith 1968: 18)

Lindesmith begins with a definition of the phenomenon he seeks to explain, which he restricts to opiate addiction on the grounds that other forms of addiction seem likely to be produced by different causes. He studied a considerable number of cases of individuals suffering from opiate addiction, often as a result of hospital treatment. He begins with the hypothesis that a person becomes addicted whenever 'he knows what drug he is getting and has been getting it long enough to cause withdrawal distress on removal' (Lindesmith 1937:2). However, this idea soon had to be abandoned in the face of negative evidence. He continued to modify and refine his hypothesis in this way until it fitted all the cases he had studied and the study of new cases did not contradict it. At that point he declared his theory to be established, though recognizing that negative cases could appear in the future, at which point revision of the theory would be necessary. His final hypothesis takes the critical causal factor in addiction to be 'using the drug for the consciously understood purpose of alleviating the withdrawal symptoms' (Lindesmith 1937:3).

Donald Cressey provides another explicit instance of the application of analytic induction in his work on financial trust violation. A student of Lindesmith, Cressey sets out to identify the necessary and sufficient conditions of trust violation, in keeping with 'the assumption of proper scientific method and generalization by determining whether a definable sequence of events is always present when trust violation is present and never present when trust violation is absent' (Cressey 1950: 739).

Cressey takes over Lewin's distinction between systematic and genetic causation (Lewin 1936), a distinction that is analogous to Znaniecki's concern with the study of closed, or semi-closed, systems. Analytic induction is concerned with systematic causation, with causal relations occurring within semi-closed systems, not with external factors that bring such systems into existence or affect their operation.

Cressey provides a detailed summary of the steps involved in analytic induction:

First, a rough definition of the phenomenon to be explained is formulated. Second, an hypothetical explanation of that phenomenon is formulated. Third, one case is studied in light of the hypothesis with the object of determining whether the hypothesis fits the facts in that case. Fourth, if the hypothesis does not fit the facts, either the hypothesis is re-formulated or the phenomenon to be explained is re-defined, so that the case is excluded. This definition must be more precise than the first one. Fifth, practical certainty may be attained after a small number of cases has been examined, but the discovery by the investigator or any other investigator of a single negative case disproves the explanation and requires a re-formulation. Sixth, this procedure of examining cases, re-defining the phenomenon and re-formulating the hypothesis is continued until a universal relationship is established, each negative case calling for a re-definition or a re-formulation. Seventh, for purposes of proof, cases outside the area circumscribed by the definition are examined to determine whether or not the final hypothesis applies to them. This step is in keeping with the observation that scientific generalizations consist of descriptions of conditions which are always present when the phenomenon is present but which are never present when the phenomenon is absent.

(Cressey 1953:16)

The last of these steps is not a standard feature of analytic induction, and for the moment I shall ignore it (but see Chapter 8). The process of analytic induction is summarized in Figure 1 below.

In the case of Cressey's own research, he reports how he began from a legal definition of embezzlement but found that the term was not used consistently. Therefore, he formulated his own definition of what he came to refer to as 'financial trust violation'. This was held to have occurred where a person had accepted a position of financial trust in good faith but later exploited that position. Cressey notes that 'These criteria permit the inclusion of almost all persons convicted for embezzlement and, in addition, a proportion of those convicted for larceny by bailee, forgery, and confidence game'. For data he relied on interviews with 'all the prisoners whose behavior met the criteria and who were confined at the Illinois State Penitentiaries at Joliet' (Cressey 1950:740).

In setting out to explain financial trust violation, Cressey began with a first hypothesis that

positions of financial trust are violated when the incumbent has learned, in connection with the business or profession in which he is employed, that some forms of trust violation are merely 'technical violations' and are not really 'illegal' or 'wrong'.

(Cressey 1950:741)

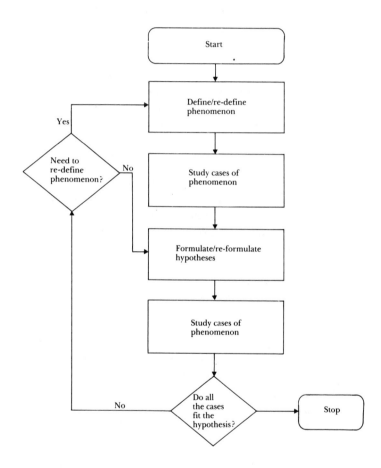

Figure 1 The process of analytic induction

However, this explanation was soon abandoned because it was found that many financial trust violators stated 'that they knew the behavior to be illegal and wrong at all times and that they merely "kidded themselves" into thinking that it was not illegal' (Cressey 1950:741).

An alternative hypothesis was developed that 'positions of trust are violated when the incumbent structures a real or supposed need for extra funds or extended use of property as an "emergency" that cannot be met by legal means' (Cressey 1950:741) This hypothesis was also soon rejected in the face of counter evidence, for example: 'persons were found who claimed that while an emergency had been present at the time they violated the trust, other, perhaps even more extreme, emergencies had been present in earlier periods and they did not violate it' (Cressey 1950:741).

The fourth hypothesis was that people violate financial trust when they incur 'financial obligations that are considered as nonsocially sanctionable and which, consequently, must be satisfied by private or secret means' (Cressey 1950:741). However, Cressey reports that

> when the cases were re-examined in light of this hypothesis it was found that in a few of them there was nothing which could be considered as financial *obligation*; that is, as a debt which had been incurred in the past and for which the person at present felt responsible. Also, in some cases there had been nonsanctionable obligations at a prior time, and these obligations had not been alleviated by means of trust violation. It became increasingly apparent at this point that trust violation could not be attributed to a single event, but that its explanation could be made only in terms of a sequence of events, a process.
>
> (Cressey 1950:741-2)

After further revisions and developments Cressey arrived at his final formulation:

> Trusted persons become trust violators when they conceive of themselves as having a financial problem which is non-shareable, have the knowledge or awareness that this problem can be secretly resolved by violation of the position of financial trust, and are able to apply to their own conduct in that situation verbalizations that enable them to adjust their conceptions of themselves as trusted persons with their

171

conceptions of themselves as users of the entrusted funds or property.

(Cressey 1950:742)

Cressey reports that this explanation fitted all the cases that he had investigated and that no new cases had emerged that challenged it.

Analytic induction provides one possible specification of Blumer's concept of inspection. It is close to Blumer's conception of science, as presented in his dissertation, and it seems likely that this was an important influence on Lindesmith (his research was carried out in the 1930s), and indirectly on Cressey. It is compatible with Blumer's account of naturalistic research in some key respects, in particular in emphasizing the importance of in-depth studies of a small number of cases rather than the statistical analysis of aggregate data.

Another account of qualitative analysis that shares much in common with Blumer's account is what Glaser and Strauss call 'grounded theorizing'.[5]

GROUNDED THEORIZING

The problem that Glaser and Strauss address is the same as that from which Blumer began his article 'What is wrong with social theory?' (Blumer 1954): the gap between social theory and empirical research; between the work of sociological theorists and that of empirical researchers. Glaser and Strauss contrast their (and implicitly Blumer's) approach to this problem with that of Robert Merton, in his famous articles on the relationship between theory and empirical research (Merton 1957). Merton poses the theorist's desire for knowledge having scope and significance against the empirical researcher's emphasis on demonstrability. He sets out to show that theory facilitates the development of empirical research beyond the production of isolated empirical generalizations; and that empirical research can, in turn, stimulate the development of theory as well as providing the means to test it. Merton's proposed solution was the development of what he called 'middle range theory': theory that is neither so abstract that it cannot be empirically tested, nor so concrete that it has little scope and significance. The development of such theory would be the result of collaboration between theorists and researchers.

Writing some eleven years after Merton, Glaser and Strauss

(1967) claim that the way in which sociologists following Merton's advice typically seek to close the gap between theory and research is to take an existing theory, derived (for example) from the work of one of the founders of sociology, and to test small parts of it as rigorously as possible, usually via quantitative techniques. Glaser and Strauss argue that this frequently involves forcing data into pre-established theoretical categories, since the theory is taken as given and unchangeable. Moreover, the procedures integral to 'rigorous testing' militate against the development of better theory since the researcher is not allowed to deviate from initial research plans, whatever data collection throws up, for fear of undermining the rigour of the test.

Glaser and Strauss's alternative solution to the problem is 'the generation of grounded theory'. By this they mean the stimulation and development of theoretical ideas by the systematic investigation of the social world, usually by means of qualitative methods. This is contrasted with 'a priori theory' produced by armchair theorizing which 'verificationist' research relies on. The purpose of grounded theorizing is both to produce effective theoretical ideas and to develop theories of wide scope and high density and integration.

Grounded theorizing is inductive rather than deductive. By its very nature, and unlike theory testing, it requires flexibility on the part of the researcher; the structure of the research – what groups and settings are investigated and by what methods, in order to find out what, and so on – cannot be specified at the start, but must be worked out as the research proceeds. And, such research involves a relaxation of the standards of evidence normally enforced in research designed to test hypotheses rigorously.

Glaser and Strauss do not simply claim that empirical research following the guidelines of grounded theory may usefully stimulate theoretical ideas, they also claim that ideas stimulated and developed in the course of empirical research are likely to be more productive and to provide a better 'fit' with the empirical world than theory produced in other ways. There seem to be two aspects to this notion of empirical fit. First, there is the claim that grounded theoretical concepts will necessarily be 'sensitizing' – that is, 'yield a "meaningful" picture, abetted by apt illustrations, that enable one to grasp the reference in terms of one's own experience' (Glaser and Strauss 1967:38-9). Second, the notion of fit refers to what they call 'plausibility'. Although they recognize that the techniques they recommend for theory generation do not test the theory with the same degree of rigour as 'verificationist techniques', they claim that grounded theory will be more plausible than *a priori* theory and, indeed, once developed is unlikely to be refuted or transformed (Glaser and Strauss 1967:4 and 253-4). They argue that for most purposes it is not necessary to go beyond the level of plausibility provided by grounded theorizing, and that the standard of rigour required in 'verification' is only necessary in special circumstances such as 'designing specific action programmes or working in rather well-developed substantive areas' (Glaser and Strauss 1967:233).

Glaser and Strauss cite Weber on bureaucracy (Weber 1946), Durkheim on suicide (Durkheim 1897/1951), and Becker on moral entrepreneurs (Becker 1963) as examples of the generation of grounded theory, but in presenting detailed accounts of grounded theorizing they concentrate, for reasons of access, on their own research, notably that concerned with the social processes surrounding dying in hospitals.

There are two major techniques that Glaser and Strauss present as central to grounded theorizing. One is the constant comparative method. This is a procedure for generating categories and their properties. Glaser and Strauss illustrate the relationships between categories and properties as follows:

> A category stands by itself as a conceptual element of the theory. A property, in turn, is a conceptual aspect or element of a category. We have, then, both categories and their properties. For example, two categories of nursing care are the nurses' 'professional composure' and their 'perceptions of social loss' of a dying patient, that is their view of what degree of loss his death will be to his family and occupation. One pro-perty of the category of social loss is 'loss rationales' – that is, the rationales nurses use to justify to themselves their percep-tions of social loss. All three are interrelated: *loss rationales* arise among nurses to explain the death of a patient whom they see as a high *social loss,* and this relationship helps the nurses to maintain their *professional composure* when facing his death.
>
> (Glaser and Strauss 1967: 36)

Glaser and Strauss's account of the constant comparative method is very close to Blumer's discussion of inspection, though much more detailed (see also Strauss 1987). It involves comparison of multiple data segments judged to belong to the same category, in such a way as to identify the central features of that category. Each incident is coded in terms of as many categories as are relevant, and all those instances assigned to a particular category are compared. In this way, a set of coherent categories is produced, along with their properties. As the analysis develops, the categories become the guiding criteria in the analysis of cases; and the categories and their properties become integrated into a theoretical core. In this process, the number of categories may decline as underlying uniformities are discovered. The analysis of cases for any particular category proceeds only until the analysis seems to be producing no new properties, to the point of what Glaser and Strauss call 'theoretical saturation'.

The other technique essential to grounded theorizing is theoretical sampling. By contrast with representative sampling, this involves choosing cases in such a way as most effectively to develop the emerging theory. There is no population specified at the outset of the research. Rather, the researcher is continually sampling the views and behaviour of different groups as the research progresses, the nature of each population and sample being determined by what is required for the further development of the theory. And the study of new cases continues, once again, only until the point of theoretical saturation. This contrasts with the procedure in random sampling, where every case within a sample has to be covered. This is an example of what Glaser and Strauss see as the relaxation of the usual standards of methodological rigour that is necessary to facilitate the generation of theory.

Theoretical sampling involves multiple comparisons of groups (though settings, times, and even individuals can also be compared) in which the researcher seeks to maximize or minimize the differences between the groups, according to her or his purposes at a particular stage of the research. Glaser and Strauss use the following example to illustrate this process:

> Visits to the various medical services were scheduled as follows: I wished first to look at services that minimized patient aware-ness (and so I first looked at a premature baby service and then at a neurosurgical service where patients were frequently coma-tose). I wished next to look at dying in a situation where expec-tancy of staff and often of patients was great and dying was quick, so I observed on an Intensive Care Unit. Then I wished to observe on a service where staff expectations of terminality

were great but where the patient's might or might not be, and where dying tended to be slow. So I looked next at a cancer service. I wished then to look at conditions where death was unexpected and rapid, and so looked at an emergency service. ... So our scheduling of types of service was directed by a general conceptual scheme – which included hypotheses about awareness, expectedness and rate of dying – as well as by a developing conceptual structure including matters not at first envisioned. Sometimes we returned to services after the initial two or three or four weeks of continuous observation, in order to check upon items which needed checking or had been missed in the initial period.

(Glaser and Strauss 1967: 59)

Glaser and Strauss argue that in the process of generating grounded theory lower-level categories usually emerge initially, more abstract ones later. The researcher typically begins by minimizing the differences between comparison groups so as to bring out the basic properties of a category; only then does he or she begin to make comparisons involving the maximization of differences so as to discover the most universal uniformities.

Two kinds of grounded theory are distinguished, differing in abstractness. Substantive theory is concerned with relatively concrete areas such as patient care, classroom interaction in schools, or race relations. Formal theory, at a more abstract level, relates to such topics as stigma, deviant behaviour, formal organizations and so on. Formal theory is usually generated from substantive theory, although it may sometimes be generated directly. Formal theories cannot simply be applied to substantive areas; rather, substantive theories must be generated for each empirical situation and selection then made among formal theories or a new one developed.

One of the criticisms sometimes levelled at Glaser and Strauss is that the approach to research they recommend is inherently non-cumulative since it is implied that every researcher must begin from scratch, ignoring all previous theory. However, Glaser and Strauss deny that this was intended, as Strauss makes clear in an article entitled 'Discovering new theory from previous theory' which appeared in a volume dedicated to Herbert Blumer (Shibutani 1970). There he shows how categories and hypotheses can be derived from existing grounded theory and that empirical investigation of these can lead to the further development of that theory, perhaps transforming it from the substantive to the formal level (see also Strauss 1987).

In summary, then, Glaser and Strauss argue that the best way to produce social theory that fits the empirical world is not to attempt rigorous testing of speculative theories, but to set out explicitly to generate grounded theory by systematic empirical research, primarily (but not necessarily exclusively, see Glaser and Strauss 1967: ch. 8) of a qualitative kind. While it is designed to develop theory, Glaser and Strauss argue that the process involves some testing too, and that it is often not necessary to engage in further testing.

In comparison with analytic induction, grounded theorizing involves more emphasis on the generation and development of theory than on its testing. Grounded theorizing also seems to differ from analytic induction in its goals. Although Glaser and Strauss are not very explicit about the status of the theory they are seeking to produce, it is clear that grounded theorizing is not intended to provide universal laws; though the findings are clearly intended to be generic, not just particularistic. In both these respects, grounded theorizing seems rather closer to Blumer's 1969 account of naturalistic research than is analytic induction.

THE PATTERN MODEL

Analytic induction and grounded theorizing are two examples of how ethnographers, some of them students of Blumer, have interpreted the concept of naturalistic research. However, there are those within the interactionist tradition who have argued that these interpretations, and other accounts of ethnographic methodology, represent a deviation from Blumer's position, resulting from the failure of modern interactionists to abandon the positivist model of theory and explanation. This argument is presented in a particularly forthright manner by Robin Williams in an important but neglected article (Williams 1976).

Williams notes Blumer's argument in his 1969 article (Blumer 1969a) that methods must respect the nature of the social world, and draws the conclusion from this that 'methods of empirical enquiry are to be assessed in terms of their power to deliver up the social world as the social world is constituted in symbolic interactionist metatheory' (Williams 1976:117).

In short, then, according to Williams, Blumer privileges ontology over epistemology, and he conceptualizes the ontology of the social world in terms of symbolic interactionism.

In this respect, Williams contrasts Blumer's views with the deductive-nomological model of explanation which 'shows stubborn disregard for questions of ontology ... and substitutes for these questions a standard for knowledge that is independent of claims for the peculiarity or special character of any particular discipline's view of the world' (Williams·1976:119). [6]

Williams argues that many symbolic interactionists, instead of treating their ontological assumptions as the guiding light, have sought to reconcile these with a positivistic view of methodology: 'symbolic interactionists seem ... to have been engaged in a complicated juggling act whereby Blumer's ontology has often been maintained apparently alongside a model of theory and explanation that is not compatible with such an ontology' (Williams 1976:120). Williams is particularly scathing about arguments for methodological and theoretical triangulation, such as those of Norman Denzin (Denzin 1978). According to Williams, participant observation 'best fits the requirements of symbolic interactionist respect for the empirical world' (Williams 1976:126). Participant observation is 'the necessary and sufficient method for symbolic interactionist research' (Williams 1976:127).

As a replacement for the deductive-nomological model of explanation, Williams advocates what he calls the 'pattern model' (following Kaplan 1964 and Diesing 1972). [7] He provides the following account of this model:

> The most important feature of this model of explanation is that explanations which exhibit this form will make no strict demarcation between description and explanation ... the activity of describing the relation between one action and others in a context is equivalent to interpreting or explaining the meaning of that action. ... [Furthermore,] the objectivity of ... descriptions/explanations cannot be decided upon by examining any single piece of evidence: neither can appeal be made to the way in which any single piece of evidence was collected. Rather, the whole pattern has to be examined with respect to its more or less inclusive character. Making a study more objective then would consist in filling in more detail of

the patterns of activity and meaning that both articulate and relate particular themes to others.

(Williams 1976:128-9)

Diesing's use of the pattern model of explanation occurs in his discussion of what he calls the 'holistic' approach to social science research, in which the whole – a community, an organization, an individual's life, and so on – is assumed to have an 'organic unity' (Diesing 1972:128). The aim of this approach is to discover the character of that unity. This is, of course, quite close to the conception of the case study in Chicago sociology. The process of analysis in holistic research, which Diesing sees as including participant observation research in sociology and anthropology, is the derivation of 'themes' that seem to characterize the case. The relationships among these themes are then studied in order to build a model of the case. It is in terms of this model that particular features of the case are explained, according to how they fit into the pattern mapped by the model. He cites the example of Becker and Geer's explanation of medical students' use of the term 'crock':

> The interns see themselves as gaining valuable experiences by treating actual cases. Certain cases exhibit routine symptoms but no recognizable underlying organic disease. Examination of these cases yields no experience in treating disease, since the cases have no disease. The interns perceive these cases as a waste of their valuable time and express their resentment by a derogatory term. In this case the pattern consists of a conflict between expectations and actual tasks, with the resulting emotion expressed in the term 'crock'. ... Becker and Geer go on to explain the use of [this] term ... further by noting that these patients were also disliked because they gave the student no opportunity to assume medical responsibility. The term is thereby connected to another theme, the desire to assume responsibility, and to another conflict, that between students and faculty over the allocation of responsibility. If these new themes and relations in turn prove puzzling, one explains them by tracing out more and more of the pattern. If one wishes to explain the students' expectations of gaining experience and assuming responsibility, one traces the development of these beliefs in the earlier years of medical school. They appear as solutions to the problems facing

179

medical students, problems that are set by the curriculum, the hierarchical organization of the school, and patterns of communication among students.

(Diesing 1972:158)

Williams claims that it is in the context of the pattern model of explanation, as outlined by Diesing, that Blumer's idea of sensitizing concepts finds its rightful place. Such concepts are not preliminary to the development of the definitive concepts that are required for deductive-nomological explanations (as Denzin 1978 suggests, for example): they are adequate as they stand in terms of the pattern model. Such concepts, and this type of model, fit the nature of the social world in a way that the positivist view of explanation does not.

On the basis of his commitment to the pattern model, Williams criticizes grounded theorizing and analytic induction as inappropriate to symbolic interactionist ontology. And it is true that the pattern model seems closer to Blumer's 1969 account of naturalistic research than analytic induction and perhaps even than grounded theorizing. Particularly important is the way that explanation is sought in the detail of patterns of action, not by abstracting from concrete complexity in search of context-independent principles.[8] Williams argues that explanation should stay closer to the commonsense interpretations of participants than analytic induction and grounded theorizing do, and, as we saw, this also seemed to be a requirement placed on naturalistic research by Blumer.

CONCLUSION

It is quite clear that Blumer's 1969 conception of naturalistic inquiry was modelled on the Chicago studies of the 1920s and 1930s. For example, it is striking how much his account of naturalistic research, even in 1979, emphasizes the collection and analysis of human documents rather than participant observation.[9] Blumer regards such research as providing valuable understanding of the social world, unlike much of the work of quantitative researchers. This is because it respects the nature of that world, which the indiscriminate application of quantitative method does not. However, it is only relatively late, in 1969, that Blumer provides a discussion of the character of naturalistic research. Even then, his account is sketchy. To compensate for this, I have examined not only Blumer's account but also three more detailed specifications of the logic of qualitative analysis: analytic induction, grounded theorizing, and the pattern model of explanation. In the next chapter I shall assess the viability of naturalistic research in these various forms.

Chapter Eight

AN ASSESSMENT OF NATURALISTIC RESEARCH

In earlier chapters I have presented Blumer's methodological writings in the context of the development of US sociology during the first half of this century, and against the background of pragmatist philosophy and nineteenth-century discussions of the relation between the natural and social sciences. In this final chapter I want to assess Blumer's arguments, and in particular his proposal for naturalistic research. The central question I shall address is an apparently simple one: does naturalistic research solve the dilemma that Blumer identified as facing social science? And if not, how might that dilemma be resolved?

I shall begin by evaluating Blumer's own account of naturalistic research, before assessing analytic induction, grounded theorizing, and the pattern model of explanation.

BLUMER'S ACCOUNT

I have emphasized that Blumer's methodological writings were very much a reaction against growing trends in US sociology away from case-study research. Where case study is concerned with documenting the interrelationships among a large number of factors in a particular instance, by the late 1930s the dominant approach was one which sought relationships among a smaller number of variables applying across a large number of cases. In case study much reliance was placed on qualitative conceptualization of variables, since for many of the variables no quantitative treatment seemed to be available that would remain true to the complex nature of the features under study. However, the dominant approach came to involve quantitative representation of variables and statistical analysis of data, almost as a matter of course.

Blumer's attitude towards quantitative method was not simple. It derived from two sources. On the one hand, he argued that that method is founded on a misconception about the nature of science: the assumption that a scientific approach requires the operationalization and quantification of sociological concepts. On the other hand, his critique of quantitative research was also based on his doubts about whether scientific method, as currently conceived, could be applied successfully in the social sciences, given the nature of human social action. While in his dissertation Blumer distinguishes these two arguments, in his later discussions he does not. Furthermore, the complexity of his attitude towards quantitative research renders the intended status of naturalistic research uncertain. Sometimes Blumer writes as if it were a complement or corrective to the use of the quantitative method: perhaps as a necessary preliminary serving to produce a conceptual framework that will later allow the effective application of a quantitative or hypothetico-deductive approach.[1] However, his predominant position seems to be that naturalistic research is a self-sufficient alternative to mainstream sociological work. This is the prevailing emphasis in Blumer's 1969a article, and it is the way that his work has usually been interpreted by qualitative researchers.

Two questions must be asked of naturalistic research if we are to discover whether it resolves Blumer's dilemma. First: does it meet the criteria of science? Second: does it match the assumptions of symbolic interactionism?

DOES NATURALISTIC RESEARCH SATISFY SCIENTIFIC CRITERIA?

Blumer's statements about whether naturalistic research can meet scientific criteria are genuinely puzzling. On most occasions (for example, Blumer 1928, 1939, and 1979), he declares that sociology cannot meet these criteria since universal laws are not available in the field of social phenomena, and because social phenomena are individually distinct and their accurate description relies on the experience and judgement of the observer. On at least one occasion, however, Blumer expressed the belief that naturalistic research does match scientific criteria:

[it] permits the scholar to meet all of the basic requirements of an empirical science: to confront an empirical social world that is available for observation and analysis; to raise abstract problems with regard to that world; to gather necessary data through careful and disciplined examination of that world; to unearth relations between categories of such data; to formulate propositions with regard to such relations; to weave such propositions into a theoretical scheme; and to test the problems, the data, the relations, the propositions, and the theory by renewed examination of the empirical world.

(Blumer 1969a:48)

Blumer makes this claim despite the fact that his account of naturalistic research in this 1969 article is very similar to what in 1928 he had described as the 'historical' approach, which he had contrasted with science, and whose claim to produce sound knowledge he had severely criticized, though not entirely rejected.

In order to answer the question of whether Blumer's naturalistic method satisfies scientific criteria, we must be clear about the nature of those criteria. As we saw in Chapter 6, Blumer's most detailed treatment of this issue is to be found in his dissertation. He argued there that the function of science is to provide the basis for social control by identifying universal laws, and its logical features include the comparative method, conceived as the logic of experimentation. It involves the 'breaking up' of reality, ignoring what is idiosyncratic in favour of what is general. The procedural core of science from this point of view is captured in Peirce's account of the hypothetico-deductive method.[2] The starting-point is some puzzling phenomenon, perhaps an exception to an existing scientific law. The first phase of inquiry is the development of plausible theoretical ideas, including reconstructions of existing theories, to account for the anomaly. Following this process, which Peirce calls abduction, is the deductive phase, in which these theoretical ideas are developed and specific hypotheses are derived from them. In the final phase, which Peirce refers to as induction, those hypotheses are tested in particular cases, controlling for other factors. In this process, the data must be publicly accessible and the phenomena studied repetitive, not unique.

Whether Blumer remained committed to this conception of science is not clear. Later on in his career there were signs that he did not. However, he does not offer any alternative definition. For the moment I shall treat the hypothetico-deductive method as the defining criterion of science.

Significantly, in his 1969 article Blumer criticizes the use of the hypothetico-deductive method in sociology, on the grounds that the premises on which hypothesis-testing takes place have not themselves been subjected to test. He argues that those who apply this method in sociology often fail to recognize that its use depends on assumptions about the nature of the phenomena under study, and that as a result the assumptions on which it relies are often false. These false assumptions arise from lack of familiarity on the part of the researcher with the phenomena he or she is studying. It is the provision of such acquaintance with social phenomena, and the overturning of stereotypes, that is one of the major functions of naturalistic research. A key assumption for Blumer here is that the social world is diverse, and that simply being a member of a society does not give one sufficient familiarity with all its parts.

The argument that the hypothetico-deductive method is defective because it does not involve the direct testing of all the assumptions made by the researcher is similar to the criticisms of speculative theorizing made by inductivists such as Bacon, Newton, and Mill. It also recalls Dilthey's rejection of the use of hypotheses in the human sciences. However, it seems to me that this argument cannot withstand scrutiny. It runs against the critical commonsensism that I ascribed to Blumer in Chapter 5. It effectively assumes that we have direct knowledge of reality, and this is an idea that is very difficult to defend.[3] As we saw, Peirce argued, convincingly in my view, that there could be no absolutely certain foundation for our knowledge. And without such a foundation we can never test all the assumptions on which an inquiry is based. In testing any one assumption we necessarily rely on others, and their uncertain validity introduces uncertainty into the interpretation of the test. We are faced with an infinite regress here.

However, Blumer's argument can be developed in a more limited way that is more convincing. It can be contrasted with the views of Karl Popper, one of the most influential advocates of the hypothetico-deductive method. Popper argues that it does not matter where hypotheses come from, or what assumptions they involve: what is crucial is that they are open to falsification and that they are tested rigorously, since through this process any errors will be eliminated (Popper 1959, 1963, and 1972).

This argument is open to at least two major criticisms: one concerned with the efficiency of the hypothetico-deductive method, the other with its effectiveness. First, as Rescher (1978) points out, if natural scientists over the past three hundred years had paid no attention to the initial plausibility of hypotheses it would be difficult to explain the success of the natural sciences during that period. After all, for any research problem there would have been a very large number of hypotheses that could have been selected for testing, only a small number of which were actually tested. The success rate of natural scientists in finding what, from our vantage point anyway, have been very fruitful hypotheses would be very surprising if their selection of hypotheses had been random or haphazard. Contrary to Popper, it seems likely that the success of the natural sciences has arisen in part from the felicitous selection of hypotheses on substantive grounds. Charles Peirce believed that instinct played, and should play, an important part in scientists' selection of hypotheses: that we have an instinct to choose the right hypothesis. It seems that for Peirce this instinct arose from our commonsense knowledge of the world. We saw that he believed that we must necessarily take most of that knowledge for granted, and that there were reasons for believing that much of it was approximately true.

We can interpret Blumer's argument as a variant of Peirce's. The only additional element required is the assumption, which Blumer makes explicit, that within large complex societies commonsense is subculturally differentiated. What is commonsense knowledge in one group will not be so in another, or at least the area of overlap will be limited. Furthermore, these diverse subcultures are adapted to their particular social niches. If, therefore, we want to investigate a particular social world, Blumer argues, we should begin by exploring the commonsense knowledge of the people who inhabit that world. Naturalistic research is particularly well suited to tapping such commonsense knowledge. By doing this, Blumer's argument might run, we are much more likely to avoid unrealistic assumptions and therefore to select productive hypotheses than if we relied on our own commonsense knowledge, which in most cases is likely to be attuned to a quite different situation from that which we are investigating.

The second argument against Popper's conception of the hypothetico-deductive method represents a more severe challenge. Here it is not just the efficiency with which false hypotheses are eliminated that is at issue, but also the reliability of the procedure in eliminating only false hypotheses, and giving us grounds for treating those hypotheses that are corroborated as more likely to be true. In other words, the ability of the hypothetico-deductive method, even in the form of the experiment, to eliminate incorrect and only incorrect hypotheses is questioned.[4]

The problem is as follows: faced with the apparent falsification of a hypothesis we cannot know for certain which part of the theory under test has been falsified. Such apparent falsification can occur even when the theory is true, because all testing of hypotheses rests upon theoretical assumptions. If one of these assumptions were false, the evidence might suggest that the hypothesis was false when in fact it was true. As I argued earlier, this reliance on theoretical assumptions when testing hypotheses presents us with a potentially infinite regression: to assess the assumptions we relied on in testing a hypothesis we would need to rely on others, and to test those others we would have to depend on yet others, and so on.

The consequence of this problem is that not only can we not show with certainty that a hypothesis is true, as Popper himself emphasized, but neither can we reject a hypothesis with certainty. This lays the basis for another possible justification for Blumer's recommendation of naturalistic research. To the extent that the testing system may involve leakage of bad hypotheses into the domain of scientific knowledge, any strategy we have that might increase the chances of our initial theoretical ideas being true becomes especially valuable. If we can screen hypotheses before testing them, weeding out those that make unrealistic assumptions about the area of the social world to which the hypothesis relates, this may not only increase the efficiency but also the effectiveness of the hypothetico-deductive method.

Of course, the value of naturalistic research in this respect depends on the assumption that commonsense knowledge, culturally differentiated or otherwise, is likely to be true; that it is a product of an evolutionary process in which it comes to represent accurately the particular circumstances in which a group lives. And this is not as obviously reasonable an assumption as Blumer and the pragmatists imply. There does seem to me to be a fundamental problem with pragmatism here. Peirce is primarily concerned with science and philosophy, and his assumption that we are dealing with a 'community of inquirers' dedicated to the pursuit of truth is perhaps not too unreasonable in that context. However, James, Dewey, Mead, and Blumer focus on commonsense inquiry in the context of practical, everyday life. Here the idea that discovering the truth is a pre-eminent concern is more questionable. At some times and in some places it may be, but in others it is not. Furthermore, not only does it seem likely that many beliefs are not produced or used as a basis for instrumental activity, in which they would be opened up to test, but also we know that instrumental success is not always dependent on truth nor does truth necessarily produce instrumental success.

Blumer's criticism of the hypothetico-deductive method has only limited force, then, but his recommendation of naturalistic research might be justified in terms of increasing the efficiency, and perhaps even the effectiveness, of the application of that method. In this context it would be a preliminary to the application of the hypothetico-deductive method. However, while Blumer recognizes the latter method might be legitimately employed following a period of exploratory research, in fact he rejects it as a component of naturalistic research on the grounds that it still: 'forces (...) data into an artificial framework that seriously limits and impairs genuine empirical analysis (...). It does not pin down in an exact way the nature of the analytical elements in the empirical social world nor does it ferret out in an exacting manner the relation between these analytical elements' (Blumer 1969a:43).

It seems clear, then, that Blumer does not believe that naturalistic research does or should involve the use of the hypothetico-deductive method. Nor, in his view, should it be a preliminary to the use of that method.

It is on the grounds that they fail to incorporate the hypothetico-deductive method that Blumer's methodological recommendations have often been criticized. For example, in a methodological critique of symbolic interactionism, and of Blumer in particular, Joan Huber argues that naturalistic research allows a distinctive kind of bias to intrude into research. She claims that because it is concerned with inducing descriptions and theories from data and with documenting the perspectives of participants, there is a strong likelihood that the views of the researcher and of the people researched will bias the findings. This is because, rather than setting out to test a hypothesis that can turn out to be right or wrong, naturalistic researchers rely on developing theory out of the process of participant observation. They claim that in this process the nature of the social world is discovered. But Huber argues that since no explicit and rigorous testing of hypotheses takes place, no control is exerted over the influence of the researcher's or participants' perspectives.

In his response to Huber, Blumer argues that naturalistic research does, or at least can, involve the testing of hypotheses. He states that

> There is no reason why the investigator who follows the symbolic interactionist approach cannot test his assertions and hypotheses about his empirical world by a careful, continuous examination of that world; his position is no different from that of Darwin or scores of competent ethnographers [a reference to anthropology]. The investigator who is sincere and sensitive to empirical observation is in the same position to find that his given ideas are untenable ... as is the researcher operating with a 'prior construction of logically-related propositions'.
>
> (Blumer 1973:798)

However, neither here nor elsewhere is Blumer clear about the nature of the process of testing that he claims is involved in naturalistic research. He seems to place faith in the idea that by 'going directly to the social world' and examining it we will discover its nature. I think he sees any fixed procedure as a barrier to such discovery because it impairs the flexibility of the researcher. The latter must be free to adapt to, to be moulded by, the world. In my view, though, while exploration, flexibility, and creativity are necessary, the idea that if one adopts a flexible attitude towards the world in one's interactions with it, one will come to discover its nature amounts to a naive form of realism. It underestimates the potential for bias and error. Not only is hypothesis-testing an essential element of the process of scientific discovery, but the most effective form of hypothesis testing is the hypothetico-deductive method. Although that method might not be a sufficient condition of sustained, successful scientific inquiry, in my view it is a necessary condition.

Like Huber, McPhail and Rexroat (1979 and 1980) also criticize

Blumer's methodological work on the grounds that it fails to recognize the centrality of the hypothetico-deductive method to sociological methodology. However, where Huber assigns the weaknesses she identifies in Blumer's methodology to the influence of pragmatism, these authors charge Blumer with misinterpreting Mead.[5] They claim that Mead viewed scientific method in terms of the application of experimental logic (see also McKinney 1955 and Kohout 1986). And elsewhere McPhail argues that Blumer's own account of symbolic interactionism provides the basis for an experimental rather than a naturalistic approach (McPhail 1979).

In his reply to McPhail and Rexroat, Blumer emphasizes once again that naturalistic research involves hypothesis-testing. Furthermore, he stresses that 'Mead did *not* see "scientific method" as a *special* kind of knowledge-producing procedure, or as a type of inquiry associated only with experimental science. To the contrary, he viewed scientific method as merely the extension of reflective intelligence' (Blumer 1980:415). Here Blumer may be arguing that naturalistic research involves the informal hypothesis-testing to be found in everyday life, rather than the hypothetico-deductive method as it is found in experimental sciences. However, while Mead and the other pragmatists certainly believed that science was a development of the practice of everyday problem-solving, rather than an entirely different procedure, they *did* regard it as a more rigorous form of that practice. They believed that science, through its employment of the hypothetico-deductive method, offered a more effective means of problem-solving than those used in everyday life. The reliance of naturalistic method on informal forms of hypothesis-testing rather than on the hypothetico-deductive method is difficult to justify from this perspective.[6]

Blumer's rejection of the hypothetico-deductive method as a component of naturalistic research probably stems from recognition of the problems involved in applying that method to the study of the social world. In his discussions of the 'problem of the concept' (Blumer 1928, 1940, and 1954), Blumer accepts that science, defined in terms of the hypothetico-deductive method, requires concepts that render decisions about whether or not particular phenomena are instances of the concept to be relatively clear and consensual. However, as we saw, he puts forward some reasons – the need to rely on judgement based on social context and the individual distinctiveness of social phenomena – that suggest that definitive concepts are impossible in the social sciences. It may be for these reasons that he believes the hypothetico-deductive method not to be appropriate in social research. I shall discuss each of them briefly.

Verstehen

While Blumer recognizes that even the observation of physical phenomena involves inference, in my view, like nineteenth-century advocates of *Verstehen*, he still underestimates the problems involved in such observation. It does not just require the use of a space–time framework, but also additional assumptions about the physical world. Even in the relatively simple case of measuring length with a ruler, for example, we make assumptions about the properties of rigid bodies (both in relation to the thing being measured and the ruler).[7]

Much the same is true of describing social phenomena. Here too we rely on assumptions, this time about the social world. Just as in the case of measuring length we infer from the alignment of the end of the object with some point on the ruler to the object's possession of a certain length, so in observing social behaviour we infer, albeit for the most part subconsciously, from the location and movement of physical objects – a pattern of body movement, a facial expression, an utterance, and so on – to action descriptions. In both cases we are using a category system plus some operational rules for assigning phenomena to categories that rely on theoretical assumptions about the phenomena concerned. Whereas the one is certainly more difficult to do reliably than the other, we should not assume that the nature of social phenomena precludes reliable observation.

Our difficulties may simply reflect the current weakness of our theoretical assumptions, a weakness that Blumer himself emphasized. Blumer certainly does not establish that there is something intrinsic to the observation of social phenomena that makes disagreement more likely than in the observation of physical phenomena. It is not obvious that there is anything about the 'subjective' character of social actions that makes their identification, in principle, any more problematic than the description of physical properties like mass, magnetism, or radioactivity. The properties that we ascribe to physical objects are no more strictly observable than those we assign to people.

Distinctiveness of social phenomena

At first sight the argument about the distinctiveness of social phenomena is even less convincing than the argument about *Verstehen*, since all phenomena, including physical objects and events, are unique. However, there is more to Blumer's argument than this. He claims that, unlike natural phenomena, social phenomena cannot be assigned to classes on the basis of common properties. And the implication is, I think, that this stems from the creative and indeterminate character of human behaviour: because the social world does not display deterministic relations, social phenomena do not fall neatly into categories showing common features, but only into more loosely defined, probabilistic groupings. Moreover, in many cases it does seem to be true that social phenomena cannot be rigorously classified on the basis of rules specifying necessary and sufficient conditions for their allocation to conceptual categories.[8]

However, it is worth noting that this is not a problem that is unique to the social sciences. It is also to be found, for example, in biological taxonomy, where various solutions have been developed, some of them quantitative (Sokal and Sneath 1963; Ridley 1986). Clearly, what is required is exploration by sociologists of the various strategies available for dealing with these problems. Blumer's proposal of sensitizing concepts constitutes one such strategy. But he tells us very little about the nature of such concepts and how they can be refined and developed. If sensitizing concepts provide only 'a direction in which to look', are they not necessarily vague, and how could they be refined and tested? Furthermore, how could they be developed without their meaning departing from that of their commonsense counterparts? Blumer provides little discussion of these problems, nor do the Chicago studies that he regards as exemplars of naturalistic research provide explicit illustrations of the process of concept development.

In summary, then, Blumer rules out the hypothetico-deductive method as inappropriate in naturalistic research, and he points to some serious problems facing its application. However, in my view he is unwise to assume that these problems are insurmountable, or that they derive simply from the nature of the social world. Although the sociological positivists' assumption that these problems can be resolved by fiat is surely misguided, their confidence in our ability to discover solutions to them is not necessarily misplaced.

Blumer insists that naturalistic research involves the testing of hypotheses, but he is not clear about what form this takes. Although hypothesis-testing of some kind may be involved in naturalistic research, there is no mention in Blumer's account of the systematic selection of cases to develop and test hypotheses.[9] Nor is there any suggestion of the explicit modification of the definition of the phenomenon to be explained, which is so central to analytic induction; and Blumer seems likely to reject such re-definition on the grounds that it moves sociological concepts away from commonsense meanings.

If we look at the studies that Blumer takes as exemplars of naturalistic research – notably, *The Polish Peasant* and other Chicago studies – we find that there is little evidence of hypothesis-testing. These studies simply present the results of analysis as a picture of the phenomena under investigation. This certainly departs from the requirement of the hypothetico-deductive method that the process of hypothesis-testing be explicit and open to replication by others. In reply to McPhail and Rexroat, Blumer argues, citing several of the Chicago studies, that naturalistic studies are 'presented in such a form as to definitely allow other research scholars to reexamine what is claimed by the original investigator, to see whether the account is empirically correct' (Blumer 1980a:413). But, as we saw in Chapter 3, this is simply not so. The Chicago studies provide descriptions and explanations of aspects of the social world with little explicit attention to methodology, and little information is provided about the process by which the findings were produced.

On balance, it seems clear that naturalistic research does not meet the criteria of science as Blumer defined these in 1928. I want to turn now to the other aspect of Blumer's dilemma, and to ask whether naturalistic research, as presented by Blumer, matches the assumptions of symbolic interactionism.

IS NATURALISTIC RESEARCH CONSISTENT WITH SYMBOLIC INTERACTIONISM?

From one point of view the answer to this question is straightforwardly positive. Symbolic interactionism portrays the social world as generated by social interaction among people; interaction that itself produces, and is shaped by, participants' interpretations of the world. Furthermore, this process of interaction is formative and creative, it is not composed of automatic responses to stimuli. The flexible character of naturalistic research, its emphasis on discovering the *perspectives* of participants and on observing the process of social interaction, would seem to be designed to capture the complex and fluid character of the social world, as portrayed by symbolic interactionism.

There is also another aspect of this match between naturalistic research and symbolic interactionism. To the extent that naturalistic inquiry is simply a refinement of the methods of inquiry and analysis that we all use in everyday life – talking to people, watching what happens, acting on our interpretations and monitoring the results, reading relevant documents, and so forth – naturalistic research has a reflexive relationship to the social world: it is not only attuned to the nature of that world, but in itself exemplifies that world (Hammersley and Atkinson 1983). In this kind of research, like other forms of social interaction, the behaviour of the researcher is not governed by rules (such as the protocol of the hypothetico-deductive method) but develops as it proceeds, responding to the changing situation by changing itself.

The only doubt about the compatibility between naturalistic research and symbolic interactionism arises from the apparent inconsistency between commonsense realism and symbolic interactionism. McPhail and Rexroat (1979) pointed to what they call an 'ontological paradox' in Blumer's writings: a conflict between his realist account of the process of research in which the nature of the world is *discovered*, and, using my terms, the phenomenalism of symbolic interactionism, in which meanings are portrayed as *constructions*, not reflections of some independent reality. However, as I argued in Chapter 5, this inconsistency can be resolved with only minor modifications to symbolic interactionism. We can recognize that different interpretations of the same thing can be made, without denying that if those interpretations are accurate they must correspond in relevant respects to the phenomena described.

In summary, then, Blumer's account of naturalistic research does seem to match the assumptions of symbolic interactionism, at least once the conflict between his phenomenalist metatheory and realist methodology has been resolved. However, it is clear that his account of naturalistic research was not intended to match the hypothetico-deductive method, nor does it do so. Furthermore, although he claims that it involves the testing of hypotheses, he does not explain how this is achieved.

ANALYTIC INDUCTION

In many respects, analytic induction seems to match Blumer's original conception of the requirements of science quite closely. It is the most explicit, and coherent, attempt to apply the hypothetico-deductive method within the qualitative research tradition.

However, there are some respects in which analytic induction deviates from the hypothetico-deductive method. That method is concerned with discovering both necessary and sufficient conditions for the occurrence of some phenomenon. And Lindesmith and Cressey explicitly claim to identify necessary and sufficient conditions. But, as Robinson (1951) points out, as formulated, if not always as practised, analytic induction allows the identification only of necessary and not of sufficient conditions. Cases are selected for study where the phenomenon to be explained occurs. But in order to identify sufficient conditions we must also investigate cases where the conditions specified by the hypothesis are known to hold in order to find out whether or not the phenomenon occurs there. Robinson provides a useful diagram to illustrate this limitation:

Figure 2 The distribution of cases

	Effect present	Effect absent
Cause present	a	b
Cause absent	c	d

Source: Derived from Robinson 1951

Analytic induction selects cases in the left-hand column, and modifies the theory or the definition of the phenomenon to be explained until all cases are in the top cell (a) and none are in the bottom (c). However, the possibility remains that there are cases in cell b. In other words, there may be cases where the conditions specified occur but the phenomenon itself is not produced. Hence, only necessary and not sufficient conditions are identified.[10]

Robinson argues that if analytic induction were modified to include investigation of cases where the conditions held, this would transform it into enumerative induction. He also claims that statistical sampling techniques should be applied in selecting cases; and he argues that doing this would reveal that the results are probabilistic rather than universal. (However, he accepts the goal of seeking to reduce the number of exceptions – that is, the number of cases in cells b and c – as far as possible.)

The first part of Robinson's argument is convincing. The investigation of cases where the conditions specified by the hypothesis occur is an essential element of the hypothetico-deductive method since it provides for the identification of sufficient conditions. To meet this criticism analytic induction would have to be modified in the manner indicated in Figure 3.

Robinson is surely correct too in claiming that we should not insist on finding perfect correlations between putative cause and effect. However, contrary to what he implies, this does not require us to formulate our theoretical claims in probabilistic terms. We can use evidence of less than perfect correlation to support universal claims: on the grounds that the exceptions arise from extraneous variables that we have not been able to control. Even in an experiment, control is rarely perfect; and we should not operate on the assumption that it can or will be, especially not in non-experimental research.

Robinson's argument that if analytic induction were to investigate sufficient as well as necessary conditions it would be transformed into enumerative induction is quite misleading. As we saw, one of the most important features of analytic induction is that it involves re-definition of the phenomenon to be explained, in an attempt to make it a causally homogeneous category. It is only by doing this that we can identify necessary conditions. Most quantitative research is concerned with discovering the relative contributions of a whole range of factors to the production of some category of phenomena that is defined independently of those factors.[11] In this sense, it is concerned with identifying sufficient, but not necessary factors. It is accepted that the effects of concern can be caused by factors other than those being studied (see Heise 1975:4-5, and Hirsch and Selvin 1973). If we reconstruct the practice of analytic induction so that it involves the search for necessary and sufficient conditions, that would render it true to its own principles and to the hypothetico-deductive method, not bring it into line with enumerative induction.

Robinson's recommendation that we apply statistical sampling techniques in the selection of cases is also misguided. The number

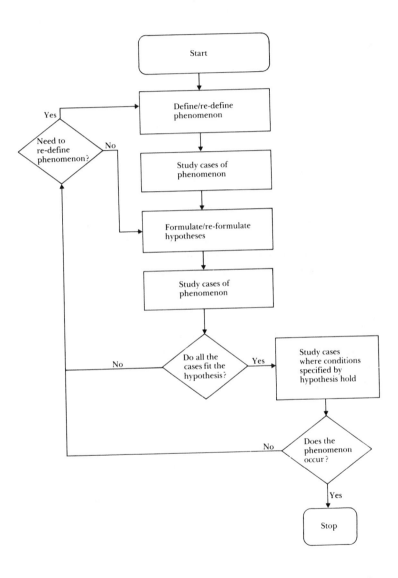

Figure 3 Analytic induction modified

of cases to which a law, universal or probabilistic, applies – past, present, and future – is infinite; and statistical sampling techniques cannot be used to draw conclusions about infinite populations (Selvin 1965; Willer 1967). Instead of statistical sampling techniques, what is required, surely, is the selection of cases in such a way that relevant extraneous factors are controlled. In this spirit, replying to Robinson, Lindesmith urges the study of crucial cases where the theory is most likely to be falsified (Lindesmith 1952). This is certainly what is necessary, though it is not clear that this strategy was implemented in Lindesmith's or Cressey's studies; and its implementation is not straightforward in non-experimental research – it can be very difficult to find the cases that are required to provide effective testing of a hypothesis in this kind of research.

Analytic induction requires some modification, then, to bring it into line with the hypothetico-deductive method, and to enable it to achieve its goal of identifying necessary and sufficient conditions. However, these modifications are within the spirit of that technique. It fares less well, however, in relation to the other horn of Blumer's dilemma. Although it has been used to study subjective factors and the processes by which particular types of social phenomena are produced, its commitment to the discovery of universal ('deterministic') relationships clearly represents a major departure from symbolic interactionism. Furthermore, in order to apply analytic induction effectively it seems likely that we require definitive rather than merely sensitizing concepts. In both these respects, then, analytic induction runs counter to key assumptions of symbolic interactionism.

GROUNDED THEORY

I have argued that the essence of analytic induction is the hypothetico-deductive method, the logic of the experiment in the broad sense used by Blumer (1928) and Znaniecki (1934). This is conceived as the method of the natural sciences; and analytic induction studies are intended as applications of this method to the study of the social world (Lindesmith 1937). Grounded theorizing is a more complex case. As we shall see, Glaser and Strauss are equivocal about whether or not grounded theorizing is a self-sufficient application of the hypothetico-deductive method.

In an early article Glaser presents the constant comparative

198

method as a codification and systematization of the more informal inspection of data which is common in qualitative research, through which theoretical ideas are generated and developed. In the constant comparative method, this informal coding of data is replaced by systematic coding similar to that involved in research concerned with theory-testing. However, Glaser contrasts this method with both quantitative theory testing and with analytic induction on the grounds that it is not designed to test hypotheses: 'the approach presented here cannot be used for provisional testing as well as discovering theory, since the collected data ... are not coded extensively enough to yield provisional tests. ... The data are coded only enough to generate, hence to suggest, theory' (Glaser 1965:438). Glaser recommends that 'partial testing of the theory, when necessary, is left to more rigorous, usually quantitative, approaches which come later in the scientific enterprise' (Glaser 1965:438).

The emphasis in *The Discovery of Grounded Theory* (Glaser and Strauss 1967) is slightly different, despite the fact that Glaser's earlier paper is incorporated largely unchanged. Here grounded theorizing is contrasted with verification studies, and it is argued that for many purposes rigorous testing of the conclusions produced by grounded theorizing is not required (Glaser and Strauss 1967:4 and 233). The implication is that grounded theorizing itself involves hypothesis testing, albeit of a less rigorous kind than that found in quantitative research. However, the nature of this process of testing is not clarified. It is not clear why we have good reason to believe that properly developed grounded theory should not only be dense, well-integrated, and plausible, but also true.

Strauss's most recent book on qualitative analysis moves even further in this direction, declaring that grounded theorizing is 'designed especially for generating and *testing* theory' (Strauss 1987:xi; my emphasis). It seems that grounded theorizing is now regarded as a self-sufficient approach, though Strauss insists that 'there is no logical or any sensible reason' for opposing qualitative against quantitative approaches, and suggests that they might be combined (Strauss 1987:2).

Some of what Strauss says about grounded theorizing makes clear that he sees it as employing the hypothetico-deductive method:

Scientific theories require first of all that they be conceived, then elaborated, then checked out. Everyone agrees on that.

What they do not always agree on are the exact terms with
which to refer to those three aspects of inquiry. The terms
which we prefer are induction, deduction, and verification.
Induction refers to the actions that lead to the discovery of an
hypothesis. ... Deduction consists of the drawing of
implications from hypotheses or larger systems of them for
purposes of verification. The latter term refers to the
procedures of verifying, whether that turns out to be total or a
partial qualification or negation. All three processes go on
throughout the life of the research project. Probably few
working scientists would make the mistake of believing these
stood in simple sequential relationship.

(Strauss 1987:11-12)

Here Strauss adopts a model of the research process that is very close
to Peirce's conception of the hypothetico-deductive method
(though the terminology is different), and he indicates his
indebtedness both to Peirce and to Dewey's book *Logic: the Theory of
Inquiry*, which drew heavily on Peirce. It seems that, from Strauss's
point of view, rather than grounded theorizing representing an early
stage in the process of scientific inquiry – to be completed by later
rigorous, quantitative testing (as Glaser had suggested earlier) – it
involved all phases of the process of inquiry, including testing
(verification). Strauss is quite explicit about this:

[in grounded theorizing] ... the theory is not just discovered
but *verified*, because the provisional character of the linkages –
of answers and hypotheses concerning them – gets checked
out during the succeeding phases of inquiry, with new data and
new coding.

(Strauss 1987:17)

Once again, though, Strauss does not tell us the nature of the
process of correction of hypotheses that he believes is built into
grounded theorizing. In the case of analytic induction, hypotheses
are compared with new cases that they claim to explain, and are
modified if they do not fit. In quantitative research, hypotheses are
tested by investigating whether the relationships they predict are to
be found in a large number of cases, controlling as far as possible
for relevant extraneous variables. With grounded theorizing,
however, the situation is less clear.

In some respects the procedures that Glaser and Strauss recommend do match the hypothetico-deductive method. In discussing their research on awareness contexts and the treatment of dying patients in hospital they state that:

Clearly, a substantive theory that is faithful to the everyday realities of the substantive area is one that is carefully *induced* from diverse data gathered over a considerable period of time. This research ... is directed in two ways – toward discovering new concepts and hypotheses, and then continually testing these emerging hypotheses under as many diverse conditions as possible.

(Glaser and Strauss 1965:261)

Theoretical sampling, involving in this case the selection of locales in which the value of the variable 'patient awareness' is different, represents an attempt to identify the consequences of such variation using comparative analysis.

Glaser and Strauss's approach also matches the hypothetico-deductive method in its commitment to mapping causal relationships, though it is not clear whether these are assumed to be universal or probabilistic. They claim that there are 'characteristic modes of interaction that result from each type of awareness context' (Glaser and Strauss 1965:269).[12] The claim that causal relations are identified in grounded theorizing is basic to Glaser and Strauss's concern with producing a theory that gives those involved in the dying situation practical control over events:

the theory must provide controllable variables with *much explanatory power*: they must 'make a big difference' in what is going on in the situation to be changed. We have discovered one such variable – awareness contexts. As we have reiterated many times, much of what happens in the dying situation is strongly determined by the type of awareness context within which the events are occurring.

(Glaser and Strauss 1965:270)

Although grounded theorizing matches the hypothetico-deductive model in these respects, in others it does not. First, Glaser and Strauss do not provide us with details about the hypotheses that were tested and the evidence used in those tests. The result is that close replication by others is not possible. In fact, their books have a very similar structure to those of the early Chicago studies and other forms of contemporary ethnography, in which the focus is primarily on the findings rather than on the process of research.[13] Second, as we have seen, Glaser and Strauss are quite explicit in *The Discovery of Grounded Theory* and especially in Glaser's earlier article (Glaser and Strauss 1967; Glaser 1965) that grounded theorizing does not involve systematic testing of hypotheses controlling for all other relevant factors; and there is nothing in the strategies recommended in Strauss's more recent text to suggest a change in this respect. Furthermore, as a procedure for selecting cases for study, theoretical sampling is designed to identify sufficient, not necessary, conditions. And, as with Blumer's account, a notable absence here is the procedure of re-defining the phenomenon to be explained in order to achieve a causally homogeneous category.

A third deviation of grounded theorizing from hypothetico-deductive method is the concern to map the complexity of social situations. Strauss comments that 'the basic question facing us is how to capture the complexity of [the] reality ... we study, and how to make convincing sense of it', and he continues that '... a theory, to avoid simplistic rendering of the phenomena under study, must be conceptually dense' (Strauss 1987:10). This represents a contrast with analytic induction. As Turner has emphasized, following Znaniecki, analytic induction attempts to identify a semi-closed system of variables and to specify the relationships among those variables (Turner 1953). It is not concerned with all the major causal factors that might produce the phenomenon. For example, Lindesmith specifies the relationship between having taken opiates, the experience of the symptoms produced by withdrawal, recognition of those symptoms as withdrawal symptoms, and the future use of the drug. He does not consider the factors that lead people to take the drug in the first place, or those affecting the chances of their recognizing withdrawal symptoms, or factors affecting the availability of the drug for future use, all of which, given the validity of his own theory, would be key causal variables. It seems to me that this is an important feature of the hypothetico-deductive method: the theories tested are not concerned with identifying all the factors that might be involved in producing a phenomenon on a given occasion, or even all of the most powerful ones. Typically, the aim is to discover a small system of interrelated variables that plays a key role in the production of a type of phenomenon whenever it occurs. In its deviation from the hypothetico-deductive method here, the logic of grounded theorizing seems closer to that of quantitative research in sociology which, as I have already suggested, is also concerned with identifying sufficient rather than both necessary and sufficient conditions.

The concern of grounded theorizing with mapping the complexity of social situations seems to stem from commitment to the goal of producing practically effective theory, in the tradition of Dewey and Mead (Glaser and Strauss 1965; Fisher and Strauss 1979):

> to achieve a theory general enough to be applicable to the total picture, we have found it ... important to accumulate a vast number of *diverse* qualitative 'facts' on dying situations (some of which may be slightly inaccurate). This diversity has facilitated the development of a theory that includes a sufficient number of general concepts relevant to most dying situations, with plausible relations among these categories that can account for much everyday behavior in dying situations.
>
> (Glaser and Strauss 1965:266)

In this respect, Glaser and Strauss seem to be presenting an approach that mixes nomothetic and idiographic concerns. They wish to produce substantive theories that apply to a wide range of social phenomena, but which, at the same time, represent cases in their particular complexity. This mixed nomothetic–idiographic approach is also suggested in one of Strauss's remarks:

> Underlying some contemporary positions are the contrasting assumptions that either a social science is possible or that it is to be eschewed in favor of more humanistic versions of knowledge about human activity. Our own position is somewhere between these two extremes.
>
> (Strauss 1987:8)

As with Rickert's suggestion that many sciences, including sociology, involve a combination of nomothetic and idiographic approaches, it is not clear here what the logic of a moderate position like this would be. This is not to say that what appears to be a disjunction could not be translated into a continuum, allowing midway positions. It is simply that Strauss does not tell us how idiographic and nomothetic goals can be achieved simultaneously.[14]

In summary, although grounded theorizing matches the

hypothetico-deductive method in some respects, it deviates from it in several important ways. Furthermore, grounded theorizing also departs from the assumptions of symbolic interactionism. It assumes 'strongly determined' (Glaser and Strauss 1965:270) relationships among variables, where symbolic interactionism emphasizes the creativity and indeterminism of human action. For these reasons, grounded theorizing, like analytic induction, fails to resolve Blumer's dilemma.

I want to turn now to the third reconstruction of the logic of naturalistic research: the pattern model.

THE PATTERN MODEL

In the case of the pattern model, the aim is to describe and simultaneously to explain the features of a particular social phenomenon – whether a community, an organization, or a person's life. Explanation takes place through a feature being shown to be related to the wider context in which it occurs. This is very much the model advocated by Dilthey:

> whereas the physical sciences systematize their findings by moving to more and more abstract levels, the human studies systematize by seeing the particular fact more and more fully in its context among other facts structurally related to it.
>
> (Hodges 1952:230)[15]

Furthermore, I think one could legitimately claim that it is the closest of the three models to the method of the historian, of the anthropologist, and, indeed, of many sociological ethnographers.

As regards the criteria of science, defined in terms of the hypothetico-deductive method, it is quite clear that the pattern model does not meet these criteria. Its advocates, both those in the nineteenth century and more recent writers like Diesing and Williams, reject that conception of science as inapplicable to the human sciences. Nor do the products of this method display the explicit hypothesis-testing through the study of multiple cases selected to control for other factors that the hypothetico-deductive method requires.

Turning to the question of whether the pattern model conforms to the assumptions of symbolic interactionism, we can note that it is closer in character than either analytic induction or grounded theorizing to Blumer's 1969 account of naturalistic research, and like that account it seems to match the assumptions of symbolic interactionism quite closely. However, there is one important respect in which it deviates. Becker, whose work on medical students was taken by Diesing to exemplify the pattern model, argues that the concept of social system is central to case-study research of the kind carried out in *Boys in White* (Becker *et al.* 1961):

> The concept of social system is a basic intellectual tool of modern sociology. The kind of participant observation discussed here is related directly to this concept, explaining particular social facts by explicit reference to their involvement in a complex of interconnected variables that the observer constructs as a theoretical model of the organization.
>
> (Becker 1971:33)

This raises the question of the status of the models of an organization or community produced by this style of research. Where the historian is typically concerned with a single case valued for itself (the French Revolution, the character of Richard III, and so on), sociologists using the pattern model usually wish to claim, like Becker, that the patterns they identify persist over time as part of a social system and also that they are representative of the internal processes to be found in particular types of social organization. For example, in the case of *Boys in White* (Becker *et al.* 1961), as the subtitle indicates, the focus was 'student culture in medical school' rather than student culture in the University of Kansas Medical School in 1956-7. Generalization over time and place is implied. However, the pattern model, as detailed by Diesing and Williams and earlier writers, provides no basis for such generalization. Indeed, as we saw in Chapter 6, Blumer himself provides a strong argument against the derivation of general claims from the study of unique cases (Blumer 1928). Generalization of this kind would only be possible if we assumed the existence of stable social systems of the kind assumed by some versions of sociological functionalism. Yet symbolic interactionism emphasizes the continual potential for social change and for this reason Blumer rejects social system models (Blumer 1969a and 1975).

In short, then, the pattern model does not meet the requirements of the hypothetico-deductive method. It does conform to the assumptions of symbolic interactionism, where it is used to study a particular situation at a particular time. But it deviates from those assumptions when it is made the basis for accounts of the enduring features of situations and/or for generalizations about particular types of social situation. Most sociological work, of course, involves generalizations of these kinds.

WHAT IS TO BE DONE?

I have argued that in none of its various forms does naturalistic research resolve Blumer's dilemma. As portrayed by Herbert Blumer himself, this form of research does match the assumptions of symbolic interactionism, once McPhail and Rexroat's 'ontological paradox' has been resolved. However, it does not meet the requirements of the hypothetico-deductive method. Analytic induction, with some modifications, can meet the criteria of science as I have interpreted them here, but does not conform to key assumptions of symbolic interactionism. Grounded theorizing matches closely neither the hypothetico-deductive method nor symbolic interactionism. The pattern model satisfies symbolic interactionism only where generalization is not intended, and its proponents specifically reject the hypothetico-deductive method. Overall, it is clear, I think, that the hypothetico-deductive method and symbolic interactionism, as currently understood, are incompatible: one assumes causal relationships defined in terms of necessary and sufficient conditions and the availability of definitive concepts, the other assumes indeterminism and a fluidity in social phenomena that is compatible only with sensitizing concepts.

This is a depressing conclusion for anyone who, like me, both believes that the hypothetico-deductive method is an essential element of rational inquiry and accepts the plausibility of the central assumptions of symbolic interactionism. I have no solution to Blumer's dilemma, but in the remainder of this chapter I shall review potential responses to it. I shall not subject these to sustained examination – my primary purpose is to map the alternatives – though I shall mention what seem to me to be the main problems associated with each of them.

A common response on the part of qualitative researchers is to ignore the problem. One possible justification for 'benign neglect' is Rock's argument that it is in the nature of symbolic interactionism to generate paradoxes (Rock 1979:xii). This is because it is 'the outcome of a scholarly rejection of ordinary scholarly pursuits' (Rock 1979:1). The substance of this argument seems to be that 'a sociology which portrays society as fluid and often unknowable cannot itself be highly structured' (Rock 1979:xii). However, while I agree that we must be prepared to tolerate unresolved philosophical problems, and not allow them to block the road of inquiry, I do not believe that we can take the view that such problems are unresolvable in principle. If we were to believe that the world is simply paradoxical, there would be little point in pursuing research or any form of inquiry. Indeed, it is difficult to see how we could live on that basis. It is an instance of what Thomas Reid called 'metaphysical insanity' (Adams 1988).

Putting problem-avoidance and defeatism to one side, there are two obvious ways of trying to resolve Blumer's dilemma. One is to re-define science in terms other than the hypothetico-deductive method. The other is to abandon or substantially modify symbolic interactionism. I shall look briefly at each of these strategies.

RE-DEFINING SCIENCE

As we saw in Chapter 6, Blumer's views about the possibility of social science were ambivalent, but I suggested that the re-definition of science was the direction in which he seemed to be moving. While nowhere in his published writings does he provide a clear alternative to his 1928 account, we can draw the outlines of one possible alternative, based on the pattern model, that is close to what Blumer suggests in a number of places (notably Blumer 1956 and 1969a). As I mentioned earlier, the pattern model has strong similarities with the ideas of nineteenth-century historicists and neo-Kantians. It also parallels the work of twentieth-century critics of the covering law model of historical explanation, such as Scriven and Dray. I shall draw on both these sources.

Developing the pattern model

Obviously, in developing a pattern explanation, we begin with the phenomenon to be explained. In the example used by Diesing concerning Becker and Geer's study of medical students, the effect to be explained is as follows:

Medical students use the term 'crock' in a derogatory manner
to refer to patients who exhibit routine symptoms but no
recognizable underlying organic disease.

In order to explain this phenomenon by means of a pattern
explanation, we must look at the context in which this linguistic
practice occurs and select one or more features that can explain it.
Becker and Geer identify two possible causes:

C1. the students believe that examination of 'crocks' yields no
experience in treating disease, and the students desire such
experience.
C2. the students feel that treating 'crocks' gives them no
opportunity to exercise professional responsibility and the
students desire such opportunities.

Both of these seem plausible explanations. But in order to justify
them we need to know from what their plausibility derives. How do
we discover, and how do we justify, relations between the
explanandum and the explanans in a pattern explanation?

There are several possibilities. One is that the relations between
the elements of a pattern explanation are given by direct
apprehension. Blumer himself sometimes comes close to this
position – for example, when he argues for 'direct examination of
the social world' and claims that the categories that we use to give
conceptual order to the social world derive from our observation of
that world (Blumer 1969a:54). This point of view can also be found
in the work of another advocate of case-study method in US
sociology, Willard Waller. He draws on *Gestalt* psychology to claim
that 'there is, in some cases, a direct perception of the causal
interdependence of events' (Waller 1934:285):

perceptions assume the form of configurations and some
degree of insight into the causal processes is usually involved in
a perceptual configuration. Cause is an elementary datum of
experience, extra-mental manipulations are therefore not
necessary to establish a relation of cause and effect.

(Waller 1934:287)

Glaser and Strauss too argue at one point that 'in field work ...
general relations are often discovered *in vivo*, that is, the field worker
literally sees them occur' (Glaser and Strauss 1967:40).

A more developed version of this argument is provided by

Michael Scriven. He claims that 'one may "see" (or understand) immediately why someone or some group did something, and not require testing to be justifiably confident that this really is the reason' (Scriven 1966:252).[16] He draws an analogy between the historian using *Verstehen* and a car mechanic diagnosing a fault. What is involved is diagnostic skill. In both cases a person 'may be extremely good at identifying causes even though he does not know, let alone know how to describe, the perceptual cues he employs' (Scriven 1966:251).

However, the claim of direct apprehension of causal relations is not easy to defend against Hume's charge that what one perceives are only regularities in the occurrence of phenomena (Hume 1748). And none of these authors adheres unswervingly to it. Waller, for example, admits that insight into causes can be mistaken (Waller 1934:297). Once this is accepted the argument collapses, since where there is doubt we must rely on other means to assess claims about perceived relations. Scriven also notes that hypothesis-testing is sometimes necessary. Furthermore, his analogy with the car mechanic reveals the problem starkly. In the case of the mechanic we can tell the difference between justified and unjustified confidence in diagnostic skill because there is a relatively straightforward test of the mechanic's judgement: once he or she has carried out the repair indicated by the diagnosis, we can assess whether the fault has been remedied by finding out whether the car now goes! Although the outcome of this test is not absolutely conclusive, it provides strong evidence. Scriven suggests that the same kind of check is available in history: 'confirmation of [the historian's] judgements is often possible with the discovery of new material and serves to provide us with confidence in them when no direct confirmation is possible' (Scriven 1966:252). But this is weak evidence compared to that available in the situation of the car mechanic: the range and falsifying potential of the evidence available is typically much less for the historian. Furthermore, the judgements of historians and ethnographers are likely to be less sound than those of car mechanics precisely because the latter's experience provides a much more rigorous check on their learning.

Dilthey also sometimes wrote as if direct apprehension of the relations embedded in experience is possible, but at other times he offers a more subtle, if less clear, view. He refers to a 'drawing out' of relations that are in experience through a process of reflection.

While Dilthey sees a role here for comparative analysis, this is to facilitate the non-inferential identification of relations in experience, not to test hypotheses. However, he does not give a clear account of this process, or of how we might assess the validity of the interpretations produced. He argues that such interpretations cannot be wholly wrong because they have their origin in our immediate experience, but he accepts that they cannot achieve 'the kind of certainty of a well-supported hypothetical generalization' (Makkreel 1975:336).

The problems with Dilthey's argument emerged most clearly in his debate with the experimental psychologist Ebbinghaus. The latter argued that Dilthey's descriptive psychology went beyond description to involve hypotheses. In particular, he pointed out that we do not have access to the totality of experience at any one point in time, but only to parts of it. As a result, if it is true, as Dilthey claimed, that we must interpret the parts in the light of the whole, we are reliant on hypotheses about that whole in interpreting the parts. Dilthey replied by distinguishing between different uses of hypotheses, arguing that while the structure of experience is not an immediate given, neither is it hypothetical since, in the words of a sympathetic interpreter, 'it is possible to transcend the given without inference' (Makkreel 1975:209). But as Makkreel points out, 'the idea of mediation without inference is never fully articulated by Dilthey' (Makkreel 1975:209). One must conclude, I think, that Dilthey never resolved this problem.

An alternative approach to the assumption of direct apprehension or the non-inferential drawing out of relations is the argument that actions can be explained in terms of rationales that motivate them. William Dray offers this alternative in his defence of historical explanation against advocates of the covering law model. By a 'rationale' Dray means an account of the process of calculation that an actor went through, or might have gone through, in order to produce an action:

> in so far as we say an action is purposive at all, no matter at what level of conscious deliberation, there is a calculation which could be constructed for it: the one the agent would have gone through if he had had time, if he had not seen what to do in a flash, if he had been called upon to account for what he did after the event, &c.

> (Dray 1957:123)

In capturing this process of calculation, the rationale shows that 'what was done was the thing to have done' (Dray 1957:124). Dray argues that the identification of such rationales is very much a matter of the historian's judgement; they are not derived from universal laws.

Of course, whereas historians cannot normally ask the people they study to give their reasons for acting in the way that they did, sociologists are often in a more favourable position: they are able to elicit the accounts of participants. This is another basis on which it might be argued that we have direct access to the causal processes generating human behaviour, so that there is no need for reliance on the hypothetico-deductive method. However, to treat participants' accounts as giving us direct knowledge of causal processes is to assume that participants themselves have privileged awareness of the factors that motivate them and also of the wider social conditions and historical developments that generate those motivations. In my view, that assumption is quite plainly false. Furthermore, we must remember that accounts, whether given to researchers or to others, are constructed for particular purposes and under particular constraints. They should not be treated as reflecting reality in some unproblematic way (Dean and Whyte 1958).

Fundamentally, then, the historian and the sociologist are in the same situation: they must construct rationales on the basis of what participants say and do. These rationales are not given by the data. And we must ask: can rationales be constructed without placing reliance on assumptions about universal relationships among types of social phenomena, and/or without reliance on the hypothetico-deductive method? In response to Dray, Hempel has argued that the use of rationales to explain human behaviour relies on the assumption that actors are rational, with the nature of that rationality being specified in terms of a number of behavioural principles (Hempel 1966). An example of such principles would be the tenets of economic rationality on which micro-economic analysis is based. There has been much debate about the status of these principles. For some, they are universal laws, for others idealizations that have instrumental value. Dray would certainly reject the former interpretation, but also the latter. There are unresolved problems here.[17]

It seems to me that pattern explanations do presuppose general principles, and that these are often universals, by which I mean that they make claims about relations among types of phenomena that are assumed to hold invariably, under certain conditions. In the case of Becker and Geer's medical students, for example, the first theme (C1) is only convincing as an explanation if we assume that if people feel themselves to be in urgent need of a certain type of experience yet the activities to which they are given access do not provide that type of experience, then they will adopt a derogatory attitude towards those activities and the people associated with them.[18] Of course we recognize that other factors might interfere with the operation of this principle, but I think we can treat it as likely to be true other things being equal. Without this assumption, it is difficult to see why we would select themes C1 or C2 as potential explanations. Without reliance on assumptions about what tends to occur, how people tend to behave, in general, how could we begin to select from the huge mass of features surrounding the action we are seeking to explain those that are potential explanations?

Of course, the advocates of the pattern model might not deny reliance on assumptions about general relationships in constructing pattern explanations, yet still dispute that these generals are scientific laws, that they must have survived testing by the hypothetico-deductive method. They may simply be commonsense assumptions derived from our experience of human behaviour. And, indeed, this seems highly likely. Furthermore, reliance on such assumptions is defensible on the basis of the critical commonsensism of Peirce. However, Peirce also emphasizes the fallibility of all knowledge, including commonsense. We assume that our everyday assumptions are true, and that assumption is reasonable; but in the future any of them may come to be regarded as false, or we may need to know under what limiting conditions they hold. At such times, we would need to seek some test of them. And in doing this, it seems to me, the hypothetico-deductive method would be the obvious strategy. For most of the pragmatists, and certainly for Peirce, Dewey, and Mead, that method was the paradigm for rational inquiry. From this point of view, it seems that the pattern model and hypothetico-deductive method complement one another, rather than being alternatives.

Even if this conclusion is correct, it does not follow that the argument for the pattern model is entirely ill-founded. Indeed, I believe that that model captures the process of explaining the occurrence of particular events or features, whether physical or human, much better than the covering law model. On this view the distinction between nomothetic and idiographic approaches is not a basis for dividing the natural and social sciences. Whenever we seek to explain particular events, whether physical or social, we typically use an idiographic approach, appealing to various features of their temporal and spatial context and the process by which the event was produced. In doing this, we draw on a variety of assumptions about universals, some of which may have been tested by use of the hypothetico-deductive method, some of which may need to be tested by that method, others of which we may accept as beyond genuine doubt.

In my view, then, the pattern model certainly makes an important contribution to social science methodology, in explicating the form of explanations of particular phenomena. But it does not seem likely to resolve Blumer's dilemma. It is not self-sufficient: it relies on the hypothetico-deductive method to test assumptions where they are subject to genuine doubt. Furthermore, to the extent that it relies on assumptions about universal relationships, it conflicts with the principles of symbolic interactionism.

Other ways of redefining science

There are, of course, other ways of altering the definition of science besides developing the pattern model. We might, for example, adopt the strategy characteristic of ethnomethodology, an approach that has sometimes been regarded as closely related to the kind of naturalistic research motivated by symbolic interactionism (Denzin 1970, but see also Zimmerman and Wieder 1970; Gallent and Kleinman 1983).[19] The term 'ethnomethodology' covers a range of different concerns and approaches. But the most interesting version for present purposes proposes the following argument.

The guiding methodological theme is very much description, on analogy with the phenomenologists' concern with the rigorous description of experience (Kolakowski 1975) and the efforts of ordinary language philosophers to trace the logic implicit in everyday linguistic usage (Coulter 1979). This represents a clear break with the hypothetico-deductive method, in principle at least. At the same time, ethnomethodologists' assumptions about the nature of the social world are very close to symbolic interactionism: they stress the meaningful character of human behaviour and its indeterminism. Social actions are indexical and reflexive: they gain their meaning from the context in which they are placed, but at the same time also define that context. Given this hermeneutic circle, not only can substantive social phenomena not be brought under causal laws, they cannot even be described rigorously. However, not all is flux and relativity. Ethnomethodologists argue that since we are able to understand one another, or at least to co-ordinate our activities, we must share methods by which we produce meanings. While the indexical and reflexive character of substantive meanings prevents their rigorous description, the methods by which we as participants in the social world produce them *are* open to such description because they are trans-contextual.

An area where much ethnomethodological work has taken place is the study of the methods by which people organize conversation – for example, how turn-taking is co-ordinated. Although this research has been extremely productive, there are problems about how we establish that a particular method is employed and about the status of such claims. After all, whatever the status of the methods themselves, even a social scientist's description of interpretative methods must itself be indexical and reflexive, and therefore is not able to stand as part of an abstract body of scientific knowledge. Nor does the restriction of focus to *possible* methods by which people construct social life seem to resolve this problem (Sacks 1963). Identifying possible methods is as problematic as documenting actual methods, if not more so. There are some serious difficulties here too (Hammersley 1989).

Another strategy for resolving Blumer's dilemma is to abandon the commitment to science altogether. An influential example of this strategy is the work of Gadamer (1960).[20] He stresses the historicity of all understanding: that it takes place at a particular point in time within a language that embodies a historically constituted tradition. It is always, therefore, understanding *from a particular point of view*, it is never a simple grasping of the object. But, Gadamer argues, this is not to be viewed as a deficiency: understanding is only possible from within a tradition. There can be no presuppositionless starting-point. Understanding is *always* based on a set of prejudices, and these are neither arbitrary nor necessarily illegitimate. They arise from tradition. Furthermore, the process of understanding involves the re-evaluation of these prejudices. Understanding occurs, Gadamer suggests, through the fusion of the horizons-of-understanding of the interpreter and of those he or she is interpreting. It is this that leads to a questioning of prejudices. As a result of the historicity of understanding, there is never a single true interpretation: those who start from different prejudices may produce different interpretations. But from this point of view, the fact that our interpretation of human documents and actions rests on experience and judgement and that different observers may come to different conclusions is not regarded as a problem. It is simply a feature of our life in the world. We are no longer trying to produce universal laws or even explanations that capture some independent reality. Rather, we are seeking to develop insights that illuminate our lives.

Not surprisingly, given this perspective, Gadamer does not take the natural sciences as the model of inquiry. He argues that the human sciences are philosophical, and he suggests that the experience of art is closer to the essence of truth in the social sciences than the conception of truth characteristic of the natural sciences.[21] Furthermore, he argues that the natural sciences represent a peculiar and limited form of inquiry, hinting that they present a distorted picture even of the physical world.

Gadamer's ideas are clearly a development of the romantic and historicist ideas of the nineteenth century. Their weak point, it seems to me, is the question of how we can assess different interpretations and re-evaluate prejudices. While Gadamer denies that he is a relativist, that his position implies that any interpretation is as good as any other, it is difficult to see how he can escape a slide into relativism.

If qualitative researchers were to adopt Gadamer's position, it would require a major reconstruction of their aims and practices – though it should be said that the character of the necessary reconstruction has hardly been sketched. What it would amount to 'on the ground' is less than clear (but see Hekman 1986).

I have explored the possibility of resolving Blumer's dilemma by re-defining science or by abandoning our commitment to it. I now want to look, much more briefly, at the other possibility: changing the nature of our commitment to symbolic interactionism.

RE-DEFINING SYMBOLIC INTERACTIONISM

It seems that for Blumer abandoning or modifying symbolic

interactionism was not a reasonable option. Though he reports that as a student at Missouri he had been a behaviourist (Blumer 1977), from at least 1928 onwards to the end of his life Blumer never wavered in his belief that symbolic interactionism captured the nature of the social world. As we saw in Chapter 5, he regarded the truth of symbolic interactionism as obvious.

In my view, though, Blumer overestimates what he calls the obduracy of the empirical world, or at least the clarity of its 'messages' about our ontological assumptions. The argument that 'the manner of testing the premises [of symbolic interactionism] is to go to the empirical social world' forgets that unless we can have direct apprehension of that world, a view that Blumer certainly does not defend, our investigation will be guided by epistemological and methodological assumptions that themselves affect the answers we receive. This is strikingly evident from David Matza's account of naturalism (Matza 1969). Matza argues that this term refers to:

> the philosophical view that strives *to remain true to the nature of the phenomenon under study or scrutiny.* For naturalism, the phenomenon being scrutinized is to be considered object or subject depending on its nature – not on the philosophical preconceptions of a researcher. That specific nature commands the fidelity of naturalism. This does not mean that the nature of phenomena is readily apparent; their nature may sometimes be at issue. But the resolution of that issue must be based on experience or more rigorous empirical methods.
>
> (Matza 1969:5)

As this passage reveals, either naturalism presupposes some form of direct knowledge of the nature of phenomena, or the emphasis shifts back to methods, and once again we must argue about the capacity of different methods to capture the nature of phenomena. Although Matza means something different from the positivists by the phrase 'rigorous methods', it is not clear on what grounds he could justify his belief that the qualitative methods he advocates are better able to capture the nature of social phenomena than those of the positivists.

Much the same argument applies to Blumer's writings. The idea that we can make ontological claims free of epistemological assumptions is as mistaken as the belief that we can define scientific method independently of assumptions about the nature of the world that is to be studied. Effectively, Blumer seeks to justify naturalistic method in terms of symbolic interactionism and then establish the validity of symbolic interactionism on the basis of naturalistic method. The circularity of this argument is obscured by his implicit reliance on the idea that the nature of the social world can be directly apprehended.

In my view, Blumer's privileging of ontological over epistemological assumptions (Williams 1976) is the most serious defect of his methodological work. Blumer takes symbolic interactionism as a relatively fixed and certain body of knowledge about the nature of human social life. Yet, for example, there has been much debate about the precise nature and implications of Mead's social psychology, much of it critical of Blumer's interpretation.[22] Much more important, though, Blumer's own account of symbolic interactionism is vague and uncertain at key points. We can identify several problems, for example:

1 Although Blumer recognizes that much action is routinized and institutionalized, he takes conscious, deliberate action as the paradigm case. He does so on the grounds that however routinized a pattern of action may be it can always be reconstructed through the actor reconsidering her or his situation and devising a new line of action. However, while this is true, it does not imply that our routine, institutionalized behaviour is produced in the same way as actions that are the product of conscious deliberation.[23] Furthermore, Blumer sometimes seems to imply that the only alternative to symbolic interactionism is a crude stimulus – response psychology. Yet this is not the case. Indeed, there seems to be a continuum from reflex models through to the most rationalistic accounts of choice behaviour. In my view the various models within this range need exploring (see van Parijs 1981).

2 Blumer's social psychology is incomplete in a rather crucial respect. I refer to the neglect of motivation. Although Blumer stresses the active character of human behaviour, we get little sense of the motives that generate it. Thomas's attempt to deal with this issue in the form of 'the four wishes' has fallen from favour within interactionism. If anything has replaced it, it is Goffman's notion of the presentation of self (Goffman 1959). What is missing, it seems to me, is the attempt to locate human

motivation within the context of the study of animal behaviour generally, without reducing it to claims about instincts. This was integral to the work of Mead (Baldwin 1986), and we now have a much more sophisticated body of research about animal behaviour than was available in his time. There is also a macro side to this issue. The effect of Blumer's emphasis on process and creativity is that it is difficult to see what generalizations could be developed about the effects of particular types of social structure on human behaviour. It is not that Blumer denies the effects of macro factors, but that his view of human action provides little basis for macro theories.[24]

3 Blumer tends to present interpretative schemas as merely a potential constraint on human action: he recognizes that much human behaviour is guided by such schemas, but underlines the fact that they may be changed by an actor at any time. But we need to recognize that creative interpretations and the development of new action strategies are only possible within the framework provided by existing interpretative schemas. This is a point that is very much in the spirit of Mead, and it would surely have been accepted by Blumer. However, in his efforts to counter crude determinism, Blumer tends to treat the individual, the group, and/or the process of interaction as producing meanings and strategies *ex nihilo*. He plays down the role of the social and cultural resources used in that process of production. We surely need to develop our understanding of how new interpretations and strategies arise out of existing interpretative frameworks and action routines.

4 Blumer makes a strong case for the role of interpretation and decision-making processes in social life. However, the relationship between these and the psychological and social factors operating on people's behaviour is left vague. He argues, for example, that social structural factors 'set the conditions for but do not determine' action (Blumer 1962:146). And he himself makes claims about the effects of such factors – for example in his research on films where he refers not just to their impact but also to the mediating effects of the character of local communities. Similarly, in his work on urbanization and industrialization, he claims that these are

'two of the most fundamental forces shaping modern society' (Blumer 1959:17). These claims imply that we may expect to discover probabilistic relations between social structural variables and patterns of action, and that these could be fruitfully investigated. This idea is hinted at by Blumer himself in his dissertation. He argues that since statistical method is:

> interested in securing a 'correlation' in the activity of the aggregate, and not a 'universal' holding true in all instances, [it] tacitly recognizes a complexity, variability or uniqueness of the instances. When used as a final form of understanding, it must be regarded as a way of meeting the condition of uniqueness by attempting to secure propositions about the aggregate and not about the individual members
>
> (Blumer 1928:47-8).

In other words on the basis of symbolic interactionism's emphasis on the indeterminism of human action one could make a plausible case for the importance of statistical analysis, certainly as against the search for universal laws. By contrast, it is not at all clear that symbolic interactionism provides a strong justification for the study of individual cases as a basis for constructing theories, since it offers no grounds for generalizing from such cases. Yet, on the basis of symbolic interactionism, Blumer rejects variable analysis in favour of case study as a means of discovering generic relations.

My point in this brief discussion has not been to mount a full-scale critique of symbolic interactionism, nor to dismiss its value, but simply to indicate that it requires further development, and perhaps even radical change at some points. At the very least, it must not be taken as fixed and given. In particular it must not be treated as an article of faith constitutive of a qualitative research paradigm.

Even if we were to accept the validity of symbolic interactionism, and what I have said does not deny it, we might still adopt an instrumentalist position and argue that good explanations can be produced by crude theories which do not capture all the subtleties of social interaction. Blumer seems to take it as given that such theories cannot produce adequate explanations. This is not obviously true, however; and it seems unwise to rule out such theories on the grounds that they do not capture the full complexity of social life as we experience it. Surely, all theories must fail in this respect, since they involve abstraction and the treatment of individual cases as instances of a general type. Furthermore, instrumentalism is, after all, by no means alien to pragmatism.

I have no solution to Blumer's dilemma, but it seems to me that in seeking a solution we must neither take the nature of science for granted, as the positivists did, nor take symbolic interactionist assumptions about the nature of the human social world as beyond doubt, as Blumer and many qualitative researchers do. We need to work on both fronts simultaneously, examining and if necessary modifying whatever is genuinely questionable.

CONCLUSION

My aim in this book has been to demonstrate that there are some serious, unresolved methodological problems at the heart of qualitative research. In the past 200 years there has been recurrent debate about these issues, and the range of questions and arguments explored has been wide. However, there has been a tendency in recent years to ignore the problems, and to forget the diversity of views adopted by both advocates and critics of qualitative method. It is only by recognizing and facing Blumer's dilemma that we have any chance of resolving it. While I am certainly not advocating that all social research stops until we have found a solution, I do believe that we must, as a matter of urgency, explore ways of resolving this dilemma, and that in doing this we must be prepared to question both our assumptions about science and those about the nature of the social world. We need to rethink the methodological foundations of social research. I take that to be the spirit of Herbert Blumer's message.

NOTES

INTRODUCTION

1 There is now a considerable literature on qualitative method in sociology: see the annotated bibliography in Hammersley and Atkinson 1983. More recent texts include: Burgess 1984a; Lofland and Lofland 1984; and Taylor and Bogdan 1984. There is also a growing literature dealing with qualitative method in particular substantive fields, especially education and medicine: Guba 1978; Bogdan and Biklen 1982; Hammersley (ed.) 1983; Burgess (ed.) 1984b, 1984c, 1985a and 1985b; Miles and Huberman 1984; Goetz and Lecompte 1984; Parse *et al.* 1985; Woods 1986.

2 Qualitative method is a loose collection of approaches, and even its boundaries with quantitative research are not well defined. For this reason my summary of it in this paragraph can only be approximately accurate.

3 Influential Chicago studies include: Becker *et al.* 1961 and 1969, Becker 1963, Davis 1963, Glaser and Strauss 1965, Goffman 1959 and 1961. See also the methodology texts, produced by Strauss (Glaser and Strauss 1967 and Schatzman and Strauss 1973) and the methodological articles in Becker 1971.

4 I have explored these issues in a number of articles: Hammersley 1985, 1986, 1987a and 1987b.

5 Schnadelbach (1984) has pointed out how distorted our view of nineteenth-century philosophy has become, some of those tendencies that were dominant becoming obscured by the attention that we give today to Marx, Nietzsche, and Kierkegaard.

CHAPTER 1 PHILOSOPHY AND THE HUMAN SCIENCES IN THE NINETEENTH CENTURY

1 Manicas (1987) traces the history of the term 'natural science' to Hobbes's *Leviathan,* but the term 'natural philosophy' continued to

be used for what we today would call 'natural science' into the nineteenth century.

2 On nineteenth-century trends in philosophy and their treatment of these questions, see Passmore 1966. Manicas 1987 traces the development of debates about the relationship between the natural and social sciences.

3 Blumer himself locates his methodological position in these terms, claiming that pragmatism, the philosophical tradition that he adopts, takes from each and supersedes both (Blumer 1969a and 1980b; Verhoeven 1980:9). Furthermore, some criticisms of his interpretation of Mead are framed in the same way, accusing him of both idealism (or nominalism) and realism (Lewis 1976; McPhail and Rexroat 1979; Lewis and Smith 1980).

4 I shall employ several other terms in the following discussion that are often used in diverse and even conflicting ways, such as 'positivism', 'romanticism', and 'historicism'. I shall give broad characterizations of their meaning, but they must not be taken to represent clearly demarcated sets of claims or well-defined philosophical movements. The aim is to give a broad picture of the philosophical scene in the nineteenth and early twentieth centuries, and this rules out the inclusion of much qualifying detail. For discussions of the meanings of these terms, see in the first instance the entries in Edwards 1967.

5 Lange's book is primarily concerned with challenging these assumptions.

6 In fact neither Bacon nor Descartes were as extreme as the common view of them, as inductivist and deductivist respectively, suggests. On Bacon, see Quinton 1980; on Descartes, see Rée 1974.

7 For useful introductions to German philosophy in the nineteenth-century, see Ermarth 1978, ch.1, and Schnadelbach 1984.

8 It is important to note, though, that Hegel regarded his own work as scientific: he rejected the view that science involved piecemeal, empirical investigation.

9 On the meanings of positivism, see Halfpenny 1982. Other useful accounts of positivism are to be found in Passmore 1966, Kolakowski 1972, and Bryant 1985.

10 Sociology was the only human science listed in Comte's classification. This was a source of debate between Comte and Mill, the latter arguing for the importance of psychology.

11 On Mill's canons: see Quinton 1980 for their origins in Bacon; Cohen and Nagel 1934 and Mackie 1967 for discussions of Mill's account. One of Mill's most important opponents was the scientist William Whewell, who advocated a version of the hypothetico-deductive method against Mill's inductivism. See Ducasse 1951, Strong 1955, and Butts 1973. In his dissertation, Blumer rejects Baconian inductivism, citing Whewell to the effect that the success of induction depends on 'having the right idea to start with' (Blumer 1928:16).

12 Biology was also an important model for Comte, being the next most

complex of the sciences to sociology, and the one on which the latter depended most directly: see Turner 1986.

13 The term 'historicism' seems to date from the early years of the twentieth century, and began its life as a term of abuse, a connotation it still retains in some usages: Schnadelbach 1984: 34. It is also used in a variety of ways: see Lee and Beck 1954 and Rand 1964. None the less, it is a useful term to summarize a number of strands associated together in nineteenth-century thought. Iggers 1968 provides a detailed account.

14 It would be a mistake, however, to view historicism as simply a rejection or upturning of the values of the Enlightenment. It is better seen as a development of some elements of Enlightenment thought, combined with other influences.

15 There are some parallels here and elsewhere between Herder and Franz Boas, the anthropologist and critic of racism. See in particular Boas 1938. For accounts of Herder's views generally, see Gillies 1945, Wells 1959, and Nisbet 1970. Berlin 1976 provides an excellent brief account.

16 There are similarities here with the alleged preoccupation of interactionist sociology of deviance with the exotica of 'nuts, sluts and perverts' (Liazos 1972).

17 Some historicists were much closer to idealism than others. Droysen's writings, for example, represent a synthesis of the historical school and Hegel. He criticized Ranke's claim to document 'what actually happened' as proposing a false objectivity, and argued that the historian must interpret events of the past from the point of view of her/his own nation and religion.

18 The precise mixture of these various influences, and the changes in Dilthey's views over time, are a matter of some controversy: see Jensen 1978. For general accounts of Dilthey's thought, see Hodges 1952, Kluback 1956, Tuttle 1969, Makkreel 1975, Ermarth 1978, and Plantinga 1980.

19 Dilthey was not just a philosopher, he was also a practising historian of ideas. One of his major works was a biography of Schleiermacher, in which he sought to reconstruct Schleiermacher's perspective and the socio-historical milieu in which he had lived, using letters, diaries, and other personal documents as well as published sources. There are obvious parallels here with life history work in twentieth-century anthropology and Chicago sociology.

20 On neo-Kantianism, see Windelband 1894, Cassirer 1930, Passmore 1966, and Willey 1978. The best introductions to Rickert's ideas are Rickert 1929 and Burger 1976. For a discussion of the influence of neo-Kantianism on modern US sociology, see Bergner 1981. A neo-Kantian discussion of methodology that seems to have been important for Blumer is Cassirer 1923. Blumer suggests that 'the reading of this book is essential for everyone who hopes to understand the theory of the formation of scientific concepts' (Blumer 1928:349). It seems likely that what Blumer had in mind

here was Cassirer's rejection of the positivist idea that science is simply a description of sense-data, in favour of an emphasis on the role of theory even in the construction of scientific data. However, Cassirer also emphasizes the role of quantification in science, and, like other neo-Kantians, he rejects reliance on ontological arguments about the nature of reality in favour of epistemological arguments about the conditions required for the achievement of scientific knowledge. His position is close in many respects to that of the conventionalists.

21 I shall not discuss political science since this seems to have had little impact on thinking about the methodology of qualitative research. The major development in this field in the early twentieth century was the decline of the old political philosophy tradition in favour of more empirical appoaches, predominantly but not entirely quantitative in character (Purcell 1973). However, the older tradition was never entirely extinguished. And its criticisms of the new quantitative research are strikingly similar to those of Blumer; though they retain a commitment to the concept of natural law that he would not accept (see for example Storing 1962: 41-3).

22 These writers were much more influential in the nineteenth century than what is today the much better-known reaction against classical political economy of Karl Marx. The similarities between the two approaches are important, both seek to place economic behaviour in socio-historical context, but of course Marx was much more strongly influenced by Hegel than by the historical school.

23 There are affinities here with the 'multiple realities' of Schutz.

24 There is considerable room for disagreement about the character of Weber's concept of causal adequacy. For an illuminating account, see Turner and Factor 1981.

25 Leach (1957) suggests that the major stimulus to what he calls Malinowski's 'obsessional empiricism' was the philosophy of William James. For useful accounts of the history of anthropology, see Harris 1969 and Kuper 1973.

CHAPTER 2 PRAGMATISM

1 Lewis (1976) claims that Ellwood and thereby Dewey were the major influences on Blumer's symbolic interactionism. However, Blumer denies that Ellwood had much influence on him. He claims that, owing to his contact with Max Meyer, another teacher at Missouri, he was a 'simon-pure behaviorist' before he reached Chicago (Blumer 1977). For an interesting discussion of Ellwood's attitude towards social research, see Bernard 1936.

2 Unlike most other pragmatists Peirce did not adopt a phenomenalist stance. He was a realist, though he did not believe that we have immediate or certain knowledge about reality. For useful accounts of pragmatism, see Passmore 1966, Ayer 1968, Rucker 1969, Morris

1970, Scheffler 1974, Fisch 1977, Kuklick 1977, and Smith 1978. Interpretations of the pragmatist movement and of the thought of individual pragmatists involve many controversial points. My account here cannot be more than a crude sketch.

3   Bain's concept of belief prefigures the approach of twentieth-century social psychologists to the concept of attitude, treating it as a disposition to behave in particular ways (Defleur and Westie 1963 and Fleming 1967). The link was probably through pragmatism and W. I. Thomas.

4   In this sense he was a precursor of Popper's fallibilism: see Rescher 1978 and Almeder 1980. This commitment to fallibilism is more important than his argument that inquiry should begin from genuine doubts: he did in fact recognize that scientists search for problems on the basis of 'feigned doubt', see Scheffler 1974. On Peirce generally, see Goudge 1950, Feibleman 1960, Murphey 1961, Apel 1970, Skagestad 1981, and Hookway 1985. Skagestad 1985 provides a useful review of Peirce scholarship, providing references for many of the alternative interpretations.

5   For a sympathetic but critical assessment of Peirce's argument about the superiority of science in 'fixing belief', see Scheffler 1974.

6   While Peirce's philosophy cannot be described as positivist (contra Kolakowski 1972), there are some similarities between Peirce's pragmatic maxim and both Bridgman's operationalism and the logical positivists' verification principle. Although the wider philosophical context in which these ideas were located were very different, in many respects their influence on social science converged. Operationism had considerable impact on US psychology and sociology in the early decades of the twentieth century; it was one of the trends that Blumer opposed. See Chapters 4 and 5.

7   James frequently travelled to Europe and was in contact with many of the leading figures in psychology and philosophy, especially in Germany. On James, see Perry 1935, Bird 1986, and Myers 1986. For a brief account, see Jones 1985.

8   There is a strong parallel here with neo-Kantian views.

9   This argument may seem to undermine my characterization of Dewey as a phenomenalist. However, it does not get to the heart of the issue. Realists can agree that we distinguish *within* our experience between that which we take to represent reality and that which we believe to be illusion, while still claiming that there is an independent reality whose character we are trying to discover. This, indeed, was Peirce's position. The term 'reality' frequently comes to be used by pragmatists to refer to what we take to be reality in everyday life. In this way, the concept of experience can often play much the same role for the pragmatist as does the concept of reality for the realist. Many pragmatists advocate viewing philosophical issues from the standpoint of our involvement in practical affairs; and it seems to me that in our practical everyday lives we cannot but be realists, or adopt a view whose implications for action are equivalent to those of

realism. In this way, in my view, pragmatists, and for that matter historicists and neo-Kantians, often illegitimately trade on realism, while yet denying it. For general accounts of Dewey's views, see Ayer 1968, Rucker 1969, Morris 1970, Scheffler 1974, and Thayer 1985.

10 Even more than with most authors, any account of Mead's thought is a reconstruction and alternatives are possible. Compare, for example, Miller 1973, Joas 1985, and Baldwin 1986. See also Mead 1964a and b, Strauss 1964, Cook 1972 and 1974, and Campbell 1985.

11 This stimulated and paralleled the shift by Meyer, Watson, and others to behaviourism.

12 There is a parallel here with Simmel's conception of cultural forms.

13 On Mead's views about scientific method, see McKinney 1955.

14 He was there at the same time as Dewey and Mead, but the extent and nature of the contact between them is not known. Coser 1971 and Bierstedt 1981 provide useful overviews of Cooley's work. See also Jandy 1942.

CHAPTER 3 CHICAGO SOCIOLOGY

1 Symptomatic of this is the fact that Chicago was one of the few universities in the USA where the works of Marx and Lenin were studied, a fact that was of considerable importance for the intellectual development of some members of the Chicago department, particularly Louis Wirth (Reiss 1966). For general accounts of Chicago sociology of the 1920s and 1930s, see Faris 1967, Carey 1975, Bennett 1981, Bulmer 1984, Harvey 1987, and Smith 1988. See also Kurtz 1984 for an annotated bibliography.

2 For introductions to Thomas, see Thomas 1966, Bennett 1981, and Bulmer 1984.

3 See also Merton's testimony of the importance of the book outside of the immediate circle of Chicago influence. He claims that it was the source of his own interest in content analysis (Merton 1983).

4 Thomas was dismissed following newspaper reports that he had been discovered in a hotel with the wife of an army officer. He was prosecuted under charges relating to prostitution and false registration in a hotel, but the charges were dismissed. There is a suspicion that this scandal was engineered to embarrass his wife, who was involved in Henry Ford's peace campaign.

5 In this sense Park and Thomas are closer to Hegel, Comte, and Spencer than to Mill and Mach. On Park, see Park 1967, Matthews 1977, and Raushenbush 1979.

6 In their *Introduction to the Science of Sociology*, Park and Burgess use the terms 'realism' and 'nominalism' to refer to the contrast between methodological collectivism and individualism. Lewis and Smith (1980) have sought to link this issue to the debate about realism and phenomenalism, but in my view the two questions are independent.

7 Simmel's essay 'The metropolis and mental life' was particularly

important for the development of the Chicagoans' concern with urban sociology.

8 See Zerubavel (1980), who draws a contrast between the substantive concerns of the Chicago sociologists (though he seems to exempt Blumer) and the formal sociology of Simmel, arguing for the importance of the latter.

9 The idea of the city of Chicago as a social laboratory predates Park (see Oberschall 1972:238).

10 Another appropriate analogy here is the mosaic. See Becker 1966.

11 Members of the department varied in their views about the relationship between sociology and social work. Thomas had adopted an interested but critical attitude towards social work, Burgess, Wirth, Shaw and others were closely involved with social work agencies. Others, particularly Park, distanced themselves from such organizations. However, most accepted the view that sociology should be at least partially autonomous from practical concerns of this kind.

12 I do not intend to imply that ethnographers today pay sufficient attention to methodological issues. Indeed, as I explained in the Introduction, this book is motivated by the belief that they do not. However, they do give methodological issues more attention than did the early Chicagoans.

13 A striking exception is the work of Erving Goffman.

14 A taxi dance hall was a dance hall where women danced with patrons for money, taking a 'fare' for each dance.

15 Interestingly, while Thomas and Znaniecki provide little information about the life history they present in *The Polish Peasant*, they do offer some methodological assessment of it and of the information contained in the letters that they analyse. For example, they consider the issue of the functions that peasant letters were intended to serve and how these affected what was written.

16 Another reason may have been the philosophically, and indeed sociologically, unsophisticated nature of many of the students. Anderson's entry to the field knowing very little about method or theory (Anderson 1983) seems to have been only an extreme case of what was common. In an interview with Jennifer Platt in 1982, Blumer comments that Chicago doctoral students in the 1920s (and he cites Thrasher as an example) were 'not very sophisticated about methodology' (Platt 1982: line 103).

17 See Shibutani 1970 and Lyman 1984 for discussions of some of this work.

18 There were some disagreements between Ogburn and Park, not only over the proper role of statistics in sociology but also about the value of psychoanalysis. Ogburn had been psychoanalysed, and encouraged students to become familiar with the work of Freud. Park was antagonistic towards psychoanalysis. In this, as in other matters, Burgess occupied a position midway between the two of them and played a mediating role. Blumer, however, was much closer to the position of Park on both issues.

CHAPTER 4 CASE STUDY VERSUS STATISTICS: THE RISE OF SOCIOLOGICAL POSITIVISM

1   Statistical method was not a new approach in the 1920s even in the United States; it had been in use, with varying degrees of sophistication, for some time. Indeed, Bernard suggests that by this time it was already the dominant method: 'By 1910 the quantitative procedure had definitely won the battle over the other contestants in the field, and one [had to] play with statistics if he wished to be regarded as definitely in the sociological game' (Bernard 1931-2:208). This may be something of an exaggeration, but it makes the point that the idea that statistical method was *the* scientific method did not first arise in the 1930s.

2   In some respects the distinction between case study and statistical method is a version of the neo-Kantian distinction between idiographic and nomothetic approaches. However, very often case study was regarded as laying the basis for a nomothetic science, much in the manner that Boas regarded what he called 'historical method' as providing the foundation for the discovery of laws.

3   At the time the statistical data available did not deal with attitudes. One of the important boosts to the application of statistical techniques in the 1930s and 1940s was the development of attitude measurement techniques; though by no means everyone agreed that these techniques were successful.

4   Ogburn was primarily responsible for arranging that the quotation from Lord Kelvin, 'When you cannot measure your knowledge is meagre and unsatisfactory', was engraved on the new social sciences building at Chicago when it was opened in 1929.

5   For Einstein's own views on this issue, which seem to have changed over time but which were always fundamentally realist, see Margenau (1949) and Frank (1949). Bridgman (1949) criticized Einstein for failing to meet positivist requirements in his formulation of the general theory of relativity.

6   Blumer reviewed Lundberg's book *Social Research* for the *American Journal of Sociology* in 1930, and later the two engaged in a face-to-face debate at a meeting of the American Sociological Society (Bierstedt 1959). Blumer 1940 and Lundberg 1942 present the arguments from that debate.

7   Pearson's book *The Grammar of Science* (Pearson 1911) had an enormous impact in Britain and the United States. In one of his articles Bain suggests that every sociologist should read Pearson's book 'at least once a year' (Bain 1930:377).

8   See also McKinney 1954 on the 'convergence' between Mead and Lundberg, and Lundberg's reply (Lundberg 1954). Other sociological positivists also drew on pragmatism (see Bain 1932). Mead's ideas became quite well known in the 1930s and 1940s, as result of the publication of *Mind, Self and Society*, and of the other volumes of lecture notes (Mead 1932, 1934, 1936, 1938). Read Bain is reported

to have quipped that at this time it was 'the mode to be a Meadian' (Adler 1968:36)

9   See also Bain 1929a. For a different view of the implications of arguments about the complexity of the social world for the applicability of quantitative method, from another advocate of that method, see Chapin 1920:393.

10 In reviewing Lundberg's methodological views many years later, Adler, in many ways a supporter of sociological positivism, argues that Lundberg took over phenomenalism without recognizing that it was fundamentally incompatible with science:

> While it may not be possible to prove the real existence of this or any other part of the outside world to the philosophers' satisfaction, the denial of its reality will lead to freeway accidents, to lots of other trouble, and finally to the psychiatrist's couch. Sociology, like any other science, must avoid the cloud-cuckoo land of individual and collective hallucination.
>
> (Adler 1968:38)

11 Ironically, Lundberg himself frequently uses the phrase 'the essence of science' (see Lundberg 1929 *passim*). Thomas and Znaniecki (1927:105) also reject reference to essences, but this seems at odds with their methodological approach, particularly that of Znaniecki (see Znaniecki 1934).

12 As we saw in the previous chapter, this also seems to have been Dewey's view.

13 This is in line with the views of many positivist philosophers at the time about the concept of causality (Frank 1934).

14 Bain applies some of the same criticisms to the questionnaire research he did with Lundberg, arguing in favour of the observation of behaviour rather than reliance on self-reports (Bain 1928).

15 An important landmark was the work of the Chicago psychologist Thurstone in developing attitude scales (Thurstone 1928).

16 See Platt 1986 for qualification of claims about the dominance of this version of sociology.

17 MacIver developed these arguments later in his book *Social Causation* (MacIver 1942).

18 Znaniecki's enumerative induction corresponds to the simple enumeration rejected by Bacon and Mill.

CHAPTER 5 AGAINST THE TREND: BLUMER'S CRITIQUE OF QUANTITATIVE METHOD

1   Interestingly, it would indicate an area of agreement between Blumer and Lundberg, both would presumably believe that Copernicanism represented a change in the universe! In fact, Blumer's rejection of realism seems to me to be a rejection of naïve realism, of the idea that the world is simply how we see it to be.

2 Apart from Faris, Park was the Chicago faculty member with whom Blumer had closest contact in the 1920s and early 1930s. As regards Thomas, Blumer has described his own work as an attempt to combine the perspectives of Mead and Thomas (Helle 1981).

3 In his Ph.D. thesis Blumer provides accounts and assessments of these and twenty-three other psychologists and social psychologists. It should be noted that he is by no means uncritical of these authors, even of Mead.

4 Blumer makes clear that symbolic interactionism does not imply that human behaviour is always well-constructed to achieve its purposes:

> The fact that the human act is self-directed or built up means in no sense that the actor necessarily exercises excellence in its construction. Indeed, he may do a very poor job in constructing his act. He may fail to note things of which he should be aware, he may misinterpret things that he notes, he may exercise poor judgment, he may be faulty in mapping out prospective lines of conduct and he may be half-hearted in contending with recalcitrant dispositions. Such deficiencies in the construction of his acts do not belie the fact that his acts are still constructed by him out of what he takes into account.
>
> (Blumer 1966a:537)

5 As we have seen, this idea is to be found not just in Mead but also in Park and James.

6 Something like this idea is built into Mead's conception of sociality. See Chapter 2.

CHAPTER 6 BLUMER'S CONCEPT OF SCIENCE

1 It is significant, however, that whereas the positivists take twentieth-century physics as their model of natural science, Blumer selects pre-twentieth-century examples and lays particular emphasis on biology.

2 However, where Rickert treats history as a form of science, Blumer excludes it, defining science in terms of the generalizing method, though he emphasizes that this is merely a 'matter of definition' (Blumer 1928:5).

3 Blumer emphasizes that the achievement of universal laws is a lengthy process and that much preliminary work is necessary before it can be accomplished.

4 However, he does suggest that 'perhaps the great genius of social science will be he who (likely by means of a new conceptual ordering of human behaviour) will bring significant activity within the realm of laboratory experimentation' (Blumer 1928: 33).

5 Even as late as 1939, Blumer declares that 'the ultimate test of the validity of scientific knowledge is the ability to use it for purposes of social control' (Blumer 1939:70). This whole section of Blumer's

dissertation throws interesting light on his critique of quantitative research, discussed in the previous chapter: it becomes clear that he was questioning *both* the concept of science involved in this research *and* the proposal to apply the logic of natural scientific method (even correctly understood) to the investigation of the social world.

6   Blumer criticizes some formulations of the comparative method in social psychology for their reliance on the idea of 'Baconian induction', according to which laws emerge 'from the mere process of gathering facts and grouping them together'. He comments that 'no procedure is less likely to result in the isolation of the universals which science seeks' (1928:355).

7   In an interview with Jennifer Platt in 1982 Blumer repeated this point. In discussing the case-study method, he asks: 'Can a purely imaginative literary account of some human experience or happening be superior as a scheme of analysis? If one takes a great writer – Dostoevsky, Shakespeare or what not – can they, through their fabrication of an occurrence, make a deeper effective analysis of some form of human experience or group action?' Platt asks what his answer is to this question and he replies: 'I don't have any. What I'm more interested in is that this whole question of the possibility of the case method as a type of research procedure ought to be addressed in those terms. I don't know the answer' (Platt 1982:lines 63-9).

CHAPTER 7 BLUMER'S ALTERNATIVE: NATURALISTIC RESEARCH

1   For an interesting discussion of this tension, see Rock 1973. For other accounts of naturalism, see Lofland 1967 and Denzin 1971.

2   Blumer's account of inspection here is close in some respects to Dewey's discussion of the experimental approach to everyday inquiry:

> The rudimentary prototype of experimental doing for the sake of knowing is found in ordinary procedures. When we are trying to make out the nature of a confused and unfamiliar object, we perform various acts with a view to establishing a new relationship to it, such as will bring to light qualities which will aid in understanding it. We turn it over, bring it into a better light, rattle and shake it, thump, push and press it, and so on. The object as it is experienced prior to the introduction of these changes baffles us; the intent of these acts is to make changes which will elicit some previously unperceived qualities, and by varying conditions of perception shake loose some property which as it stands blinds or misleads us.
>
> (Dewey 1929:87)

As is clear from this extract, more than Blumer, Dewey emphasizes manipulation rather than just inspection. And as we saw, he regards the contrast between manipulation and observation as the key difference between modern and ancient science.

3   Here there seems to be a contrast with Blumer's concern to preserve commonsense meanings.

4   Lindesmith's work was carried out when he was a graduate student, under the supervision of Blumer. There are other examples of analytic induction – for example Angell 1936, Becker 1963 (on becoming a marijuana user), Bloor 1978, and Katz 1983. I have focused on the studies of Lindesmith and Cressey because these are the most distinctive and best-documented cases.

5   Strauss was a student of Blumer.

6   For a diametrically opposed account of Blumer's attitude to the hypothetico-deductive method, see Rauma 1981.

7   It should be noted, however, that while both Diesing and Williams cite Kaplan in arguing that the pattern model represents an alternative to the deductive-nomological model, this is not the way Kaplan presents it:

> I put forward the two models (pattern and deductive models), not to insist that there are two kinds of explanation – and especially not that in behavioral science the explanations are of a different kind from those in other sciences – but to acknowledge that there are two different reconstructions of explanation (different at least in formulation if not in substance), and that both may serve a useful purpose in methodology.
>
> (Kaplan 1964:332-3)

8   This links to Rock's (1973) argument that interactionism exhibits a concern to preserve and represent social phenomena in their full complexity. There are certainly hints of this in Blumer's later work, and it forms a sharp contrast to his account of science in 1928 which requires the 'breaking up' of reality. This concern with representing reality in its fullness is shared with some nineteenth-century historicists and also has affinities with William James's radical empiricism.

9   In 1928 Blumer classed 'personal observation' with literature and folklore in its value as a source of social psychological data, declaring that it is 'obviously too unstandardized a method to warrant any consideration' (Blumer 1928:426).

CHAPTER 8 AN ASSESSMENT OF NATURALISTIC RESEARCH

1   See, for example, his reply to McPhail and Rexroat (Blumer 1980a:414). In his dissertation Blumer emphasizes the need for such exploratory research (Blumer 1928:11-12).

2   This conception of scientific method can be traced back to William Whewell and beyond: see Madden 1960 and Butts 1973. It is often contrasted with inductivism, the attempt to derive laws or general

patterns from the data themselves without use of hypotheses. However, the differences between the hypothetico-deductive method and inductivism are not as great or as clear as is sometimes supposed. See Quinton's (1980) discussion of the work of Francis Bacon, often regarded as the key figure in the development of inductivism.

3 The major twentieth-century advocates of the idea of the direct knowledge of phenomena have been the logical positivists. For a description of the collapse of this aspect of their doctrine, see Suppe 1974.

4 Popper does recognize these problems, but he gives them less attention than they deserve. For a good introductory account of Popper's ideas, see Magee 1973.

5 These and other criticisms of Blumer's interpretation of Mead have led to an extensive debate. See Bales 1966, Blumer 1966b, Lewis 1976, Blumer 1977, McPhail and Rexroat 1979, Blumer 1980a, McPhail and Rexroat 1980, Johnson and Shifflet 1981, Stewart 1981. Given the ambiguity to be found in Mead's published work (Blumer in Verhoeven 1980; Fine and Kleinman 1986), the fact that scientific methodology was not his central concern, and the different conceptions of scientific method held by the interpreters, it is hardly surprising that there is disagreement. In part, this disagreement reflects the conflict between the Chicago and Iowa schools of symbolic interactionism, on which see Meltzer et al. 1975, Couch and Hintz 1975, and Couch et al. 1986. In my view, whether Blumer's interpretation of Mead is correct is less important than the validity of his methodological arguments and the value of his proposals.

6 Dewey's account of the scientific method in *Experience and Nature* (Dewey 1925) is similar in some respects to Blumer's discussion of naturalistic research; though it is important to note that he emphasizes replication. However, in *The Quest for Certainty* and *Logic: the Theory of Inquiry* Dewey contrasts the hypothetico-deductive method of modern science with the more informal and less powerful approaches characteristic of ancient science and everyday life (see Chapter 2). An alternative interpretation of Blumer's argument here is suggested by his comment that Mead 'could readily see scientific method in historical studies' (Blumer 1980a:415). Here, as elsewhere, Blumer may be suggesting the re-definition of science to include the historical method, with naturalistic research as an example of the latter. I shall explore this possibility later.

7 The situation is much more complex even in other areas of physics: for example in the observation of sub-atomic particles (see Watkins 1986).

8 For a discussion of these problems in one area, see Scarth and Hammersley 1986.

9 In his 1969 account he does not even mention the search for negative cases as an element of naturalistic research. While this *is* mentioned elsewhere, even then there is little indication of what is involved or of how it can be achieved (Blumer 1981; Verhoeven 1980).

10 Robinson's criticism does not apply to Cressey's formulation of analytic induction; and Robinson points out that in practice both Lindesmith and Cressey did investigate cases in cell b. However, in my view there is little evidence that they did this effectively. Lindesmith provides little information, and Cressey only investigated cases where conditions held in earlier periods of his informants' lives, relying on retrospective data.

11 In his study *Suicide*, Durkheim (1897) states the aim of achieving causally homogeneous types of suicide. However, he is unable to follow this through because he does not study individual suicides but relies on official data about suicide rates. Later quantitative studies have rarely sought to achieve causally homogeneous categories for dependent variables. For an attempt to develop analytic induction along the lines suggested by Robinson, see Miller 1982.

12 However, in a footnote they note that the interactional modes characteristic of one context may also occur in other contexts 'but in less empirically significant form or magnitude' (Glaser and Strauss 1965:10). This seriously weakens their analysis, particularly since we are given no account of how frequency of occurrence was assessed or of what 'empirical significance' means.

13 This is also true of analytic induction studies, but Lindesmith and Cressey do state the hypotheses that were tested and provide much of the evidence.

14 Rickert discusses this issue, though in my view he does not provide a satisfactory resolution. See Rickert 1929 and Bryant 1985.

15 Dilthey put this approach into practice in his study of Schleiermacher.

16 It is not entirely clear whether Scriven is claiming that we literally see causal relations. He may be arguing that often we are confident enough in our commonsense inferences of causation to rely on them and that such reliance may often be justified. I shall assume for the sake of argument that he is adopting the former position. I deal with the weaker, but more plausible, view implied by the alternative interpretation later.

17 For discussions of the status of micro-economic assumptions, see Caldwell 1982 and 1984. Like Dray, Weber also seeks a third position (see Manicas 1987).

18 It should be noted that explaining the medical students' use of the concept of 'crock' was not the major concern of Becker *et al.* On the contrary, use of 'crock' was taken as an indicator of the centrality of the values of clinical experience and professional responsibility to the perspectives of medical students in the clinical years. The purpose of their research was primarily descriptive: to document the character of the changes in medical students' perspectives as they progressed through medical school. Doing this on the basis of a study of medical students at a particular institution at a particular time, however, raises the problems of generalization that I mentioned earlier.

19 For a detailed account of ethnomethodology and references to the literature, see Heritage 1984.

20 For useful discussions of Gadamer's work, see Weinsheimer 1985 and Warnke 1987. For an excellent brief account, see Anderson *et al* 1986.

21 Blumer's raising of the question of the status of fictional accounts (see Chapter 7) represents a move towards this sort of position, but it is very unlikely that he would have endorsed much of Gadamer's point of view.

22 See the references in note 5.

23 The same problem arises with Dray's conception of rationales. What causal status can we give to the calculation that the actor 'would have gone through if he had had time' or to what he or she would have said 'when called upon to account ... after the event' (Dray 1957:123)? Blumer's tendency to assume that meaning depends on consciousness has been a key element of the criticisms of his interpretation of Mead. For Mead, consciousness only arises when a problem is faced, and consciousness is not necessary for meaning to be present. On this view, much human action is meaningful but not conscious.

24 There has been much debate about the relationship between interactionism and macro theory. Many critics and some defenders have claimed that interactionism leaves no room for macro theory (Reynolds and Reynolds 1973; Rock 1979). Others have argued that there is no intrinsic incompatibility between the two (Maines 1977; Stryker 1980). Indeed, Lyman has claimed that Blumer himself has made an important contribution to macro theory in the field of race relations (Lyman 1984).

REFERENCES

Adams, T. (1988) 'The commonsense tradition in America: E.H. Madden's interpretations', *Transactions of the Charles S. Peirce Society* 24, 1: 1-31.

Adler, F. (1968) 'Comments on Lundberg's sociological theories', in A. de Grazia, R. Handy, E. C. Harwood, and P. Kurtz (eds.) *The Behavioral Sciences*, Great Barrington, Mass.: The Behavioral Research Council.

Adler, P. A. and Adler, P. (1987) *Membership Roles in Field Research*, Newbury Park, Cal.: Sage.

Allport, G. (1942) *The Use of Personal Documents in Psychological Science*, New York: Social Science Research Council.

Almeder, R. (1980) *The Philosophy of Charles S. Peirce*, Oxford: Blackwell.

Anderson, N. (1923) *The Hobo: the Sociology of the Homeless Man*, Chicago: University of Chicago Press. 2nd edn, 1961.

—— (1975) 'Introduction' to 1961 edn of Anderson 1923.

—— (1983) 'A stranger at the gate: reflections on the Chicago School of Sociology', *Urban Life* 11, 4: 396-406.

Anderson, R. J., Hughes, J. A., and Sharrock, W. W. (1986) *Philosophy and the Human Sciences*, London: Croom Helm.

Angell, R. C. (1936) *The Family Encounters the Depression*, New York: Scribner's Sons.

—— (1945) 'A critical review of the development of the personal document method in sociology: 1920-40', in L. Gottschalk, C. Kluckhohn, and R. C. Angell (eds) (1945) *The Use of Personal Documents in History, Anthropology and Sociology*, New York: Social Science Research Council.

Apel, K. O. (1970) *Charles S. Peirce: from Pragmatism to Pragmaticism*, English translation, Amherst, Mass.: University of Massachusetts Press, 1981.

Ashworth, P. D., Giorgi, A., and de Koning, A. J. J. (eds) (1986) *Qualitative Research in Psychology*, Pittsburgh, Pa.: Duquesne University Press.

Athens, L. (1984) 'Blumer's method of naturalistic inquiry: a critical appraisal', in N. K. Denzin (ed.) *Studies in Symbolic Interaction*, vol. 5, Greenwich, Conn.: JAI Press.

Ayer, A. J. (1968) *The Origins of Pragmatism*, London: Macmillan.

Bain, R. (1928) 'An attitude on attitude research', *American Journal of Sociology* 33: 940-57.

—— (1929a) 'The concept of complexity in sociology: I and II', *Social Forces* 8: 222-31 and 369-78.

—— (1929b) 'The validity of life histories and diaries', *Journal of Educational Sociology* 3: 150-64.

—— (1930) 'Theory and measurement of attitudes and opinions', *Psychological Bulletin* 27: 359-79.

—— (1932) 'Behavioristic technique in sociological research', *Publications of the American Sociological Society* 26: 155-64.

Baker, P. J. (ed.) (1973) 'The life histories of W. I. Thomas and Robert E. Park', *American Journal of Sociology* 79, 2: 243-60.

Baldwin, J. D. (1986) *George Herbert Mead: a Unifying Theory for Sociology*, Newbury Park, Cal.: Sage.

Bales, R. F. (1966) 'Comment on Herbert Blumer's paper', *American Journal of Sociology* 71: 547-8.

Batiuk, M. E. (1982) 'Misreading Mead: then and now', *Contemporary Sociology* 11: 138-40.

Bauman, Z. (1978) *Hermeneutics and Social Science*, London: Hutchinson.

Beck, L. W. (1967) 'Neo-Kantianism', in P. Edwards (ed.) *The Encyclopaedia of Philosophy*, New York: Macmillan.

Becker, H. S. (1958) 'Problems of inference and proof', *American Sociological Review* 23, 6: 652-60.

—— (1963) *Outsiders: Studies in the Sociology of Deviance*, New York: Free Press.

—— (1966) 'Introduction' to the reprint of C. R. Shaw (1930) *The Jack-Roller*, Chicago: University of Chicago Press.

—— (1970) 'Dialogue with Howard S. Becker: an interview conducted and prepared by Julius Debro', *Issues in Criminology* 5, 2: 159-79.

—— (1971) *Sociological Work: Method and Substance*, London: Allen Lane.

Becker, H. S., Geer, B., Hughes, E. C., and Strauss, A. (1961) *Boys in White*, Chicago: University of Chicago Press.

—— (1969) *Making the Grade*, New York: Wiley.

Benjamin, A. C. (1955) *Operationism*, Springfield, Ill.: Thomas.

Bennett, J. (1981) *Oral History and Delinquency*, Chicago: University of Chicago Press.

Bergner, J. (1981) *The Origins of Formalism in Social Science*, Chicago: University of Chicago Press.

Berlin, I. (1976) *Vico and Herder*, London: Hogarth Press.

Bernard, L. L. (1919) 'The objective viewpoint in sociology', *American Journal of Sociology*, 25: 288-325.

—— (1931-2) 'An interpretation of sociological research', *American Journal of Sociology* 37: 203-12.

—— (1936) 'The great controversy; or both heterodoxy and orthodoxy in sociology unmasked', *Social Forces* 14: 64-72.

Bhaskar, R. (1978) *A Realist Theory of Science*, 2nd edn, Brighton: Harvester.

Bierstedt, R. (1959) 'Nominal and real definitions in sociological theory', in L. Gross (ed.) *Symposium on Sociological Theory*, New York: Harper & Row.

—— (1981) *American Sociological Theory*, New York: Academic Press.

Bird, G. (1986) *William James*, London: Routledge & Kegan Paul.

Bleicher, J. (1980) *Contemporary Hermeneutics*, London: Routledge & Kegan Paul

Bloor, M. (1978) 'On the analysis of observational data: a discussion of the worth and uses of inductive techniques and respondent validation', *Sociology*, 12, 3: 545-52.

Blumer, H. (1928) 'Method in social psychology', unpublished Ph.D. dissertation, University of Chicago.

—— (1930) 'Review of Lundberg's *Social Research*', *American Journal of Sociology*, 35: 1101-11.

—— (1931) 'Science without concepts', *American Journal of Sociology* 36: 513-15.

—— (1933) *Movies and Conduct*, New York: Macmillan.

—— (1937) 'Social psychology', in Emerson P. Schmidt (ed.) *Man and Society*, Englewood Cliffs, NJ: Prentice-Hall.

—— (1939) *Critiques of Research in the Social Sciences: 1 An Appraisal of Thomas and Znaniecki's 'The Polish Peasant in Europe and America'*, New York: Social Science Research Council.

—— (1940) 'The problem of the concept in social psychology', *American Journal of Sociology* 45: 707-19.

——(1948) 'Public opinion and public opinion polling', *American Sociological Review* 13: 542-54.

—— (1954) 'What is wrong with social theory?', *American Sociological Review* 19: 3-10.

—— (1955) 'Attitudes and the social act', *Social Problems*, III.: 59-65.

—— (1956) 'Sociological analysis and the "variable"', *American Sociological Review* 21: 683-90.

—— (1959) 'The study of urbanization and industrialization: methodological deficiencies', *Boletim de Centro Latin-Americano de Pesquisas de Ciencias Sociais* 2, 2: 17-34.

—— (1962) 'Society as symbolic interaction', in A.M. Rose (ed.) *Human Behavior and Social Processes*, Boston: Houghton Mifflin, pp. 179-92.

—— (1964) 'Industrialization and the traditional order', *Sociology and Social Research* 48: 129-38.

—— (1966a) 'Sociological implications of the thought of George Herbert Mead', *American Journal of Sociology* 71: 535-44.

—— (1966b) 'Reply to Bales', *American Journal of Sociology* 71: 547-8.

—— (1966c) 'Foreword' to S.T. Bruyn, *The Human Perspective in Sociology*, Englewood Cliffs, NJ: Prentice-Hall.

——(1967a)'Ernest W. Burgess 1886-1966', *American Sociologist* 2: 163-4.

—— (1967b) 'Reply to Woelfel, Stone and Farberman', *American Journal of Sociology* 72: 411-12.

—— (1969a) 'The methodological position of symbolic interactionism', in Blumer 1969b.

—— (1969b) *Symbolic Interactionism: Perspective and Method*, Englewood Cliffs, NJ: Prentice-Hall.

—— (1973) 'A note on Symbolic Interactionism: reply to Huber', *American Sociological Review* 38: 797-8.

—— (1975) 'Symbolic interpretation and the idea of social system', *Revue Internationale de Sociology/International Review of Sociology* 11: 1-2, 3-12.

—— (1976) 'A tri-fold test of all sociological approaches', *Wisconsin Sociologist* 13, 4: 107.

—— (1977) 'Comment on Lewis's "The classic American pragmatists as forerunners to Symbolic Interactionism"', *Sociological Quarterly* 18, 285-9.

—— (1979a) *An Appraisal of Thomas and Znaniecki's 'The Polish Peasant in Europe and America'*, New Brunswick: Transaction Books (first published in 1939).

—— (1979b) 'Comments on "George Herbert Mead and the Chicago tradition of Sociology"', *Symbolic Interaction* 2, 2: 21-2.

—— (1980a) 'Mead and Blumer: the convergent methodological perspectives of social behaviorism and symbolic interactionism', *American Sociological Review* 45: 409-19.

—— (1980b) 'Conversation with Herbert Blumer: I', *Symbolic Interaction* 3: 113-28.

——(1981) 'Conversation with Herbert Blumer: II', *Symbolic Interaction* 4, 2: 273-95.

—— (1982) 'George Herbert Mead', in B. Rhea, *The Future of the Sociological Classics*, London: Allen & Unwin.

—— (1983) 'Going astray with a logical scheme: review of Lewis and Smith', *Symbolic Interaction* 6, 1: 127-37.

Blumer, H. and Hauser, P. (1933) *Movies, Delinquency and Crime*, New York: Macmillan.

Boas, F. (1938) 'Living philosophies II: an anthropologist's credo', *Nation* 147: 201-4.

—— (1940) *Race, Language and Culture*, New York: Free Press.

Bogardus, E. S. (1933) 'A social distance scale', *Sociology and Social Research* 17: 265-71.

—— (1950) 'The sociology of Charles A. Ellwood', *Sociology and Social Research* 34, 5: 365-73.

Bogdan, R. C. and Biklen, S. K. (1982) *Qualitative Research for Education*, Boston: Allyn & Bacon.

Bogdan, R. C. and Taylor, S. (1975) *Introduction to Qualitative Research Methods: a Phenomenological Approach to the Social Sciences*, New York: Wiley.

Bonfantini, Massimo A. (1985) 'The two souls of the young Peirce', *Semiotica* 55, 3/4.

Boring, E. G. (1929) *A History of Psychology*, New York: Appleton-Century-Crofts (2nd edn).

Bottomore, T. and Nisbet, R. (1978) *A History of Sociological Analysis*, London: Heinemann.

Bridgman, P. W. (1928) *The Logic of Modern Physics*, New York: Macmillan.

—— (1949) 'Einstein's theories and the operational point of view', in P. A. Schilpp (ed.) *Albert Einstein: Philosopher-scientist*, vol.2, LaSalle, Ill.: Open Court.

Bruun, H. H. (1972) *Science, Values and Politics in Max Weber's Methodology*, Copenhagen: Munksgaard.

Bruyn, S. T. (1966) *The Human Perspective in Sociology: the Methodology of Participant Observation*, Englewood Cliffs, NJ: Prentice-Hall.

Bryant, C. G. A. (1985) *Positivism in Social Theory and Research*, London: Macmillan.

Buban, S. I. (1986) 'Studying social process: the Chicago and Iowa schools revisited', in C. J. Couch, S. L. Saxton, and M. A. Katovich (eds) *Iowa School, Studies in Symbolic Interaction*, Supplement 2, A and B, Greenwich, Conn.: JAI Press.

Bulmer, M. (1984) *The Chicago School of Sociology*, Chicago: University of Chicago Press.

Burger, T. (1976) *Max Weber's Theory of Concept Formation*, Durham, NC: Duke University Press.

Burgess, E. W. (1927) 'Statistics and case studies as methods of sociological research', *Sociology and Social Research* 12: 103-20.

—— (1930) 'Discussion', in C. R. Shaw (1930) *The Jack-Roller*, Chicago: University of Chicago Press.

—— (1945) 'Sociological research methods', *American Journal of Sociology* 50: 474-82.

Burgess, R. G. (1984a) *In the Field*, London: Allen & Unwin.
—— (1984b) (ed.) *The Research Process in Educational Settings*, Lewes: Falmer.
—— (1984c) (ed.) *Field Methods in the Study of Education*, Lewes: Falmer.
——(1985a) (ed.) *Issues in Educational Research*, Lewes: Falmer.
—— (1985b) (ed.) *Strategies of Field Research*, Lewes: Falmer.
Butts, R. E. (1973) 'Whewell's logic of induction', in R. Giere and R. S. Westfall (eds) *Foundations of Scientific Method in the Nineteenth Century*, Bloomington: Indiana University Press.
Cahnman, W. J. (1964) 'Max Weber and the methodological controversy in the social sciences', in W. J. Cahnman and A. Boskoff (eds) *Sociology and History: Theory and Research*, New York: Free Press.
Caldwell, B. (1982) *Beyond Positivism: Economic Methodology in the Twentieth Century*, London: Allen & Unwin.
—— (ed.) (1984) *Appraisal and Criticism in Economics*, Boston: Allen & Unwin.
Campbell, J. (1982) 'Review of Lewis and Smith: *American Sociology and Pragmatism*', *Transactions of the Charles S. Peirce Society* 18, 1: 105-8.
—— (1983) 'Mead and pragmatism', *Symbolic Interaction* 6, 1: 155-64.
—— (1985) 'George Herbert Mead: philosophy and the pragmatic self', in M. G. Singer (ed.) (1985) *American Philosophy*, Royal Institute of Philosophy Lecture Series 19, Cambridge: Cambridge University Press.
Cardwell, J. D. (1971) *Social Psychology: a Symbolic Interactionist Perspective*, Philadelphia, Pa.: F. A. Davis.
Carey, J. (1975) *Sociology and Public Affairs: the Chicago School*, Beverly Hills, Cal.: Sage.
Cassirer, E. (1923) *Substance and Function*, English translation, New York: Dover, 1953.
—— (1930) 'Neo-Kantianism', *Encyclopaedia Britannica*, XVI, 14th edn.
Cavan, R. S. (1928) *Suicide*, Chicago: University of Chicago Press.
—— (1983) 'The Chicago School of Sociology: 1918-1933', *Urban Life* 11: 407-20.
Cavan, R. S., Hauser, P., and Stouffer, S. (1930) 'Note on the statistical treatment of life history material', *Social Forces* 9, 2: 200-3.
Chapin, F. S. (1920) *Field Work and Social Research*, New York: Century.
—— (1935) 'Measurement in sociology', *American Journal of Sociology* 40: 476-80.

—— (1939) 'Definition of definitions of concepts', *Social Forces* 18, 2: 153-60.

Cohen, M. and Nagel, E. (1934) *Introduction to Logic and Scientific Method*, London: Routledge & Kegan Paul.

Comte, A. (1970) *Introduction to Positive Philosophy*, Indianapolis, Ind.: Bobbs-Merrill (revised translation of the first 2 chs of Comte's *Cours de philosophie positive*, 1830-42).

Cook, G. A. (1972) 'The development of G. H. Mead's social psychology', *Transactions of the Charles S. Peirce Society* VIII, 3: 167-86.

—— (1974) 'Review of D. Miller: *George Herbert Mead*', *Transactions of the Charles S. Peirce Society* X, 4: 253-60.

Cooley, C. H. (1922) *Human Nature and the Social Order*, New York: Scribner's Sons (1st edn 1902; 2nd edn, reprinted, New York: Schocken Books, 1964).

—— (1926) 'The roots of social knowledge', *American Journal of Sociology* 32, 1: 59-79 (reprinted in Cooley 1930/1966).

—— (1928) 'Case study of small institutions as a method of research', *Publications of the American Sociological Society* 18: 147-55.

—— (1930) *Sociological Theory and Social Research*, New York: Holt (reprinted, New York: Kelley, 1966).

Coser, L. A. (ed.) (1965) *Georg Simmel*, Englewood Cliffs, NJ: Prentice-Hall.

—— (1971) *Masters of Sociological Thought*, New York: Harcourt, Brace Jovanovich (2nd edn, 1977).

Cottrell, L. (1980) 'George Herbert Mead: the legacy of social behaviorism', in R. L. Merton and M. W. Riley (eds) *Sociological Traditions from Generation to Generation*, Norwood, NJ: Ablex.

Couch, C. J. (1984) 'Symbolic interaction and generic sociological principles', *Symbolic Interaction* 7, 1: 1-13.

—— (1986) 'Questionnaires, naturalistic observation and recordings', in C. J. Couch, S. L. Saxton, and M. A. Katovich (eds) *Iowa School, Studies in Symbolic Interaction*, Supplement 2, A and B, Greenwich, Conn.: JAI Press.

Couch, C. J. and Hintz, R. A. (1975) (eds) *Constructing Social Life*, Champaign, Ill.: Stipes.

Couch, C. J., Saxton, S. L., and Katovich, M. A. (eds) (1986) *Iowa School, Studies in Symbolic Interaction*, Supplement 2, Parts A and B, Greenwich, Conn.: JAI Press.

Coulter, J. (1979) *The Social Construction of Mind*, London: Macmillan.

Cressey, D. (1950) 'The criminal violation of financial trust', *American Sociological Review* 15: 738-43.

—— (1953) *Other People's Money*, Glencoe, Ill.: Free Press.

Cressey, P. G. (1932) *The Taxi Dance Hall*, Chicago: University of Chicago Press.

—— (1983) 'The methodology of the taxi-dance hall: an early account of Chicago ethnography from the 1920s', M. Bulmer (ed.) *Urban Life* 12: 109-19.

Dallmayr, F. and McCarthy, T. A. (eds) (1977) *Understanding and Social Inquiry*, Notre Dame, Ind.: University of Notre Dame Press.

Danziger, K. (1979) 'The positivist repudiation of Wundt', *Journal of the History of the Behavioral Sciences* 15: 205-30.

Davis, F. (1963) *Passage through Crisis: Polio Victims and their Families*, Indianapolis, Ind.: Bobbs-Merrill.

—— (1982) 'On the "symbolic" in symbolic interaction', *Symbolic Interaction* 5, 1: 111-26.

Day, R. and Day, J. V. (1977) 'A review of the current state of negotiated order theory: an appreciation and critique', *The Sociological Quarterly* 18, 1: 126-42.

Dean, J. P. and Whyte, W. F. (1958) 'How do you know if the informant is telling the truth?', *Human Organization* 17, 2: 34-8.

Defleur, M. L. and Westie, F. R. (1963) 'Attitude as a scientific concept', *Social Forces* 42: 17-31.

de Grazia, A., Handy, R., Harwood, E. C., and Kurtz, P. (eds) (1968) *The Behavioral Sciences: Essays in Honor of George A. Lundberg*, Great Barrington, Mass.: The Behavioral Research Council.

Denzin, N. K. (1970) 'Symbolic interactionism and ethnomethodology', in J.D. Douglas (ed.) *Understanding Everyday Life*, Chicago: Aldine.

—— (1971) 'The logic of naturalistic inquiry', *Social Forces* 50: 166-82.

—— (1978) *The Research Act*, 2nd edn, New York: McGraw-Hill.

Dewey, J. (1925) *Experience and Nature*, Chicago: Open Court.

—— (1929) *The Quest for Certainty*, New York: Pedigree Books, 1980.

—— (1938) *Logic: the Theory of Inquiry*, New York: Henry Holt.

Diesing, P. (1972) *Patterns of Discovery in the Social Sciences*, London: Routledge & Kegan Paul.

Dilthey, W. (1894) *Descriptive Psychology and Historical Understanding*, English translation, The Hague: Nijhoff, 1977.

—— (1976) *Selective Writings*, Cambridge: Cambridge University Press.

Diner, S. (1975) 'Department and discipline: the department of sociology and the University of Chicago, 1892-1920', *Minerva* 13: 514-53.

Dodd, S. C. (1942) *Dimensions of Society: a Quantitative Systematics for the Social Sciences*, New York: Macmillan.

Douglas, J. D. (ed.) (1970) *Understanding Everyday Life*, Chicago: Aldine.

Dray, W. (1957) *Laws and Explanation in History*, London: Oxford University Press.

—— (ed.) (1966) *Philosophical Analysis and History*, New York: Harper & Row.

Ducasse, C. J. (1951) 'Whewell's philosophy of scientific discovery', *Philosophical Review* 60: 56-69 and 213-34.

Durkheim, E. (1897) *Suicide*, English translation, New York: Free Press, 1951.

Edwards, P. (1967) *The Encyclopaedia of Philosophy*, New York: Macmillan.

Ellwood, C. A. (1930) 'The uses and limitations of behaviorism in sociology', *Publications of the American Sociological Society* 24: 74-82.

—— (1931) 'Scientific method in sociology', *Social Forces* 10: 15-21.

—— (1933) *Methods in Sociology: a Critical Study*, Durham, NC: Duke University Press.

Emerson, R. M. (ed.) (1983) *Contemporary Field Research*, Boston: Little, Brown.

Ermarth, M. (1978) *Wilhelm Dilthey: the Critique of Historical Reason*, Chicago: University of Chicago Press.

Fann, K. T. (1970) *Peirce's Theory of Abduction*, The Hague: Martinus Nijhoff.

Faris, E. (1928) 'Attitudes and behaviour', *American Journal of Sociology* 34: 271-81.

—— (1937) 'The social psychology of George Herbert Mead', *American Journal of Sociology* 43: 391-403.

Faris, R. E. L. (1967) *Chicago Sociology 1920-32*, Chicago: University of Chicago Press.

Faught, J. (1980) 'Presuppositions of the Chicago School in the work of Everett C. Hughes', *American Sociologist* 15: 72-82.

Feibleman, J. K. (1960) *Introduction to the Philosophy of Charles S. Peirce*, London: Allen & Unwin, republished, M.I.T. Press, 1970.

Filstead, W. J. (1970) *Qualitative Methodology: Firsthand Involvement with the Social World*, Chicago: Markham.

Fine, G. A. and Kleinman, S. (1986) 'Interpreting the sociological classics: can there be a "true" meaning of Mead?', *Symbolic Interaction* 9,1: 129-46.

Fisch, M. (1977) 'American pragmatism before and after 1898', in R. W. Shahan and K. R. Merrill (eds) *American Philosophy*, Norman, Okla.,: University of Oklahoma Press.

—— (1986) *Peirce, Semeiotic, and Pragmatism: Essays by Max H. Fisch*, K. L. Ketner and C. J. W. Kloesel (eds) Bloomington, Ind.: Indiana University Press.

Fisher, B. and Strauss, A. (1978a) 'The Chicago Tradition and social change: Thomas, Park and their successors', *Symbolic Interaction*, 1, 2: 5-23.

—— (1978b) 'Interactionism', in T. Bottomore and R. Nisbet (eds) *A History of Sociological Analysis*, London: Heinemann.

—— (1979) 'George Herbert Mead and the Chicago tradition of sociology', *Symbolic Interaction* 1,1: 9-26 and 2,1: 9-20.

Fleming, D. (1967) 'Attitude: the history of a concept', *Perspectives in American History* 1,2: 87-365.

Foote, N. (1962) 'Identification as the basis for a theory of motivation', *Sociological Quarterly* III: 107-13.

Frank, L. K. (1934) 'Causation: an episode in the history of thought', *Journal of Philosophy* 31, 16: 421-28.

Frank, P. (1949) 'Einstein, Mach and logical positivism', in P. A. Schilpp (ed.) *Albert Einstein: Philosopher-scientist*, vol.1, LaSalle, Ill.: Open Court.

Frazier, E. F. (1931) *The Negro Family in Chicago*, Chicago: Chicago University Press.

Frisby, D. (1981) *Sociological Impressionism: a Reassessment of Georg Simmel's Social Theory*, London: Heinemann.

—— (1987) 'The ambiguity of modernity: Georg Simmel and Max Weber', in W. J. Mommsen and J. Osterhammel (eds) *Max Weber and his Contemporaries*, London: Allen & Unwin.

Fuhrman, E. R. (1978) 'Images of the discipline in early American sociology', *Journal of the History of Sociology* 1, 1: 91-116.

Gadamer, H-G. (1960) *Truth and Method*, English translation, London: Sheed & Ward, 1975.

Gallent, M. J. and Kleinman, S. (1983) 'Symbolic interactionism versus ethnomethodology', *Symbolic Interaction* 6, 1: 1-18.

Geyl, P. (1955) *Debates with Historians*, The Hague: Martinus Nijhoff.

Giddings, F. H. (1924) *The Scientific Study of Human Society*, Chapel Hill, NC: University of North Carolina Press.

Gillies, A. (1945) *Herder*, Oxford: Blackwell.

Glaser, B. G. (1965) 'The constant comparative method of qualitative analysis', *Social Problems* 12: 436-45; reprinted in G. J. McCall and J. L. Simmons (eds) *Issues in Participant Observation*, Reading, Mass.: Addison Wesley, 1969.

Glaser, B. G. and Strauss, A. L. (1965) *Awareness of Dying*, Chicago: Aldine.

—— (1967) *The Discovery of Grounded Theory*, Chicago: Aldine.

—— (1968) *Time for Dying*, Chicago: Aldine.

Goetz, J. and Lecompte, M. (1984) *Ethnography and Qualitative Design in Educational Research*, New York: Academic Press.

Goffman, E. (1959) *The Presentation of Self in Everyday Life*, New York: Doubleday.

—— (1961) *Asylums: Essays on the Social Situation of Mental Patients and Other Inmates*, New York: Doubleday.

Gorman, R. (1977) *The Dual Vision: Alfred Schutz and the Myth of Phenomenological Sociology*, London: Routledge & Kegan Paul.

Gottschalk, L., Kluckhohn, C. and Angell, R. C. (1945) *The Use of Personal Documents in History, Anthropology and Sociology*, New York: Social Science Research Council.

Goudge, T. A. (1950) *The Thoughts of C. S. Peirce*, Toronto: University of Toronto Press.

Gregory, F. (1977) *Scientific Materialism in Nineteenth Century Germany*, Dordrecht: Reidel.

Guba, E. (1978) *Toward a Methodology of Naturalistic Inquiry in Educational Evaluation*, Los Angeles: Center for the Study of Evaluation, University of California Los Angeles Graduate School of Education.

Halfpenny, P. (1982) *Positivism and Sociology*, London: Allen & Unwin.

Hammersley, M. (ed.) (1983) *The Ethnography of Schooling*, Driffield: Nafferton.

—— (1985) 'From ethnography to theory: a programme and paradigm for case study research in the sociology of education', *Sociology* 19, 2: 244-59.

—— (1986) 'Measurement in ethnography', in M.Hammersley (ed.) *Case Studies in Classroom Research*, Milton Keynes: Open University Press, pp. 49-60.

—— (1987a) 'Ethnography and the cumulative development of theory', *British Educational Research Journal* 13, 3: 283-96.

—— (1987b) 'Ethnography for survival? a reply to Woods', *British Educational Research Journal* 13, 3: 309-17.

—— (1989) 'The methodology of ethnomethodology', unpublished.

Hammersley, M. and Atkinson, P. (1983) *Ethnography: Principles in Practice*, London: Tavistock.

Hanson, N. (1970) 'Hypotheses Fingo', in R. E. Butts and J. W. Davies (eds) *The Methodological Heritage of Newton*, Toronto: University of Toronto Press.

Harre, R. and Secord, P. F. (1972) *The Explanation of Social Behaviour*, Oxford: Blackwell.

Harris, M. (1969) *The Rise of Anthropological Theory*, London: Routledge & Kegan Paul.

Harvey, L. (1987) *Myths of the Chicago School of Sociology*, Aldershot: Gower.

Hayner, N. (1936) *Hotel Life*, Durham, NC: University of North Carolina Press.

Healey, W. (1923) 'The contribution of case studies to sociology', *Publications of the American Sociological Society* 18: 147-55.

Heise, D. R. (1975) *Causal Analysis*, New York: Wiley.

Hekman, S. J. (1986) *Hermeneutics and the Sociology of Knowledge*, Cambridge: Polity Press.

Helle, H. J. (1981) 'A conversation between Herbert Blumer and Horst J. Helle', published 1983 in Italian in *Sociologia della Communicazione* 2, 3: 199-215.

Hempel, C. G. (1965) *Aspects of Scientific Explanation*, New York: Free Press.

—— (1966) 'Explanation in science and history', in W. Dray (ed.) (1966) *Philosophical Analysis and History*, New York: Harper & Row.

Hennis, W. (1987) 'A science of man: Max Weber and the political economy of the German historical school', in W. J. Mommsen and J. Osterhammel (eds) *Max Weber and his Contemporaries*, London: Allen & Unwin.

Herbst, J. (1965) *The German Historical School in American Scholarship*, Ithaca, NY: Cornell University Press.

Heritage, J. (1984) *Garfinkel and Ethnomethodology*, Cambridge: Polity Press.

Hinkle, R. C. and Hinkle, G. J. (1954) *The Development of Modern Sociology*, New York: Random House.

Hirsch, T. and Selvin, H. (1973) *Principles of Survey Analysis*, New York: Free Press.

Hodges, H. A. (1949) *Wilhelm Dilthey: an Introduction*, 2nd edn, London: Routledge & Kegan Paul.

—— (1952) *The Philosophy of Wilhelm Dilthey*, London: Routledge & Kegan Paul.

Hookway, C. (1985) *Peirce*, London: Routledge & Kegan Paul.

Huber, J. (1973a) 'Symbolic interactionism as a pragmatic perspective: the bias of emergent theory', *American Sociological Review* 38: 274-84.

—— (1973b) 'Reply to Blumer: but who will scrutinize the scrutinizers?', *American Sociological Review* 38: 798-800.

—— (1973c) 'The emergency of emergent theory', *American Sociological Review* 39: 463.

Huff, T. E. (1984) *Max Weber and the Methodology of the Social Sciences*, New Brunswick, NJ: Transaction Books.

Hughes, H. M. (1980) 'Robert Ezra Park: the philosopher-newspaperman-sociologist', in R. K. Merton and M. W. Riley (eds) *Sociological Traditions from Generation to Generation*, Norwood, NJ: Ablex.

Hume, D. (1748) *Enquiries Concerning the Human Understanding*, L. A. Selby-Bigge (ed.), Oxford: Oxford University Press, 1962.

Iggers, G. (1965) 'The dissolution of German historicism', in R. Herr and H. T. Parker (eds) *Ideas in History*, Durham, NC: Duke University Press.

—— (1968) *The German Conception of History: the National Tradition of Historical Thought from Herder to the Present*, Middletown, Conn.: Wesleyan University Press.

James. W. (1890) *The Principles of Psychology*, 2 vols, New York: Dover, 1950.

—— (1899) 'On a certain blindness in human beings', in *Talks to Teachers of Psychology*, New York: Henry Holt; reprinted, New York: Dover, 1962.

—— (1907) *Pragmatism: a New Name for Some Old Ways of Thinking*, New York: Longmans, Green.

—— (1909) *The Meaning of Truth*, New York: Longmans, Green.

—— (1912) *Essays in Radical Empiricism*, New York: Longmans, Green.

Jandy, E. C. (1942) *Charles Horton Cooley: his Life and his Social Theory*, New York: Dryden Press.

Jensen, B. E. (1978) 'The recent trend in the interpretation of Dilthey', *Philosophy of the Social Sciences* 8: 409-38.

Joas, H. (1985) *G. H. Mead: a Contemporary Re-examination of his Thought*, Cambridge: Polity Press.

—— (1987) 'Symbolic interactionism', in A. Giddens and J. Turner (eds) *Social Theory Today*, Cambridge: Polity Press.

Johnson, G. D. and Shifflet, P. A. (1981) 'George Herbert Who? a critique of the objectivist reading of Mead', *Symbolic Interactionism* 4: 143-55.

Johnson, J. M. (1975) *Doing Field Research*, New York: Free Press.

Jones, P. (1985) 'William James', in M. G. Singer (ed.) *American Philosophy*, Royal Institute of Philosophy Lecture Series 19, Cambridge: Cambridge University Press.

Joynson, R. B. (1974) *Psychology and Common Sense*, London: Routledge & Kegan Paul.

Kaplan, A. (1964) *The Conduct of Inquiry*, New York: Chandler.

Katovich, M. (1984) 'Symbolic interaction and experimentation: the laboratory as a provocative stage', in N. K. Denzin (ed.) *Studies in Symbolic Interaction*, vol.5, Greenwich, Conn.: JAI Press.

Katovich, M. A., Saxton, S. L., and Powell, J. O. (1986) 'Making naturalism work in the laboratory', in C. J. Couch, S. L. Saxton, and M. A. Katovich (eds) *Iowa School, Studies in Symbolic Interaction*, Supplement 2, Greenwich, Conn.: JAI Press.

Katz, J. (1983) 'A theory of qualitative methodology: the social system of analytic fieldwork', in R. M. Emerson (ed.) *Contemporary Field Research*, Boston: Little, Brown.

Kluback, W. (1956) *Wilhelm Dilthey's Philosophy of History*, New York: Columbia University Press.

Knight, D. (1986) *The Age of Science: the Scientific World View in the Nineteenth Century*, Oxford: Blackwell.

Kohout, F. J. (1986) 'George Herbert Mead and Experimental Knowledge', in C. J. Couch, S. L. Saxton, and M. A. Katovich (eds.) *Iowa School, Studies in Symbolic Interaction*, Supplement 2, Greenwich, Conn.: JAI Press.

Kolakowski, L. (1972) *Positivism*, Harmondsworth: Penguin.

—— (1975) *The Search for Certitude*, New Haven, Conn.: Yale University Press.

Korner, S. (1955) *Kant*, Harmondsworth: Penguin.

Krausser, P. (1968) 'Dilthey's revolution in the theory of the structure of scientific inquiry and rational behavior', *Review of Metaphysics* 22: 262-80.

Krieger, L. (1977) *Ranke: the Meaning of History*, Chicago: University of Chicago Press.

Kroeber, A. (1935) 'History and science in anthropology', *American Anthropologist* 37: 539-69.

Kroner, R. (1914) *Kant's 'Weltanschauung'*, English translation, Chicago: University of Chicago Press, 1956.

Kuhn, M. H. (1964) 'Major trends in symbolic interaction theory in the past twenty-five years', *Sociological Quarterly* 5: 61-84.

Kuklick, B. (1977) *The Rise of American Philosophy*, New Haven, Conn.: Yale University Press.

—— (1984) 'The ecology of sociology' (a review of Lewis and Smith 1980), *American Journal of Sociology* 89: 1433-40.

Kuper, A. (1973) *Anthropologists and Anthropology: the British School 1922-72*, London: Allen Lane.

Kurtz, L. R. (1984) *Evaluating Chicago Sociology*, Chicago: University of Chicago Press.

Landesco, J. (1929) *Organized Crime in Chicago: part III of the Illinois Crime Survey, 1929*, Chicago: Illinois Association for Criminal Justice; reprinted Chicago, University of Chicago Press, with an introduction by M. H. Haller, 1968.

Lange, F. (1865) *The History of Materialism*, English translation, London: Routledge, 1925.

Langlois, C. V. and Seignobos, C. (1898) *Introduction to the Study of History*, English translation, London: Duckworth.

Lauer, R. H. and Handel, W. H. (1977) *Social Psychology: the Theory and Application of Symbolic Interactionism*, Boston: Houghton Mifflin.

Lazarsfeld, P. F. and Robinson, W. S. (1940) 'The quantification of case studies', *Journal of Applied Psychology* 24: 817-25.

Lazarsfeld, P. F., Berelson, B., and Gaudet, H. (1948) *The People's Choice*, New York: Columbia University Press.

Leach, E. R. (1957) 'The epistemological background to Malinowski's empiricism', in R. Firth (ed.) *Man and Culture: an Evaluation of the Work of Bronislaw Malinowski*, London: Routledge & Kegan Paul.

Leary, D. E. (1979) 'Wundt and after: psychology's shifting relations with the natural sciences, social sciences and philosophy', *Journal of the History of the Behavioral Sciences* 15: 231-41.

Lee, D. E. and Beck, R. N. (1954) 'The meaning of "historicism"', *American Historical Review* 59, 3: 568-77.

Leiter, K. (1980) *A Primer in Ethnomethodology*, New York: Oxford University Press.

Levine, D. (1971) 'Introduction' to G. Simmel (1971) *On Individuality and Social Forms*, Chicago: University of Chicago Press.

Lewin, K. (1936) 'Some social and psychological differences between the United States and Germany', *Character and Personality* 4: 265-93.

Lewis, J. D. (1972) 'Peirce, Mead and the objectivity of meaning', *Kansas Journal of Sociology* 8: 111-22.

—— (1976) 'The classic American pragmatists as forerunners to symbolic interactionism', *Sociological Quarterly* 17: 347-59.

—— (1977) 'Reply to Blumer', *Sociological Quarterly* 18: 291-2.

Lewis, J. D. and Smith, R. L. (1980) *American Sociology and Pragmatism: Mead, Chicago Sociology and Symbolic Interactionism*, Chicago: University of Chicago Press.

—— (1983) 'Putting the symbol in symbolic interactionism: a rejoinder', *Symbolic Interaction* 6, 1: 165-74.

Liazos, A. (1972) 'The poverty of the sociology of deviance: nuts, sluts and perverts', *Social Problems* 20: 102-20.

Lindeman, E. C. (1924) *Social Discovery*, New York: Republic.

Lindesmith, A. (1937) *The Nature of Opiate Addiction*, Chicago: University of Chicago Libraries.

—— (1952) 'Comment on W. S. Robinson's "The logical structure of analytic induction"', *American Sociological Review* 17: 492-3.

—— (1968) *Addiction and Opiates*, Chicago: Aldine.

Lindesmith, A., Strauss, A., and Denzin, N. K. (1977) *Social Psychology*, New York: Holt, Rinehart & Winston, 5th edn.

Lobkowicz, N. (1967) *Theory and Practice: History of a Concept from Aristotle to Marx*, Notre Dame, Ind.: University of Notre Dame Press.

Lofland, J. (1967) 'Notes on naturalism in sociology', *Kansas Journal of Sociology* 3: 45-61.

—— (1971) *Analyzing Social Settings*, Belmont, Calif.: Wadsworth.

Lofland, J. and Lofland, L. (1984) *Analyzing Social Settings*, 2nd edn, Belmont, Calif: Wadsworth; 1st edn by J. Lofland (1971).

Lofland, L. (ed.) (1980) 'Reminiscences of classic Chicago: the Blumer-Hughes talk', *Urban Life* 9: 251-81.

—— (1983) 'Understanding urban life: the Chicago legacy', *Urban Life* 11, 4: 491-511.

Lukes, S. (1973) *Emile Durkheim: his Life and Work*, London: Allen Lane.

Lundberg, G. A. (1929) *Social Research: a Study in Methods of Gathering Data*, New York: Longmans, Green; 2nd edn, 1942.

—— (1933) 'Is sociology too scientific?', *Sociologus* 9: 298-322.

—— (1936) 'Quantitative methods in social psychology', *American Sociological Review* 1: 38-54.

—— (1938) 'The concept of law in the social sciences', *Philosophy of Science* 5: 189-203.

—— (1939a) 'Contemporary positivism in sociology', *American Sociological Review* 4, 1: 42-55.

—— (1939b) *Foundations of Sociology*, New York: Macmillan; partial reprint, New York: McKay, 1964.

—— (1942) 'Operational definitions in the social sciences', *American Journal of Sociology* 47: 427-43.

—— (1947) *Can Science Save Us?* New York: Longmans, Green & Co.

—— (1949) 'Applying the scientific method to the social phenomena', *Sociology and Social Research* 34: 3-12.

—— (1954) 'Methodological convergences between Mead, Lundberg, and Parsons', *American Journal of Sociology* 60: 182-4.

—— (1955) 'The natural science trend in sociology', *American Journal of Sociology* 61, 3: 191-202.

—— (1960) 'Quantitative methods in sociology: 1920-1960', *Social Forces* 39: 19-24.

—— (1964) *Foundations of Sociology*, New York: McKay.

Lyman, S. M. (1984) 'Interactionism and the study of race relations at the macro-sociological level: the contribution of Herbert Blumer', *Symbolic Interaction* 7, 1: 107-20.

Lynd, R. S. (1939) *Knowledge for What?* Princeton, NJ: Princeton University Press.

McDermott, J. J. (ed.) (1973) *The Philosophy of John Dewey*, volume 1 *The Structure of Experience*, New York: California Books.

MacIver, R. M. (1931) 'Is sociology a natural science?', *Publications of the American Sociological Society* 25: 25-35.

—— (1942) *Social Causation*, New York: Ginn & Co.; 2nd edn, New York: Harper & Row, 1964.

MacIver, R. and Page, C. (1949) *Society: an Introductory Analysis,* New York: Rinehart.

Mackenzie, B. D. (1977) *Behaviourism and the Limits of Scientific Method,* London: Routledge & Kegan Paul.

Mackie, J. L. (1967) 'Mill's methods of induction', in P. Edwards (ed.) *The Encyclopaedia of Philosophy,* New York: Macmillan.

McKinney, J. C. (1954) 'Methodological convergence of Mead, Lundberg and Parsons', *American Journal of Sociology* 59: 565-74.

—— (1955) 'Mead and the philosophy of science', *Philosophy of Science* 22: 264-71.

—— (1957) 'Methodology, techniques and procedures in sociology', in H.Becker and A. Boskoff (eds) *Modern Sociological Theory in Continuity and Change,* New York: Holt, Rinehart & Winston.

—— (1966) *Constructive Typology and Social Theory,* New York: Appleton-Century-Crofts.

McPhail, C. (1979) 'Experimental research is convergent with symbolic interaction', *Symbolic Interaction* 2, 1: 89-94.

McPhail, C. and Rexroat, C. (1979) 'Mead vs Blumer: the divergent methodological perspectives of social behaviorism and symbolic interactionism', *American Sociological Review* 44: 449-67.

—— (1980) 'Ex cathedra Blumer or ex libris Mead', *American Sociological Review* 45: 420-30.

Madden, E. H. (1960) *Theories of Scientific Method: the Renaissance through the Nineteenth Century,* Seattle, Wash.: University of Washington Press.

Magee, B. (1973) *Popper,* Glasgow: Fontana/Collins.

Maines, D. (1977) 'Social organization and social structure in symbolic interactionist thought', *Annual Review of Sociology* 3: 235-59.

—— (1986) 'Researching form and process in the Iowa tradition', in C. J. Couch, S. L. Saxton, and M. A. Katovich (eds) *Iowa School, Studies in Symbolic Interaction,* Supplement 2, Greenwich, Conn.: JAI Press.

Makkreel, R. (1975) *Dilthey: Philosopher of the Human Studies,* Princeton, NJ: Princeton University Press.

Malinowski, B. (1967) *A Diary in the Strict Sense of the Term,* London: Routledge & Kegan Paul.

Mandelbaum, M. (1964) *Philosophy, Science and Sense Perception,* Baltimore, Md.: Johns Hopkins University Press.

Manicas, P. T. (1987) *A History and Philosophy of the Social Sciences,* Oxford: Blackwell.

Margenau, H. (1949) 'Einstein's conception of reality', in P. A. Schilpp (ed.) *Albert Einstein: Philosopher-scientiest,* vol. 1, LaSalle, Ill.: Open Court.

Marshall, G. (1982) *In Search of the Spirit of Capitalism: an Essay on Max Weber's Protestant Ethic Thesis*, London: Hutchinson.

Matthews, F. H. (1977) *Quest for an American Sociology: Robert E. Park and the Chicago School*, Montreal: McGill-Queen's University Press.

Matza, D. (1969) *Becoming Deviant*, Englewood Cliffs, NJ: Prentice-Hall.

Mead, G. H. (1917) 'Scientific method and the individual thinker', in J. Dewey *et al*, *Creative Intelligence: Essays in the Pragmatic Attitude*, New York: Henry Holt.

—— (1930) 'Cooley's contribution to American social thought', *American Journal of Sociology* 35, 5: 693-706.

—— (1932) *The Philosophy of the Present*, Chicago: Open Court.

—— (1934) *Mind, Self and Society*, Chicago: Chicago University Press,

—— (1936) *Movements of Thought in the Nineteenth Century*, Chicago: University of Chicago Press.

—— (1938) *The Philosophy of the Act*, Chicago: University of Chicago Press.

—— (1964a) *George Herbert Mead: Selected Writings*, A. Reck (ed.), Chicago: University of Chicago Press.

—— (1964b) *On the Social Psychology of George Herbert Mead*, A. L. Strauss (ed.), Chicago: University of Chicago Press; 1st edn, 1956.

—— (1982) *The Individual and the Social Self*, D. Miller (ed.), Chicago: University of Chicago Press.

Meltzer, B. and Petras, J. (1970) 'The Chicago and Iowa schools of symbolic interactionism', in T. Shibutani (ed.) *Human Nature and Collective Behavior: Papers in Honor of Herbert Blumer*, Englewood Cliffs, NJ: Prentice-Hall.

Meltzer, B., Petras, J., and Reynolds, L. (1975) *Symbolic Interactionism: Genesis, Varieties and Criticism*, London: Routledge & Kegan Paul.

Menger, C. (1883) *Problems of Economics and Sociology*, English translation, Urbana, Ill.: University of Illinois Press, 1963.

Merton, R. K. (1957) *Social Theory and Social Structure*, Glencoe, Ill.: Free Press.

—— (1967) *On Theoretical Sociology*, New York: Free Press.

—— (1983) 'Florian Znaniecki: a short reminiscence', *Journal of the History of the Behavioral Sciences* 19: 123-6.

Merton, R. K. and Riley, M. W. (1980) *Sociological Traditions from Generation to Generation*, Norwood, NJ: Ablex.

Miles, M. B. and Huberman, M. (1984) *Qualitative Data Analysis*, Beverly Hills, Cal.: Sage.

Mill, J. S (1974) *Collected Works of John Stuart Mill*, vol. 8: *A System of Logic*, Books 4-6, Toronto: University of Toronto Press.

—— (1969) *Autobiography*, London: Oxford University Press.

Miller, D. L. (1973) *George Herbert Mead: Self, Language and the World*, Austin, Texas: University of Texas Press.

Miller, S. I. (1982) 'Quality and quantity: another view of analytic induction as are search technique', *Quality and Quantity* 16: 281-95.

Mills, P. J. (1982) 'Misinterpreting Mead' (a review of Lewis and Smith 1980), *Sociology* 16: 116-31.

Mischel, T. (1970) 'Wundt and the conceptual foundations of psychology', *Philosophy and Phenomenological Research* 31: 1-26.

Mommsen, W. J. and Osterhammel, J. (eds) (1987) *Max Weber and his Contemporaries*, London: Allen & Unwin.

Morris, C. (1970) *The Pragmatist Movement in American Philosophy*, New York: Braziller.

Mowrer, E. (1927) *Family Disorganization*, Chicago: University of Chicago Press.

Mullins, N. C. (1973) *Theory and Theory Groups in Contemporary American Sociology*, New York: Harper & Row.

Murphey, M. G. (1961) *The Development of Peirce's Philosophy*, Cambridge, Mass.: Harvard University Press.

Murphy, G. (1949) *Historical Introduction to Psychology*, London: Routledge & Kegan Paul (5th edn).

Myers, G. (1986) *William James: his Life and Thought*, New Haven, Conn.: Yale University Press.

Needham, J. (1951) 'Human laws and the laws of nature in China and the West', *Journal of the History of Ideas* 12: 3-32 and 194-231.

Nisbet, H. B. (1970) *Herder and the Philosophy and History of Science*, Cambridge: Modern Humanities Research Association.

Oakes, G. (1987) 'Weber and the Southwest German School: the Genesis of the Concept of the Historical Individual', in W. J. Mommsen and J. Osterhammel (eds) *Max Weber and his Contemporaries*, London: Allen & Unwin.

Oberschall, A. (1972) 'The institutionalization of American sociology', in A. Oberschall (ed.) *The Establishment of Empirical Sociology*, New York: Harper & Row.

Ogburn, W. F. (1927) 'Sociology and statistics', in W. F. Ogburn and A. Goldenweiser (eds) *The Social Sciences and their Interrelations*, Boston: Houghton Mifflin.

—— (1930) 'The folkways of a scientific sociology', *Publications of the American Sociological Society* 24: 1-11.

—— (1932) 'Statistics and art', *Journal of the American Statistical Association*, 27: 1-8.

Outhwaite, William (1975) *Understanding Social Life: the Method Called Verstehen*, London: George Allen & Unwin.

—— (1983) *Concept Formation in Social Science*, London: Routledge & Kegan Paul.

Palmer, R. E. (1969) *Hermeneutics*, Evanston, Ill.: Northwestern University Press.

Palmer, V. M. (1928) *Field Studies in Sociology: a Student's Manual*, Chicago: University of Chicago Press.

Papineau, D. (1987) *Reality and Representation*, Oxford: Blackwell.

Park, R. E. (1904) *The Crowd and the Public*, English translation, Chicago: University of Chicago Press, 1972.

—— (1929) 'Sociology', in W. Gee (ed.) *Research in the Social Sciences: its Fundamental Methods and Objectives*, New York: Macmillan.

—— (1950) *Race and Culture*, Glencoe, Ill.: Free Press.

—— (1952) *Human Communities: the City and Human Ecology*, E. C. Hughes (ed.), Glencoe, Ill.: Free Press.

—— (1967) *On Social Control and Collective Behavior*, R. H. Turner (ed.), Chicago: University of Chicago Press.

Park, R. E. and Burgess, E. W. (eds) (1921) *Introduction to the Science of Sociology*, Chicago: University of Chicago Press (3rd edn 1969).

Park, R. E. and Miller, H. A. (1921) *Old World Traits Transplanted*, New York: Harper & Bros. (Main author W. I. Thomas.)

Parse, R. R., Coyne, A. B., and Smith, M. J. (1985) *Nursing Research: Qualitative Methods*, Bowrie, Md: Brady.

Passmore, J. (1966) *A Hundred Years of Philosophy*, London: Duckworth.

Pearson, K. (1892) *The Grammar of Science*, London: Adam & Charles Black, 3rd edn, 1911.

Peirce, C. S. (1934) *Collected Papers*, vol. 5, *Pragmatism and Pragmaticism*, C. Hartshorne and P. Weiss (eds), Cambridge, Mass.: Harvard University Press.

Perry, R. B. (1935) *The Thought and Character of William James*, 2 vols., Boston: Little, Brown.

Petras, J. W. (1968) *George Herbert Mead: Essays on his Social Philosophy*, New York: Teachers' College Press.

Plantinga, T. (1980) *Historical Understanding in the Thought of Wilhelm Dilthey*, Toronto: University of Toronto Press.

Platt, J. (1982) 'Interview with Herbert Blumer, 10th September, 1982', unpublished.

—— (1983) 'The development of "participant observation" method in sociology: origin, myth and history', *Journal of the History of the Behavioral Sciences* 19: 379-93.

—— (1986) 'Functionalism and the survey: the relation of theory and method', *Sociological Review* 34, 3: 501-36.

——(1987) 'The Chicago School and firsthand data', paper given at the annual conference of CHEIRON (The European Society for the History of Behavioural and Social Sciences).

Poggi, G. (1983) *Calvinism and the Capitalist Spirit*, London: Macmillan.

Popper, K. R. (1959) *The Logic of Scientific Discovery*, London: Hutchinson.

—— (1963) *Conjectures and Refutations: the Growth of Scientific Knowledge*, London: Routledge & Kegan Paul.

—— (1972) *Objective Knowledge*, Oxford: Oxford University Press.

Purcell, E. A. (1973) *The Crisis of Democratic Theory: Scientific Naturalism and the Problem of Value*, Lexington: University Press of Kentucky.

Quinton, A. (1980) *Francis Bacon*, Oxford: Oxford University Press.

Radcliffe-Brown, A. R. (1952) 'The comparative method in social anthropology', *Journal of the Royal Anthropological Institute* 81: 15-22.

Radin, P. (1933) *The Method and Theory of Ethnology*, 2nd edn, New York: Basic Books, 1966.

Rancurello, A. C. (1968) *A Study of Franz Brentano*, New York: Academic Press.

Rand, C. (1964) 'Two meanings of historicism in the writings of Dilthey, Troeltsch, and Meinecke', *Journal of the History of Ideas* 25: 503-18.

Rauma, D. (1981) 'Herbert Blumer, the scientific attitude and the problem of demarcation', in G. P. Stone and H. Farberman (eds) *Social Psychology through Symbolic Interaction*, 2nd edn, New York: Wiley, 1981.

Raushenbush, W. (1979) *Robert E. Park: Biography of a Sociologist*, Durham, NC: Duke University Press.

Reckless, W. C. (1933) *Vice in Chicago*, Chicago: University of Chicago Press.

Rée, J. (1974) *Descartes*, London: Allen Lane.

Reilly, F. (1970) *Charles Peirce's Theory of the Scientific Method*, New York: Fordham University Press.

Reiss, A. J. (1966) 'Introduction' to Wirth (1966).

—— (ed.) (1968) *Cooley and Social Analysis*, Ann Arbor, Mich.: University of Michigan Press.

Rescher, N. (1978) *Peirce's Philosophy of Science*, Notre Dame, Ind.: University of Notre Dame Press.

Reynolds, J. M. and Reynolds, L. T. (1973) 'Interactionism, complicity and astructural bias', *Catalyst* 7: 76–85

Reynolds, L. T. (1969) 'The sociology of symbolic interactionism', Ph.D dissertation, Ohio State University.

Rickert, H. (1902) *The Limits of Concept Formation in Natural Science: a Logical Introduction to the Historical Sciences*, English translation, abridged edn, Cambridge: Cambridge University Press, 1986.

—— (1929) *Science and History: a Critique of Positivist Epistemology*, English translation, Princeton, NJ: Van Nostrand, 1962.

Rickman, H. P. (1967) *Understanding and the Human Studies*, London: Heinemann.

Ridley, M. (1986) *Evolution and Classification: the Reformation of Cladism*, London: Longman.

Ritchie, A. D. (1923) *Scientific Method: an Inquiry into the Character and Validity of Natural Laws*, London: Kegan Paul, Trench, Trubner.

Robinson, W. S. (1951) 'The logical structure of analytic induction', *American Sociological Review* 16, 6: 812-18.

Rochberg-Halton, E. (1983) 'The real nature of pragmatism and Chicago sociology', *Symbolic Interaction* 6: 139-53.

Rock, P. (1973) 'Phenomenalism and essentialism in the sociology of deviance', *Sociology* 7, 1: 17-29.

—— (1979) *The Making of Symbolic Interactionism*, London: Macmillan.

Rose, A. (1962) *Human Behavior and Social Processes*, Boston: Houghton Mifflin.

Rosnow, R. L. (1981) *Paradigms in Transition: the Methodology of Social Inquiry*, New York: Oxford University Press.

Ruby, J. E. (1986) 'The origins of scientific "law"', *Journal of the History of Ideas* 47, 3: 341-59.

Rucker, D. (1969) *The Chicago Pragmatists*, Minneapolis, Minn.: University of Minnesota Press.

Runciman, W. G. (1972) *A Critique of Max Weber's Philosophy of Social Science*, Cambridge: Cambridge University Press.

Russell, B. (1925) 'Introduction' to English translation of F. Lange (1865) *The History of Materialism*, London: Routledge.

Ryan, A. (1970) *The Philosophy of John Stuart Mill*, London: Macmillan.

Sacks, H. (1963) 'Sociological description', *Berkeley Journal of Sociology* 8: 1-16.

Scarth, J. and Hammersley, M. (1986) 'Some problems in assessing the closedness of classroom tasks', in M. Hammersley (ed.) *Case Studies in Classroom Research*, Milton Keynes: Open University Press.

Schatzman, L. and Strauss, A. L. (1973) *Field Research*, Englewood Cliffs, NJ: Prentice-Hall.

Scheffler, I. (1974) *Four Pragmatists: a Critical Introduction to Peirce, James, Mead and Dewey*, New York: Humanities Press.

Schilpp, P. A. (1949) *Albert Einstein: Philosopher-scientist*, 2 vols, LaSalle, Ill.: Open Court.

Schnadelbach, H. (1984) *Philosophy in Germany: 1831-1933*, Cambridge: Cambridge University Press.

Schultz, D. P. (1960) *A History of Modern Psychology*, New York: Academic Press.

Scriven, M. (1966) 'Causes, connections and conditions in history', in W. Dray (ed.) *Philosophical Analysis and History*, New York: Harper & Row.

Selvin, H. (1965) 'Durkheim's *Suicide*: further thoughts on a methodological classic', in R. Nisbet (ed.) *Emile Durkheim*, Englewood Cliffs, NJ: Prentice-Hall.

Shalin, D. (1984) 'The romantic antecedents of Meadian social psychology', *Symbolic Interaction* 7, 1: 43-65.

Shaw, C. R. (1930) *The Jack Roller*, Chicago: University of Chicago Press; reprinted with an introduction by H. S. Becker, 1966.

—— (1931) 'Case study method', *Publications of the American Sociological Society* 21: 149-57.

Shaw, C. R. and Mckay, H. D. (1931) *Social Factors in Juvenile Delinquency*, Washington, DC: US Government Printing Office.

Shibutani, T. (ed.) (1970) *Human Nature and Collective Behavior: Papers in Honor of Herbert Blumer*, Englewood Cliffs, NJ: Prentice-Hall.

Short, J. (ed.) (1971) *The Social Fabric of the Metropolis*, Chicago: University of Chicago Press.

Sills, D. (1968) *International Encyclopaedia of the Social Sciences*, New York: Macmillan.

Simmel, G. (1905) *The Problems of the Philosophy of History*, English translation, New York: Free Press, 1977.

—— (1916-18) *Essays on Interpretation in Social Science*, English translation, Manchester: Manchester University Press, 1980.

—— (1971) *On Individuality and Social Forms*, D. Levine (ed.), Chicago: University of Chicago Press.

Simon, W. M. (1963) *European Positivism in the Nineteenth Century*, Ithaca, NY: Cornell University Press.

Simpson, G. (1954) *Man in Society*, New York: Random House.

Singer, M. G. (ed.) (1985) *American Philosophy*, Royal Institute of Philosophy Lecture Series 19, Supplement to *Philosophy* 1985, Cambridge: Cambridge University Press.

Skagestad, P. (1981) *The Road of Inquiry: Charles Peirce's Pragmatic Realism*, New York: Columbia University Press.

—— (1985) 'American Pragmatism', in G. Floistad (ed.)

Contemporary Philosophy: a New Survey, The Hague: Nijhoff.

Small, A. (1924) *Origins of Sociology*, Chicago: University of Chicago Press.

Smith, D. (1988) *The Chicago School: a Liberal Critique of Capitalism*, London: Macmillan.

Smith, J. E. (1978) *Purpose and Thought: the Meaning of Pragmatism*, New Haven: Yale University Press.

Smith, L. D. (1986) *Behaviorism and Logical Positivism*, Stanford, Cal.: Stanford University Press.

Sokal, R. R. and Sneath, P. H. A. (1963) *Principles of Numerical Taxonomy*, San Francisco, Cal.: W. H. Freeman.

Sorokin, P. (1940) 'Review of G.A. Lundberg: *Foundations of Sociology*', *American Journal of Sociology* 45: 795-8.

Spykman, N. (1925) *The Social Theory of Georg Simmel*, 2nd edn (1965), New York: Atherton Press.

Stewart, R. L. (1981) 'What George Mead should have said: exploration of a problem of interpretation', *Symbolic Interaction* 4, 2: 157-66.

Stone, G. P. and Farberman, H. (1967) 'Further comment on the Bales-Blumer dialogue', *American Journal of Sociology* 72: 409-10.

—— (eds) (1970) *Social Psychology through Symbolic Interaction*, Waltham, Mass.: Ginn-Blaisdell; 2nd edn, New York: Wiley, 1981.

Stone, G. P., Maines, D. R., Farberman, H. A., Stone, G. I., and Denzin, N. K. (1974) 'On methodology and craftsmanship in the criticism of sociological perspectives', *American Sociological Review* 39: 456-63.

Storing, H. J. (ed.) (1962) *Essays on the Scientific Study of Politics*, New York: Holt, Rinehart & Winston.

Stouffer, S. A. (1930) 'An experimental comparison of statistical and case-history methods of attitude research', Ph.D. thesis, University of Chicago; reprinted New York: Arno Press, 1980.

—— (1962) *Social Research to Test Ideas*, New York: Free Press.

Stouffer, S. A., and Lazarsfeld, P. F. (1937) *Research Memorandum on the Family in the Depression*, New York: Social Science Research Council.

Stouffer, S. A., Suchman, E. A., Devinney, L. C., Star, S. A., and Williams, R. M. (1949) *The American Soldier: Studies in Social Psychology in World War II*, vol. 1: *Adjustment During Army Life*, Princeton, NJ: Princeton University Press.

Strauss, A. L. (1964) 'Introduction' to G. H. Mead (1964) *On the Social Psychology of George Herbert Mead*, (ed.) Chicago: University of Chicago Press.

—— (1987) *Qualitative Analysis for Social Scientists*, Cambridge: Cambridge University Press.

Strauss, L. (1953) *Natural Right and History*, Chicago: University of Chicago Press.

—— (1968) 'Natural law', in D. Sills (ed.) *International Encyclopaedia of the Social Sciences*, New York: Macmillan.

Strong, E. W. (1955) 'William Whewell and John Stuart Mill: their controversy about scientific knowledge', *Journal of the History of Ideas* 16: 209-31.

Stroud, B. (1977) *Hume*, London: Routledge & Kegan Paul.

Stryker, S. (1980) *Symbolic Interactionism: a Social Structural Version*, Menlo Park, Cal.: Benjamin/Cummings.

—— (1981) 'Symbolic interactionism: themes and variations', in M. Rosenberg and R. H. Turner (eds) *Social Psychology: Sociological Perspectives*, New York: Basic Books.

Suppe, F. (ed.) (1974) *The Structure of Scientific Theories*, Chicago: University of Illinois Press.

Taylor, C. (1979) *Hegel and Modern Society*, Cambridge: Cambridge University Press.

Taylor, S. J. and Bogdan, R. (1984) *Introduction to Qualitative Research*, 2nd edn, New York: Wiley. (First edn. Bogdan and Taylor (1975).)

Thayer, H. S. (1985) 'John Dewey', in M. G. Singer (ed.) *American Philosophy, Royal Institute of Philosophy Lecture Series 19*, Cambridge: Cambridge University Press.

Thomas, W. I. (1951) *Social Behavior and Personality*, New York: Social Science Research Council; reprinted, Westport, Conn.: 1981.

—— (1966) *On Social Organization and Social Personality*, M. Janowitz (ed.), Chicago: University of Chicago Press.

Thomas, W. I. and Thomas, D. S. (1928) *The Child in America: Behavior Problems and Programs*, New York: Alfred Knopf; reprinted, New York: Johnson, 1970.

Thomas, W. I. and Znaniecki, F. (1918-20) *The Polish Peasant in Europe and America*, 5 vols, Chicago: University of Chicago Press/Boston: Badger Press; (1927) reprinted, New York: Alfred Knopf; (1958) reprinted, New York: Dover.

Thomason, B. C. (1982) *Making Sense of Reification: Alfred Schutz and Constructionist Theory*, London: Macmillan.

Thrasher, F. M. (1927a) *The Gang: a Study of 1,313 Gangs in Chicago*, Chicago: University of Chicago Press.

—— (1927b) 'The group factor', *Welfare Magazine* 18: 143.

Thurstone, L. L. (1928) 'Attitudes can be measured', *American Journal of Sociology* 33: 529-54.

Tillman, M. K. (1974) 'Review of D. Miller: *George Herbert Mead*', *Man and World* 7: 293-300.

Truzzi, M. (1974) *Verstehen: Subjective Understanding in the Social Sciences*, Reading, Mass.: Addison-Wesley.

Turner, R. H. (1953) 'The quest for universals in sociological research', *American Sociological Review* 24: 605-11.

Turner, S. P. (1986) *The Search for a Methodology of Social Science*, Dordrecht: Reidel.

Turner, S. P. and Factor, R. A. (1981) 'Objective possibility and adequate causality in Weber's methodological writings', *Sociological Review* 29, 1: 5-28.

Tursman, R. (1987) *Peirce's Theory of Scientific Discovery*, Bloomington, Ind.: Indiana University Press.

Tuttle, H. N. (1969) *Wilhelm Dilthey's Philosophy of Historical Understanding: a Critical Analysis*, Leiden: Brill.

Valle, R. and King, R. (1978) *Existential-Phenomenological Alternatives for Psychology*, New York: Oxford University Press.

van Parijs, P. (1981) *Evolutionary Explanation in the Social Sciences*, London: Tavistock.

Verhoeven, J. (1980) 'Interview with Herbert Blumer, 25th June 1980', published 1987 in Flemish in *Tijdschrift Voor Sociologie* 4: 3-29.

Waller, W. (1934) 'Insight and scientific method', *American Journal of Sociology* 40, 3: 285-97.

—— (1936) 'Discussion of G. A. Lundberg: Quantitative methods in social psychology', *American Sociological Review* 1: 54-60.

Warnke, G. (1987) *Gadamer: Hermeneutics, Tradition and Reason*, Cambridge: Polity Press.

Watkins, P. (1986) *Story of the W and Z*, Cambridge: Cambridge University Press.

Watson, J. (1913) 'Psychology as a behaviorist views it', *Psychological Review* 20: 158-79.

Weber, M. (1903-6) *Roscher and Knies: the Logical Problems of Historical Economics*, English translation, New York: Free Press, 1975.

—— (1903-17) *The Methodology of the Social Sciences*, English translation, New York: Free Press, 1949.

—— (1946) *From Max Weber: Essays in Sociology*, H. H. Gerth and C. W. Mills (eds), New York: Oxford University Press.

Weinsheimer, J. C. (1985) *Gadamer's Hermeneutics: a Reading of Truth and Method*, New Haven, Conn.: Yale University Press.

Wells, G. A. (1959) *Herder and After: a Study in the Development of Sociology*, The Hague: Mouton.

Whittaker, T. (1908) *Comte and Mill*, London: Constable.

Willer, D. (1967) *Scientific Sociology*, Englewood Cliffs, NJ: Prentice-Hall.

REFERENCES

Willey, T. E. (1978) *Back to Kant*, Detroit, Mich.: Wayne State University Press.

Williams, R. (1976) 'Symbolic interactionism: fusion of theory and research', in D. C. Thorns (ed.) *New Directions in Sociology*, London: David and Charles.

Wilson, T. P. (1970) 'Normative and interpretive paradigms in sociology', in J. D. Douglas (ed.) *Understanding Everyday Life*, Chicago: Aldine.

Winch, P. (1958) *The Idea of a Social Science*, London: Routledge & Kegan Paul.

Windelband, W. (1894) 'History and natural science', English translation, *History and Theory* 19, 2: 165-85, 1980.

Wirth, L. (1928) *The Ghetto*, Chicago: University of Chicago Press.

—— (1966) *On Cities and Social Life*, A. J. Reiss (ed.), Chicago: University of Chicago Press.

Wisdom, J. O. (1987) *Philosophy of the Social Sciences 1: a Meta-Scientific Introduction*, Aldershot: Avebury/Gower.

Wollheim, R. (1967) 'Natural law', in P. Edwards (ed.) *The Encyclopaedia of Philosophy*, New York: Macmillan.

Woods, P. (1986) *Inside Schools*, London: Routledge & Kegan Paul.

Young, P. (1932) *The Pilgrims of Russian Town*, Chicago: University of Chicago Press.

Young, P. V. (1939) *Scientific Social Surveys and Research*, Englewood Cliffs, NJ: Prentice-Hall.

Zerubavel, E. (1980) 'If Simmel were a fieldworker: on formal sociological theory and analytical field research', *Symbolic Interaction* 3, 2: 25-33.

Zilsel, E. (1942) 'The genesis of the concept of scientific law', *The Philosophical Review* 51: 245-67.

Zimmerman, D. H. and Wieder, D. L. (1970) 'Ethnomethodology and the problem of social order: comment on Denzin', in J. D. Douglas (ed.) *Understanding Everyday Life*, Chicago: Aldine.

Znaniecki, F. (1928) 'Social research in criminology', *Sociology and Social Research* 12: 307-22.

—— (1934) *The Method of Sociology*, New York: Farrar & Rinehart.

—— (1969) *Florian Znaniecki on Humanistic Sociology*, R. Bierstedt (ed.), Chicago: University of Chicago Press.

Zorbaugh, H. (1929) *The Gold Coast and the Slum*, Chicago: University of Chicago Press.

NAME INDEX

SUBJECT INDEX